MW00397430

Shopper Marketing

Shopper Marketing

Profiting from the Place Where Suppliers, Brand Manufacturers, and Retailers Connect

Daniel J. Flint

Chris Hoyt

Nancy Swift

Associate Publisher: Amy Neidlinger
Executive Editor: Jeanne Glasser Levine
Operations Specialist: Jodi Kemper
Cover Designer: Chuti Prasertsith
Managing Editor: Kristy Hart
Project Editor: Elaine Wiley
Copy Editor: Geneil Breeze
Proofreader: Debbie Williams
Indexer: Lisa Stumpf
Senior Compositor: Gloria Schurick
Manufacturing Buyer: Dan Uhrig

© 2014 by Daniel J. Flint, Chris Hoyt, and Nancy Swift
Upper Saddle River, New Jersey 07458

For information about buying this title in bulk quantities, or for special sales opportunities (which may include electronic versions; custom cover designs; and content particular to your business, training goals, marketing focus, or branding interests), please contact our corporate sales department at corpsales@pearsoned.com or (800) 382-3419.

For government sales inquiries, please contact governmentsales@pearsoned.com.

For questions about sales outside the U.S., please contact international@pearsoned.com.

Company and product names mentioned herein are the trademarks or registered trademarks of their respective owners.

All rights reserved. No part of this book may be reproduced, in any form or by any means, without permission in writing from the publisher.
Printed in the United States of America

First Printing June 2014
ISBN-10: 0-13-348142-5
ISBN-13: 978-0-13-348142-6

Pearson Education LTD.
Pearson Education Australia PTY, Limited.
Pearson Education Singapore, Pte. Ltd.
Pearson Education Asia, Ltd.
Pearson Education Canada, Ltd.
Pearson Educación de Mexico, S.A. de C.V.
Pearson Education—Japan
Pearson Education Malaysia, Pte. Ltd.
Library of Congress Control Number: 2014933848

This book is dedicated to all the shopper marketing professionals working diligently for long hours to improve the shopping experience and to all the scholars passionate about research that can assist the shopper marketing discipline.

Contents

Foreword

Few can lay claim to being both pioneers *and* futurists, but Chris Hoyt, Dan Flint, and Nancy Swift are exactly that when it comes to the exciting—and still emerging—discipline of shopper marketing. Together, they have defined shopper marketing's purpose and elucidated its full potential over the past 20 years or more.

Yes, it's been at least that long. While many trace the birth of shopper marketing to the moment at which Coca-Cola or perhaps Procter & Gamble embraced it about a decade ago, its roots actually run deeper than that. In fact, I can remember talking about placing the shopper at the center of marketing with Chris and Nancy as early as 1987. We just didn't know what to call it yet!

While the idea of putting shoppers first may sound obvious now, it wasn't always so. For years, even decades, retailers and manufacturers focused mostly on each other without much real concern for the shopper or the shopping experience. Marketing brands at retail, such as it was, was more about striking a deal between business adversaries than thinking about what shoppers might actually want or need at the store.

That changed rapidly with the advent of the Internet and the power it invested in the shopper. It accelerated further with the recognition that the retail store was not merely a channel for the distribution of products, but a highly experiential medium for marketing in its own right. It arrived with the epiphany that if accountability in marketing were the goal, then it made sense to invest marketing dollars where the cash register rang.

Shortly after I launched *The Hub Magazine* in 2004, Chris and Nancy fielded the first of a series of research studies to bring greater definition to what was then becoming known as shopper marketing. The goal was to identify its tenets and codify "best practices." The idea was to set some standards and try to help move the industry forward.

This seminal research became the foundation of an annual industry survey, *The Hub Top 20*, in which agencies and brands (both manufacturer and retailer) evaluate each other's progress against a specific set of criteria. Now in its eighth year, and with the support of Dan Flint's Shopper Marketing Forum at the University of Tennessee, *The Hub Top 20* serves as an ongoing reminder of both the promise and the complexities of achieving excellence in shopper marketing.

That search for excellence begins with this book. Chris, Dan, and Nancy have set forth, with great clarity and in fine detail, exactly what it takes to do shopper marketing—and do it right. *Shopper Marketing* is indispensable to novice and experienced shopper marketers alike. Read it, study it, and read it again. Refer back to it.

Share it, discuss it, and keep it by your side. Apply it with the same verve with which it was written. It is both a handbook for today's shopper marketer and a guidebook to the future of shopper marketing.

Tim Manners
Founder
The Hub Magazine
February 23, 2014

Acknowledgments

Shopper marketing is a discipline that has been "built" rather than "born." We wish to offer special thanks to those "builders"—some known throughout the industry for their pioneering efforts in making shopper marketing a mainstream strategy for all product marketers, regardless of size or nature of business; others perhaps less known but who nonetheless contribute to the body of knowledge through their questioning, creativity, and passion.

From the manufacturing side, thanks to A. G. Lafley, Dina Howell, and Brett Stover who brought industrywide visibility to shopper marketing and laid much of the strategic underpinnings while at P&G. Thanks to Lisa Klauser and Mike Twitty for generously sharing with the industry their research in understanding the shopper while at Unilever. A personal as well as industry thank you to Mike McMahon, Jesse Spungin, and Tammy Brumfield for demonstrating in ConAgra how the integration of shopper marketing into the organization could drive sales and ROI. Thanks also to Rick Abens, now leading Foresight ROI, and Cannon Koos, who developed shopper marketing metrics there. Thanks to Jeff Swearingen and Stephen Springfield, who championed shopper marketing at Frito-Lay, as did John Compton and Michelle Adams at PepsiCo and Mark Scott at Kimberly-Clark. Thanks to Jeff King and Bill Lardie of Anderson Merchandisers, Tim Purcell of Pilot Flying J, and Ray Kielarowski of Bush Brothers for their generous support.

Special thanks to the agencies that have taken the shopper marketing concept and, with both insight and creativity, spun it into programs that meet the needs of shoppers, retailers, and brands. Our appreciation to Ken Barnett, Paul Gustafson, Jim Holbrook, Beth Ann Kaminkow, Terry Mangano, Andy Murray, Sharon Napier, Joe Robinson, Michele Roney, Karen Sauder, Cecy Shveid, and Al Wittemen. So many of the real drivers of shopper marketing come from the agency side, and we thank them all.

Thanks to the shopper marketing evangelists—those people who saw the inherent value of shopper marketing, many very early on—and told the world about it. For adding to the knowledge base of shopper marketing we specifically want to thank Mike Bach and Bryan Gildenberg for their work at MVI/Kantar Retail, Bill Bishop of Willard Bishop Consulting, Matt Egol of Booz & Company, and John Karolefski and Linda Winick of CPG Matters. We also thank the authors Paco Underhill, Herb Sorensen, Michael Anthony, Toby Desforges, Markus Ståhlberg, and Ville Maila. A very special thanks to Tim Manners, publisher of *The Hub Magazine*, for all his efforts in advancing shopper marketing. From providing the platform for countless research surveys, to establishing the standards with *The Hub Top 20*, to interviewing and showcasing industry leaders, Tim is an indefatigable champion of shopper marketing and a great friend to all of us.

Finally, we thank Tiffany Jenkins, Chip Hoyt, and Lynn, Ryan, and Spencer Flint for being the best of sounding boards—both honest and insightful—as we worked through the challenges. Your support is invaluable.

About the Authors

Dan Flint, PhD, is the Regal Entertainment Group Professor of Business and Director/Founder of the Shopper Marketing Forum in The Department of Marketing and Supply Chain Management, The University of Tennessee, Knoxville. He is a graduate from the US Naval Academy, has a sales engineering background, and a PhD in marketing and logistics from the University of Tennessee. He has worked with many firms in the consumer goods, aerospace, industrial, and third-party logistics industries on branding, shopper marketing, marketing strategy, account management, and innovation. He works internationally often and remains active in both marketing and supply chain management associations. His research focuses on helping businesses develop a proactive customer orientation; understand what customers, consumers, and shoppers value; improve their marketing strategies; and develop more productive business-to-business connections. Dan has published in top-tier journals such as the *Journal of Marketing*, *Journal of Consumer Research*, *Journal of the Academy of Marketing Science*, *Journal of Business Logistics*, and the *International Journal of Physical Distribution and Logistics Management*. Dan currently is focused on shopper marketing, spending a great deal of time with leading CPG, agency, broker, and retailing firms.

Founder of Hoyt & Company and a CPG marketing and sales consultant for more than 35 years, **Chris Hoyt** has developed an industrywide reputation for his real-world, fact-filled, challenging, and entertaining point of view. Because Chris actually "walked the walk" in senior management positions with P&G and Clairol prior to becoming a consultant, he knows the difference between theory and practice and invariably leaves his readers significantly better equipped to deal with the realities of the current marketplace. Details at www.hoytnet.com.

Nancy Swift is vice president and co-founder of Hoyt & Company. Her extensive experience in advising consumer goods brand leaders on their sales, marketing, and trade challenges created a natural pathway for Nancy's move into shopper marketing. Her background in consumer understanding, research, and data analysis proves key to synthesizing the interrelationships of brand, retailer, and shopper essential to best practice shopper marketing. Prior to founding Hoyt & Company, Nancy was the first female Managing Director of Consulting at Ryan Partnership and a research specialist at Glendinning Associates.

Introduction

What Is This Book All About?

This book is about doing shopper marketing, with an emphasis on "doing." In it, we provide an overview of key shopper marketing concepts as well as specifics on a formal process for developing shopper marketing programs. But what is this thing called "shopper marketing" anyway? There sure seems to be a lot of attention being paid to it despite everyone you speak with seemingly having a slightly different definition. Is it merely the latest fad in brand management? Is it merely marketing to shoppers while they are in the store, something retailers have been doing all along? Is it simply what merchandisers and manufacturer account managers decide to do in each store? No, it is not any of these. Shopper marketing is a new way of looking at business relationships between brand manufacturers, retailers, and the agencies with whom they work. Although, as you will read, shopper marketing as it is referenced today has only been around since the early 2000s, it is a discipline that has evolved from and emerged out of previous brand management, account management, and retailing practices.

Shopper marketing has exploded recently having a major influence on brand manufacturers and retailers alike. Associations such as POPAI (Point of Purchasing Advertising International), P2PI (Path-to-Purchase Institute), IIR USA (US division of the Institute for International Research), and others host large annual conferences dedicated to shopper marketing. There now exists an entire industry of shopper insights research companies, shopper and retail data analytics companies, and shopper marketing program ROI (return on investment) measurement companies. As of this writing, the LinkedIn Shopper Insights and Marketing Professionals discussion group has 34,700 members. And several books have been written on the topic. However, whereas previous books provide insights to various aspects of shopper marketing, none has offered a comprehensive set of processes for actually *doing* shopper marketing. That is where we come in. This book does not replace others that have preceded it nor does it replace the exponentially expanding volume of industry reports. It complements them.

We prepared this book to help you build a firm foundation in exactly what shopper marketing is and how to leverage your firm's assets to create the best shopper marketing organization, strategies, initiatives, and plans possible that have meaningful returns on their investments. Because many firms are learning very quickly, you must learn at a faster rate to stay ahead. So hold on, there's a lot to cover that's both exciting and challenging.

We are a unique group of three authors—two consultants who have been working with the best of the best in shopper marketing since its beginning, as well as running several agencies within this space over the last 30 years, and a marketing professor who has been teaching and researching customers and marketing strategies for more than 18 years. We bring a blend of both practice and scholastic research. Collectively, drawing on our expertise and that of others with whom we interact daily, we think we present to you the most critical aspects and latest thinking on state of the art shopper marketing. You will see the shopper marketing world through the eyes of those who have lived it—what works, why, and what doesn't. The scholastic view keeps us honest, objective, and rigorous. Let's face it, a great deal of research has been done over the years on retailing, shopper behavior, consumer behavior, branding, business-to-business relationships, selling, advertising, merchandising, and so forth. We rely on this research to support our recommendations in this book—we recommend what we know works.

So you may be asking, if people like us have been working with firms on shopper marketing for years and academics have been researching aspects of what we now call shopper marketing for years, why do we need this book? Quite simply—and in this case "simply" does apply—there are two reasons. First, no one has ever pulled it all together in a systematic way sufficient enough to lay a solid foundation for shopper marketing managers. Due to this problematic situation, shopper marketing positions are being created within organizations and filled by competent people, but people who may not have the tools and process knowledge necessary to be as successful as they could be. Second, there are still only a few companies, relatively speaking, that can be classified as advanced in shopper marketing management. Our aim is to increase that number significantly. The best of the best are manufacturing companies like Coca-Cola, PepsiCo and, specifically, the Frito-Lay division, Procter & Gamble, Nestlé, Unilever, Campbell's Soup Company, and ConAgra working with retailers like Target, Kroger, Safeway, The Home Depot, and Walmart, and agencies like Mars, TracyLocke, Integer, Saatchi & Saatchi X, and brokers like CROSSMARK. They draw on data from firms like Nielsen and dunnhumby. We have worked with these firms and many more like them across a variety of consumer goods companies. We can't reveal their secrets, but the foundational processes they all rely on are sharable. Even if you work for one of these outstanding firms, you may have only recently even heard of the term "shopper marketing" and now you've been thrown into a job where you are responsible for part of it. Or maybe you work in part of the organization that is affected by shopper marketing, supply chain management for example, and you desperately need to know what's going on. For all these reasons, this book should serve as your pillow for a while. Read it, think about it, apply it, and read it again. Soon you will find that you have a solid foundation and will begin to develop your own advanced slant on aspects of shopper marketing. This foundation may do more than help you create initiatives with high ROI for your firm, but may very well save your brands from complete demise.

We adopt a strategic view of shopper marketing. It is far more than merchandising tactics. Not that the tactics are unimportant. They are important, but only if they emerge from a strategic orientation. Our objectives for this book are to help you

- Understand what shopper marketing is and is not from both the manufacturer's and retailer's point of view.
- Understand why shopper marketing is here to stay and why both retailers and manufacturers have been quick to embrace it.
- Be able to develop, manage, and motivate a best-in-class shopper marketing organization.
- Be able to develop and implement a best-in-class shopper marketing strategic plan and initiatives.
- Be able to understand the challenges and opportunities for collaboration for (a) shopper insights, (b) strategic planning, and (c) program execution, including supply chain management support for shopper marketing.
- Be able to understand measurement and ROI trade-offs involved in strategic shopper marketing.

How Is This Book Structured?

We begin with an overview of shopper marketing and lay out the basic process through which we take you. We move the discussion to focus on who the shopper really is and how we study the shopper to understand opportunities and develop insights. We then provide an overview of how retailers operate followed by a review of how consumer goods companies operate. Many people with whom we work really don't know how leadership at these two kinds of companies think and how often differences in their thinking creates tension for everyone involved. The next key topics focus on strategic planning, organizing for shopper marketing, execution issues that involve interfunctional and interorganizational coordination and collaboration, and measurement approaches.

We also present scholastic research in a unique way. At the end of most chapters, we present "Interesting Findings from Research" that provide some insights to specific, individual research studies conducted by marketing scholars that could be relevant to shopper marketing. You may not know it, but business academics at research universities around the globe spend at least 40% of their time and sometimes more conducting original research that ought to be helpful to industry. The best of this research draws upon sound theory, relies on rigorous research methods, and presents poignant findings. For more than half a century researchers have been conducting experiments, attitudinal surveys, ethnographies, interviews, and mathematical modeling to determine what works and why in all aspects of the marketing world. Not all the findings from research we offer will be relevant to you. In some cases, we present findings that are dated by business standards. We do this for a few reasons. In some cases, the findings are still valid. In other cases, we use a finding to demonstrate that a particular topic has been explored for a long time. Finally, some of the older research demonstrates how much things have changed and as such reinforces the point to conduct new research when it is warranted. However, most of what we present are merely examples from the last 10 to 15 years. There is a lot of research on shopper behavior, environmental and social cues, private label brands and brand equity, product assortments, segmentation, promotions, in-store advertising, mobile marketing, supply chain management, and so forth. Aside from the specific research findings, if you take away one key idea from the findings from research we will have been successful. That one key idea is to find a way to connect with academics conducting research relevant to your business and use them to remain abreast of current scholastic knowledge in the field. Shopper marketing is moving at too great a speed for you to waste time trying to answer questions to which we already know part or all of the answers.

Before we get started, let's remind ourselves of the environment we marketers operate within today.

What Does the Landscape Look Like Today?

Brand management does not look the same as it did 15 years ago. Brand managers now spend a great deal of time not only worried about creating brand awareness and building brand equity with consumers, but also worried about what happens along the path to purchase as consumers turn into shoppers. They worry more about what happens in the retail environment. Brand manufacturers now segment consumers, shoppers, and retailers in entirely new ways as they tease out shopper need states, modes, and profiles.

Account management for consumer brand manufacturers does not look the same as it did either. The sales side of the organization has always tried to connect with the strategies and priorities of specific strategic retailers, but today they coordinate with brand management in greater detail and spend funds on a wider variety of media choices, both inside and outside the store itself. Collaboration is at a higher strategic level than ever before.

Shopper marketing advertising agencies have come into their own. What were smaller, niche firms have now become stars of the show. Shopper marketing agencies find ways to leverage shopper insights and brand equity along the entire path to purchase to connect with precisely targeted shoppers and activate purchases at the point of sale.

Market research now involves a heavy dose of shopper insights work, which differs from consumer research. How people shop for products differs from how they consume them. Although both have always been examined, a far greater emphasis than in the past is now focused on shopper research. Some of the most interesting research is coming out of neurology and behavioral economics. Additionally, "big data," the science of data mining within large datasets (such as transaction data from retailers and loyalty programs), and the firms focused on conducting research in this space, has emerged as an industry in itself. We can now understand and target individual shoppers by the millions, whereas not so long ago we were focused on gross market segmentation—if we segmented at all.

Shoppers and shopping have changed. We now have a plethora of media choices for accessing information about products, services, and other shoppers. Social media alone presents shoppers with hundreds of options for connecting with each other, brands, and retailers. We don't need to list them all here; you know their names because you use them—Facebook, Twitter, Pinterest, Google +, LinkedIn, we could go on and on. Besides, by the time this book hits printing, there will be many more choices. Of particular note: Media space is highly fragmented, and shoppers trust no brand as much as they trust the opinions of others whom they see as "like them." Shopper marketers must tap into this social network as well as leverage and integrate all the other tools they have available, such as websites, mobile device applications, print media, cable, radio, experiential events, and so on to help brands and retailers connect with and converse with target shoppers in relevant ways.

We have different cohorts of shoppers who we must understand and to whom we must pay attention, cohorts like Millennials, multiculturals (in the United States anyway), and the growing Latino market.

All this has created a shopping environment where thematic programs and the hundreds of initiatives they spawn, such as Boxtops for Education, Back-to-School, Family Night In, helping first-time moms learn, or Game Time during the Super Bowl, are the norm. Shopping is expected to be far more experiential and in some cases social. Many of these programs involve more and more technology that does everything from entertain and educate shoppers to assist them in making purchase decisions. Brands are often expected to customize these programs for retailers such that the retailer is differentiated from nearby competitors. These shorter run, customized programs can wreak havoc on supply chain management and sometimes be quite costly. Therefore, more agile supply chains have emerged. Execution of these programs at the store level is problematic to say the least. Efforts to improve on consistent execution are significant. And finally, as the discipline becomes established, many firms are paying careful attention to the measurement of the return on investments made in shopper marketing programs.

As you can see, the marketplace for consumer goods branding, retailing, and shopping is extremely dynamic. However, successful processes for consistently developing impactful and profitable shopper marketing programs exist, and we present them in this book. We hope you gain as much out of this material as we think you will.

1

Shopper Marketing Overview

What in the world is this thing called *shopper marketing*? Is it yet another industry buzzword? Is it another name for what we have always referred to as merchandising, so just about marketing in a store? Is it a practice limited to the grocery products, consumer packaged goods, or fast moving consumer goods context since many of the examples seem to come from there? Isn't this actually more of the same stuff we already know? No, no, no, and no. However, these questions and more like them made us realize the industry needs a book and training to establish standard base-line knowledge of what shopper marketing is and how it gets done for professionals moving into shopper marketing roles. For best practitioners, shopper marketing is a corporate go-to-market strategy that impacts wide swaths of the corporation. Shopper marketing affects brand management, research (both subject matter and methodology), relationships between brand manufacturers and retailers, and, importantly, operational execution throughout retail supply/demand chains. It is important that all these constituencies have a clear and uniform understanding of what shopper marketing is and what is required to do it well. This first chapter provides an overview to get us started.

First and foremost, shopper marketing is a strategy, not a tactic. When positioned as a cross-functional corporate strategy, it provides the framework for marketing to consumers as they morph into a shopping mindset along a virtual *path to purchase* that every consumer follows en route to making a final purchase decision, whether online or in a retail store.

Let's take a deeper look at this thought because it encompasses some of the core concepts of shopper marketing:

- What is meant when we say "consumers as they morph into a shopper mindset"? A key concept of shopper marketing is that a shift in mindset occurs when a consumer moves from "I want…" or "I need…" to the decision-making process of determining where and what to buy and the accompanying trade-offs that define the value equation of purchasing. While the consumer and shopper are often the same person, the thought processes in each role are different.

- What is meant by the phrase "virtual path to purchase"? You may be familiar with the phrase *path to purchase* or *purchase funnel* or *shopper's journey* in your marketing work. Each of these, in shopper marketing, refers to the possible virtual steps that a potential shopper takes in developing a consideration set of *what* to buy and *where* to buy, researching attributes (both product and retail), and making a purchase decision. This path varies by person, by product, and by shopping occasion and is rarely linear. Also included in the shopper marketing path to purchase is the physical path that a shopper takes to effectuate the purchase itself—and the marketing opportunities to communicate with the shopper along that path.

- Frequently confused in the lexicon of shopper marketing is the difference between the shopper's virtual path to purchase and the marketing path to purchase. The virtual path to purchase refers to a decision process—essentially mapping how the shopper thinks and what decision points she uses in making the ultimate decision. The marketing path to purchase is what marketers use to segment these decision points and communicate with the shopper as she is going through her virtual path. Thus, the marketing path to purchase is relatively simple and comprises four segments: at home, en route, in store, and post-purchase. This is an important concept to understand because these four delineations enable marketers to determine what, how, and where to message. Conversely, if one attempts to do this based on the virtual path to purchase—the map of the shopper's thought processes—the result will always be consistent frustration and even paralysis because the possible permutations run into the billions. Therefore, in this book, we are always going to refer to the marketing path to purchase and use this as the basis for all marketing proposals and solutions.

- *Purchase decision* acknowledges that a decision on what a shopper ultimately decides to buy is often subject to influence along the path and, especially, at the point of sale. Thus, it is the objective of every marketer to leverage the awareness that its advertising has built by maintaining top of mind awareness of its product and benefits along the shopper's virtual path to purchase, ultimately resulting in the shopper's decision to buy its brand at the point of sale—whether online or in a brick-and-mortar store.

- Online? Even if all shopping were to go online and, hypothetically, brick-and-mortar stores were to disappear, the principles of shopper marketing would still apply. It is about meeting the needs of the shopper while in a shopper mode, not about a location. Shopper marketing goes well beyond the doors of the store. It is, in our opinion, marketing *to a shopper* not marketing *in a store*.

For retailers, shopper marketing provides the opportunity to grow sales and profits by differentiating from competing retailers on a basis other than price alone. For manufacturers, shopper marketing provides a means of "winning" at the point of sale by creating programs carefully tailored to the needs and interests of specific retailers and specific shopper segments within those retailers. The unique thing about shopper marketing is that both retailers and manufacturers have a vested interest in making it work, not only for themselves, but for each other.

Shopper marketing is not a niche nor an add-on. It has become an integral part of marketing today. It got started in response to the realization both by manufacturers and retailers that traditional marketing and merchandising approaches were no longer working—for either constituency. It has evolved to become—in the best of cases—a collaborative effort between retailer and brand to reach out and provide a superior shopping experience to the mutual target shopper.

In reality, bits and pieces of shopper marketing have been with us for a long time. Industry experts just did not name it as such, and it was not always conducted in a strategic, holistic way; the way it is today by world class shopper marketing organizations. It looks unique right now, and you must understand how it looks and why it is critical to your success—right now. Once you learn the foundational concepts, you will be able to leverage that knowledge forever—or at least as long as people shop.

A Brief History

To understand why best practice manufacturers currently position shopper marketing as they do, it is important to go back and understand how shopper marketing got started. Like most inventions, it was born out of necessity—for both product manufacturers and retailers. Toward the end of the twentieth century, manufacturers were faced with the unpleasant fact that traditional methods of getting consumers to buy their brands weren't working as effectively or as efficiently anymore. Cable TV, the Internet, and the DVR had disrupted the effectiveness and efficiency of tried-and-true network advertising. The traditional target for most product manufacturers—moms with kids—was shrinking as the population aged and family building was delayed. Additionally, these "moms with kids" were more difficult to reach with far more mothers in the workforce, more single moms, and growing ethnic diversity.

Retailers were faced with enormous challenges of their own. America was over-stored—too many stores and too few consumers—and rampant stock keeping unit (SKU) proliferation meant that there were also too many items in these stores. The catchword of the day was *channel blurring*—that is, mass availability of the same items in different channels—which prompted blast furnace competition among channels with different business models. And a host of new competitive channels were springing up and rapidly growing. Warehouse clubs, supercenters, and dollar stores—the *value discounters*—were in ascendancy. Traditional channels such as supermarkets, drug stores, and mass merchandisers saw share (and stores) decline. In fact, supermarkets lost 29 share points between 1998 and 2005,[1] and the average annual number of trips to supermarkets dropped from 85 in 1998 to 72 in 2003.[2]

Despite these issues—in fact, most likely *because* of these issues—three key building blocks for shopper marketing emerged. The first was *partnering,* a concept that recognized that manufacturer and retailer had some common interests and could benefit from a relationship that went beyond the transactional nature of buyer-seller. While the initial focus was primarily in building efficiencies, especially supply chain, this resulted in both significant collaboration and a better understanding of the issues and needs of the other. Procter & Gamble and Walmart became the most visible champions of partnering as P&G put 110 nonsales personnel in northwest Arkansas to service Walmart.

The second building block was *co-marketing,* a concept developed by Chris Hoyt in 1993 that encouraged manufacturers and retailers to work together to advertise and promote to their mutual consumer for topline growth. The premise was that the *consumer*, not cost cutting, was the strategic starting point. If they could leverage the manufacturer's reach, frequency, and brand loyalty in behalf of individual retailers to attract and hold *new consumers* and leverage the retailer's customer count and store visit frequency to sell more of the manufacturer's product to *current customers*, then both parties would benefit. They could focus on growing the pie rather than making a shrinking pie more efficient.

The third building block was retailer consolidation. One solution to the financial pressures caused by the growth of value discounters was for traditional retailers to seek out efficiencies of scale. The 1990s was a decade of retail mergers. Between 1995 and 2005, the share of the Top 10 supermarkets grew from 33% to 51%[3] of US supermarket sales. While consolidation did not prove to be a panacea, it did allow retailers the opportunity to experiment with ways to draw traffic and/or increase loyalty to their stores. Plus, the volume that these larger retailers sold made account-specific executions more likely to deliver the required return on investment (ROI) for manufacturers.

Two seminal moments are frequently credited for the birth of shopper marketing. The first was in 2003 when P&G's CEO A. G. Lafley articulated two "moments of truth" for a brand. The first moment of truth was the point at the retail shelf when a consumer would choose to buy or not buy the company's product. The second moment of truth was when a consumer first used that product and decided whether it fully satisfied his needs. This concept turned the consumer packaged goods (CPG) industry on its ear. Procter & Gamble—the largest CPG advertiser—acknowledged that, despite the advertising, product innovation, and brand loyalty that these engendered, the hand of the consumer at the retail shelf could waver. If the company could not get that consumer to buy its brand when at the retail shelf, the consumer would not have a chance to appreciate the investment the company made in innovation and quality. P&G brands now had to "win" at the point of sale—the "first moment of truth."

Meanwhile, TNS NFO, the merged market research firms of Taylor Nelson Sofres and the NFO Worldgroup that they acquired in 2003, on behalf of the Coca-Cola Retailing Research Council of North America, was busily researching and segmenting shoppers for the groundbreaking study *The World According to Shoppers* unveiled at the Food Marketing Institute (FMI) Annual Convention in 2004. The study "focused on developing a deeper understanding of the needs experienced by contemporary consumers, rather than competition among supermarkets—because in the world according to shoppers, there are many places to grocery shop."[4] This work brought the idea of meeting the needs of consumers—and understanding shopper motivations—into high relief for retailers as well as manufacturers.

It didn't take long before retailers understood they could build their own brand equity much like the brands do. Today, the fragmentation of consumer media, the ubiquitous availability of products, and the explosive change of technology advancements continues with the result that much of the power is squarely in the hands of the shopper, and she is demanding to be part of the conversation.[5]

There are real pioneers in shopper marketing—Procter & Gamble in conceptual development; Unilever in shopper understanding; Frito-Lay's segmentation work is state of the art. Food Lion and Walmart in their shopper segmentation work also come immediately to mind, but there are many more in every area of shopper marketing—all of whom have contributed greatly to making shopper marketing the mainstream go-to-market discipline that it is today.

The bottom line is that shopper marketing has become known as a more sophisticated way in which manufacturers and retailers are collaborating to develop marketing strategies and both pre-store and in-store initiatives that are wins for both. So let's see what this thing called shopper marketing really is.

Shopper Marketing Defined

Many people want to know "exactly" what shopper marketing is. Numerous definitions have been put forth, and shopper marketing is changing all of the time, and as such, its definition. Nestlé U.S.A. might have said it most directly when it defined shopper marketing once as:

"Shopper marketing is understanding how our target consumers behave as shoppers in different channels and formats and leveraging this intelligence via strategies and initiatives that result in balanced benefits to all stakeholders—our brands, our key retailers and the mutual shopper."

Although Deloitte examined numerous definitions such as this and offered its own in a report jointly developed with the Grocery Manufacturers Association (GMA), the Nestlé one is a good one, and the key is to understand what we are discussing when we say we are talking about shopper marketing.

We believe shopper marketing is the combination of *all* the influences a marketer can bring to bear on one's target shopper as he decides what, when, and where to purchase. It requires an understanding of the consumer as shopper, of what it takes to influence that shopper and the most effective means of doing so. But that's not all. It also requires an understanding of retail and how it works, of the strategies, objectives, and executional capabilities of specific retailers and how to prioritize and negotiate for mutual benefit. To work best, shopper marketing is linked to marketing and to sales and often to operations. It is integrated into brand plans and key account plans. It is budgeted and measured. And it provides a real opportunity to make good stuff happen for the brand, the retailer, and the shopper.

Because of this complexity and the need for clear understanding across different functions, that best practice shopper marketing is built on objectives and standards; it is not "liquid" nor desultory. Following are the six key objectives for shopper marketing that practitioners need to keep in mind as they develop shopper marketing initiatives:

1. Make it easy for the mutual shopper to find and buy your brands.
2. Extend the equity of your brands along the entire path to purchase.
3. Provide a source of differentiation for both your brands and participating retailers.
4. Activate purchase at the point of sale (POS) by delighting, engaging, and motivating shoppers beyond their expectations.
5. Align with the opportunities, strategies, and protocols of different channels, formats, and retailers.
6. Provide mutually balanced benefits over time to all constituents—retailer, brand, and shopper.

Let's look at these objectives in a bit more depth as they are the cornerstone of effective shopper marketing initiatives.

The first objective—make it easy for the mutual shopper to find and buy your brands—sounds so easy. In fact, as you will learn, many things stand in the way of your shopper finding your brand and then determining whether it is the right brand for her. Making it easy to find requires one to understand what issue the shopper is trying to solve—is she looking specifically for your brand or for your category or is she looking for ideas. Let's say you sell canned chili. If the shopper is looking specifically for your brand, all you have to do is make sure she knows what stores carry it, where it is within the store, and that it "pops" on the shelf. If she's looking for the chili category, you may need to direct her to your brand from the deli department or the frozen department where she might go first to buy chili. If she is looking for ideas for lunch, you may need to entice her to consider your chili when she is not even going down the aisle where it is shelved. And if she needs inspiration while shopping, you might want to tell her how good a chili omelet would taste while she is buying her eggs. Making it easy to buy means that you have answered whatever questions she might have about your product and whether it is the right choice for her at this time. Does she understand how to prepare your product or how it works? Does she have the tools to use it? Have you communicated the value of your product in terms that are relevant to the shopper? Can that shopper choose your brand with confidence and leave the store feeling like a smart shopper?

The second objective—extend the equities of your brand along the entire path to purchase—speaks to Mr. Lafley's first moment of truth. Marketing cannot be one-dimensional and certainly cannot stop at the door of the store. The shopper needs to be reminded of why she loves your brand no matter where along the path to purchase she is. Are you reminding her when she is making out her list? Are you reminding her when she is online researching products or stores or looking for coupons? Are you reminding her when she checks her smartphone for ideas or asks friends or "experts" for recommendations? In addition, are you leveraging the equities of your retailer when selling your product in the store? To do any of this, one needs to have a clear understanding of the equities that are important to your shopper and the decision points and media choices that impact her decision.

The provide a source of differentiation for both your brand and participating retailers objective means that your brand and/or your retailer stand out from the pack in the eyes of your shopper—and for a reason *other than price* alone. This can mean creating a superior shopping experience or value-added events or exclusive offers. We have seen initiatives that tie in with specific charities, celebrate local sports teams, target specific shopper segments, or support local schools. Understanding what both your brand and your retailer are already famous for can help you identify differentiation opportunities that ring true with the shopper.

Activate purchase by delighting, engaging, and motivating the mutual shopper reminds us that the goal of shopper marketing is to get the product into the shopping basket—*today*. We are most able to succeed at this when we develop an emotional connection with the shopper in addition to the rational reason to buy.

The fifth objective—align with the opportunities, strategies, and protocols of different channels, formats, and retailers—speaks to the benefits of collaboration and reminds us of the need to understand the expectations shoppers have of different channels and how this should be reflected in shopper marketing initiatives. It also reminds us to be mindful of retailer protocols, not just out of respect but to allocate spending wisely.

The final objective is to provide mutually balanced benefits over time to all constituents—retailer, brand, and shopper. In some respects, this is a self-correcting objective. When shopper marketing programs are totally brand focused, the retailer simply won't approve them; when totally retailer focused, shopper marketing funding dries up. That said, some initiatives in your plan work more to the retailer's benefit and some more to the benefit of the brand (and if they don't benefit the shopper, they don't work at all). The goal is to achieve a balance over time.

We see these objectives translated into action in various chapters throughout the book. However, these objectives are merely a foundational orientation. We need a process, or more accurately, a set of processes, to *do* shopper marketing. At the process level, this involves

1. **Opportunity identification**—Situation assessment, right targets, right insights
2. **Planning**—Right strategies, right initiatives, and right customer plan
3. **Execution**—Collaboration, agency empowerment, reporting results, supply chain and operational execution
4. **Measure-Learn-Change**—Internal, external, continuous improvement

Much of this book is dedicated to walking you through every detail of this four-stage process. So, shopper marketing is about brand manufacturers working with specific retailers to help differentiate both the manufacturer's brand and the retailer *as a brand* or destination of choice. It involves collaborating for generating insights to shoppers—consumers when in a shopping mode, collaborating on strategic intent, planning initiatives with long-term strategy in mind, creating an organization that can do this effectively, using supply chain management in a way that integrates both demand and supply management resources, and does all this with high ROI for the retailer and manufacturers in question. Yes, it is most definitely about making sales, but it is also about equity; that is, leveraging brand equity, building retailer equity.

Let's See It!

What do you see when you look at shopper marketing? When you see an initiative in the store, there are some hallmark giveaway signs. What you don't see is all the work that goes into an initiative or how each individual initiative connects with many others happening within the store at that time and planned for the future. What you *can* notice is this:

- Packaging, signage, and displays all work together to stop you in your tracks, hold your attention, and compel you to buy. It is engaging and experiential.
- The initiative usually demonstrates that this particular brand has partnered with this particular retailer for this initiative, which may include several noncompeting brands as well as a social cause of some kind such as breast cancer awareness, education, or local support. This may mean multiple logos on packaging and displays.
- The initiative demonstrates a solution to a shopper's problem, for example, snacking in a healthy way, coordinating a Super Bowl party, managing the child lunch preparation routine, fixing a home, or creating an audio-visual entertainment center in the home.

As you look at shopper marketing initiatives in practice, it is worthwhile to ask yourself how that initiative meets one or more of the shopper marketing objectives.

Eight Principles of Shopper Marketing

The eight principles of shopper marketing lay a foundation for shopper marketing and how it can successfully be integrated into the organization, especially with respect to marketing, sales, and collaboration with retail customers.

Principle 1: Top Down Understanding and Commitment

Shopper marketing involves strategic partnerships between brand manufacturers and their specific retail customers. It involves marketing platforms or themes, under which numerous initiatives are created, such as teaching the first-time mom about a specific child development stage. Within those initiatives are relevant brands communicating with target shoppers at many touchpoints inside and outside stores. These integrated marketing campaigns developed between strategic partners are at the resource level, requiring commitment from senior leaders within each partner organization. Every initiative may not require senior leadership sign-off, but the overall shopper focus, platforms, and themes do. The research, planning, execution, and measurement involved demand input—and in some cases resources—from numerous departments across multiple organizations.

Principle 2: Shopper and Business Insights

Shopper marketing today is driven significantly by shopper and business insights. Both the word "shopper" and the word "insights" are critical here. Research into shoppers is different from research into consumers. It certainly builds upon traditional consumer research and in a scholastic sense can be seen as a subset of consumer behavior research. But where consumer research traditionally focuses on what end users think about, feel, and do (i.e., cognitions, emotions, and behaviors) while consuming the product, shopper research focuses on those consumers when they are in one of numerous shopping modes. Consumer behavior at its broadest addresses attitudes, emotions, and behaviors individually and in groups: from first conceiving of a product or service need, through the entire purchase process, and on to actual consumption and disposition. There is enormous scholastic consumer behavior research available to jumpstart one's insight process, although the dynamic nature of consumer and shopping behavior does mean there is always a great deal more to learn—especially as technology and "big data" open new vistas. Although shopper marketing research tends to focus on the consumer when he is in what is referred to as *shopper mode*, the best shopper marketers understand the entire human being, with an emphasis on *being*. What are people like as they live their lives using and shopping for products? What are the needs that underlie and drive purchase? While shopper marketing does require a deep and detailed understanding of how people shop and why, it's more of a shift in focus to provide intense scrutiny to shopping but not at the expense of the entire consumption process.

The second word, "insights," has specific meaning as well. Firms focusing on shopper marketing want unique insights to their shoppers, not facts or data. For example, data that say men between the ages of 18 and 25 purchase milk and beer at a convenience store an average of two+ times per week may be a "fact;" the notion that these men see the convenience store as their refrigerators is closer to an insight. Insights get into the psyche and behavior of shoppers in a deep way. They get at what shopping *means* to people, *motivations* for certain shopping behaviors, be they conscious, or more these days, unconscious. Insights are like epiphanies or "aha!" moments.

Shopper insight development demands a triangulation of many forms of research, such as ethnography from anthropology, depth interviews from psychology and social psychology, surveys, experiments, complex observational methods, behavioral economics, and neurology. It requires a sophisticated eye toward human behavior because the low hanging fruit has been picked. Basic demographics and overall brand attitude research simply won't cut it anymore. That being said, the importance of gender differences has been shown recently through numerous industry and scholastic works involving neurology to be a powerful predictor of certain kinds of attitudes and emotions in the shopping context. Some brand manufacturers are world class at this kind of research as are several agencies. Both augment their own research with that from firms such as The Nielsen Company, Symphony IRI, Kantar Retail, dunnhumby, and consultants, for example, Deloitte, Booz and Company, and many, many more like them. There is a cottage industry of smaller shopper insight—focused firms such as Decision Insights and experts such as Michelle Adams of Marketing Brainology—just two examples of many exciting, fast growing sources of expertise in the field. Shopper insights seem to be the sexy part of shopper marketing if the sheer volume of experts, conferences, and reports is any indicator. But let us not forget that business insights play critical roles as well. We cover how insights get generated later in this book.

Principle 3: Collaboration

Let's face it, tension has long existed between retailers and manufacturers; it has existed for a long time and will likely continue to exist. Part of this is due to the different ways manufacturers and retailers view their business models, objectives, financial processes, consumer segments, and the inherent tension that comes in any supply chain when some parties have greater power than others. Conflict over the use of trade dollars has become a major and well-publicized specific point. We cover some of the details here within the chapters on how consumer goods manufacturers work and how retailers work. Our objective is not to resolve this longstanding conflict, but to describe how in some cases shopper marketing has become incredibly successful *because* the players have found constructive ways to manage this tension and develop new ways of collaborating both inside and outside the store for mutual wins. The way manufacturers and retailers—as well as other firms such as agencies, agents, and brokers—are interacting, sharing information, developing customized consumer and shopper research projects, customizing product packaging and, in some cases, even products is unique today. The coordination across programs throughout the year within specific, strategically selected partnerships is deeper than it has been in the past, demanding significantly different skill sets on the part of brand managers, account managers, front-line managers, merchandisers, retailer operations managers, and so on. Firms that embrace a strategic view of shopper marketing adopt a collaborative orientation that goes beyond words.

Align Needs and Priorities of Stakeholders

When we say that collaboration and supply chain management are key principles, what actually gets done often deals with alignment of stakeholder interests. Who are the stakeholders? Within each organization are specific departments such as marketing, sales, manufacturing, and logistics. At the organizational level, there are manufacturers, retailers, brokers, and agencies. Each has specific priorities and objectives for the short and long term. For shopper marketing to work, the difficult process of getting these all in alignment must occur first. There must be commitment from the top of each organization or programs will fail.

Help Retailers Solve Their Business Problems

Shopper marketing has primarily been a brand manufacturer-driven concept, and as such, after organizational alignment is reached, manufacturers spend significant time trying to deeply understand and resolve specific retailer problems and help manage demand appropriately with specific target shoppers. Often, it is a specific retailer problem that leads brand manufacturers to develop shopper marketing initiatives.

Share Ownership of Process and Input

While within problem resolution, managers develop processes that work uniquely for their business relationships. Ownership for input to and management of these processes must be shared. All stakeholders need to commit resources. Shopper marketing programs are not simply a manufacturer's responsibility to be "delivered to" retailers. Nor are they entirely retailer conceptualizations "demanded of" the lowest bidding vendors.

Find the Right Partners to Ensure That 1+1 > 2

Collaboration is a principle. Selecting the right partners is a process step. Manufacturers must select the right agencies, retailers, and brokers (if appropriate) with whom to work. Likewise, retailers need to select the right manufacturers and brokers with whom to work. Shopper marketing program management is far too complex and resource intensive to be done at the same level with all partners. There is plenty to go around. Managers must think carefully about their partner organizations. They ought to create specific criteria that are used to evaluate the shopper marketing partnership potential of other organizations. One set of criteria used by agencies and manufacturers to evaluate the other is *The Hub Top 20* annual survey, which asks thousands of agency personnel to rank the best manufacturer partners and manufacturers to rank the best agency partners.

If this step is taken seriously, the result is greater than the sum of its parts. Together, the partnerships generate insights and programs that neither one could have brought to the table alone.

Principle 4: Transform Need into Demand

Shopper marketing is about demand management. It is not merely about demand generation. Higher demand is not always the best solution. However, increased demand for specific offerings at specific points in time as well as the implied opposite, reduced demand for other offerings, is a key objective of shopper marketing. Shopper marketing is about closing the deal. If sales lift as well as enhanced brand equity for the manufacturer and retailer do not accrue, shopper marketing is irrelevant.

Principle 5: Strategy Then Tactics

The fifth principle of successful shopper marketing is that it is firstly strategic. Setting up a unique display in one store that combines a few complementary products for Thanksgiving or the Super Bowl and placing them on sale is a tactic and one that has been used for as long as retailing has been around. Collaborative research on specific target shoppers by a specific brand manufacturer, developing relevant insights, modifying products specifically for that retailer based on these insights, developing a number of programs that run at specific times throughout the year possibly being altered at certain stores based on regional differences, and sharing in the profits these unique programs generate, requires strategic commitment from the top of the respective organizations and strategic planning and execution. Initiatives run under thematic platforms. Strategies lead to specific tactics. They need to do so if consistent growth, significant returns on the investments, and long-term customer lifetime value are to emerge. The only way to think about shopper marketing in the long term is strategic first, then tactics.

The strategic orientation is the only one that leads to thinking about changing organizational structure to effectively plan and execute shopper marketing. Specifically, some firms place shopper marketing responsibility within sales and others within marketing. Sometimes the shopper insights component is placed within market research, sometimes sales, and sometimes brand management. There is great debate over where shopper marketing "best" fits. We have seen effective shopper marketing from all forms of organizational structures, even if most of them come from those where shopper marketing is housed in marketing departments. The point is that only a strategic orientation toward shopper marketing gets an organization thinking through the issues.

Principle 6: Measurement

If one of the hallmarks of shopper marketing is an excitement for shopper insights, another is the heated debate over measurement. Despite firms being dissatisfied with current measurement of traditional marketing efforts outside the store, such as advertising in its many forms of media, salesperson effectiveness, and now even digital, the industry has accepted less than optimal metrics that estimate reach and frequency like GRPs (gross rating points) and so forth. There has been a strong push in the last decade toward accountability though in trying to connect investments in sales and marketing to sales lift and profitability. This has proven to be a bit of a difficult nut to crack even for advanced mathematical modelers conducting marketing mix modeling because there are so many variables that affect the outcome, yet only a limited amount of time and, frankly, need to gather, analyze, and respond to the data. Shopper marketing adds another level of complexity to the problem.

The store is now considered another form of media. In reality, a retail store houses many forms of media. Yet the effectiveness of their application (in isolation or in combinations) is not yet measured well by retailers or manufacturers. When we say "not measured well" we mean not measured precisely enough. A positive aspect to this is that media in the store are closest in a temporal (i.e., time) sense to actual purchases, and so have the potential to be the most correlated marketing actions with purchase behavior. A downside is the difficulty in collecting the data to be analyzed. Marketing "audiences" need to be thought of differently in store than out because the nature of the distractions, the time spent becoming aware of and processing information, and the mindset of shoppers differ significantly from that of consumers reading a magazine in a doctor's office, watching a television show, or driving to work. But they are still most definitely an audience. The attributes we discuss and connect to all kinds of measurement issues include in-store signage, digital and otherwise, in-store product demonstrations, shelf placement, assortment, facings, packaging, solution centers, co-branding, secondary placements, and more. We address multiple ways of collecting data that attempt to capture how many shoppers actually see, process, and act on specific media—from video mining, to heat maps, and emergent GPS technology. The primary point is that firms concerned with shopper marketing are thinking a lot about measuring the short- and long-term costs and impact; that is, the ROI, of these efforts. Understand, the effort involved in effective shopper marketing programs can be significant. As such, there must be a commensurate return on these investments and an understanding of how shopper marketing spending compares to marketing alternatives. If we do not measure the effects precisely, we will draw inaccurate conclusions.

Principle 7: Supply Chain Management

A hidden key to shopper marketing success is supply chain management, yet few firms recognize this. It is nowhere near as sexy as shopper insights, but it can be far more impactful. Think about it. Let's say that Frito-Lay wants to create a special event within Kroger in partnership with DreamWorks to launch a new DVD release on a specific date nationally. At the same time, Frito-Lay wants to help Walgreens and CVS differentiate from each other through unique programs at those retailers, as well as unique programs at Walmart and Target because, after all, shopper marketing from the manufacturer's perspective is about working with specific retailers to help them differentiate themselves from their competitor retailers as well as leverage their own brand equity to effect sales and profitability. Getting unique products to specific locations cost-effectively creates all sorts of supply chain challenges. Remember, margins in consumer packaged goods are often slim. The challenges include, but are not limited to, forecasting, packaging, transportation, inventory management, in-store product display management and control, and distribution network solutions. We are now talking about the potential for far more SKUs being launched and for short periods of time in an era where SKU reduction and longer production runs are the charge. This also can result in significant interfunctional tension between marketing, sales, logistics, and production as well as interorganizational tension. We address these challenges in their own chapter in this book. For now realize that the most advanced shopper marketing organizations recognize the critical importance of agile supply chain management in executing what are now far more complex and unique programs consistently throughout the year.

Principle 8: Value for the Manufacturer, Retailer, and Shopper

The eighth principle of shopper marketing is that there is an orientation toward creating value for all parties involved. This may sound like an idealistic philosophy, but it is not. If manufacturers, retailers, and shoppers do not all feel as if shopper marketing efforts are worth it, shopper marketing will revert to traditional forms of retailing. But what does "value" mean? It just so happens that there is extensive research on what consumers, shoppers, and business organizations value from products, services, and the people/firms who provide them. Value means far more than the simplistic mid-to-low price range depiction much of marketing likes to portray. When someone says that a shopping experience or a product she has purchased is valuable or is a good value, she doesn't only mean that she obtained a lot for a little amount of money. She means that all the benefits, for example, experiential, emotional, and practical, were worth the time, effort, and money she invested in it. She means that in specific use occasions, it was worth it. Given her specific values, it was worth it. Given all other alternatives at that point in time, it was worth it. Shoppers today actually want far more input into product and service design and execution than they did in the past. And value is only determined in the eyes of the user. These concepts are often referred to as co-production and co-creation of value. We discuss these notions of value creation throughout this book.

The same holds true for retailers when they describe vendor relationships; that is, the benefits they gain by working with a specific supplier exceed the costs in time, effort, and monetary resources invested in the relationship more than the alternatives do. Similarly, manufacturers evaluate the value of their retailer relationships and segment them accordingly into strategic accounts, key accounts, and more transactional accounts. They have to because resources are limited. Shopper marketing approached strategically has the potential to increase the value each party brings to others in the relationship.

Given this set of foundational principles of shopper marketing, let's take a look at the process world-class shopper marketing organizations use to actually do shopper marketing. Although each organization has its own, internally developed processes, what we present here is a time-tested approach that captures the best of what we have observed working with companies.

A Process of Doing Shopper Marketing

This book builds on and explains the eight foundation principles through a specific four-stage process for actually doing shopper marketing. This process is depicted in Figure 1-1.

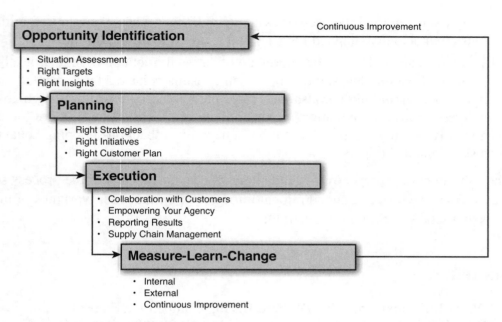

Figure 1-1 *The shopper marketing process.*

Interesting Findings from Research

As we explained in the introduction, we are including short interesting findings from hundreds of scholastic research studies at the end of many chapters. Again, not all of them will be directly relevant to you. We present them to reinforce the message that research is being conducted at universities everywhere that may be helpful to you. Here are just a few examples to get us started.

1. Shopping can be for personal motives, such as role playing (household care-giver), a diversion, fulfillment of self-gratification, learning about trends, exercise, and sensory stimulation. Shopping can be for social motives, such as social experiences outside the home, communication with others having a similar interest, peer group attraction, status and authority, and the pleasure of bargain hunting. (This study is quite old—1972! It demonstrates that we have been study-ing shopping for a while. Yet far too often, practitioners remain unaware of the research and as such, fail to leverage it.)[6]

2. The average correlation between what consumers know (objective knowledge) and what they think they know (subjective/perceived knowledge) about various products, service, and other marketing contexts is .37.[7]

3. Individuals reported themselves as shopping longer when exposed to familiar music but actually shopped longer when exposed to unfamiliar music.[8]

4. When consumers have a recreational motivational orientation, high arousal has a positive effect on pleasantness, but when consumers have a task-oriented motivational orientation, high arousal decreases pleasantness. In addition, high arousal increases consumer intentions to visit and make purchases in the store for recreationally oriented shoppers, but it has a negative impact on shopping behavior for task-oriented shoppers.[9]

The subsequent chapters cover foundational concepts and each of the process steps in great detail as well as present additional information on the inner workings of manufacturers and retailers. So let's get started!

Endnotes

1   Willard Bishop Consulting, Willard Bishop Competitive Edge, The Future of Food Retailing, industry presentation of June 1999-2006 calculations.

2   *The World According to Shoppers*, (2004), The Coca Cola Company, industry report: https://ccrrc.org/wp-content/uploads/2012/09/World_According_to_Shoppers_2004.pdf.

3   Hoyt & Co. presentation, calculated from Progressive Grocer Marketing Guidebooks, 1996-2006.

4   *The World According to Shoppers*, (2004), The Coca Cola Company, industry report: https://ccrrc.org/wp-content/uploads/2012/09/World_According_to_Shoppers_2004.pdf.

5   Hoyt & Co. presentation based on annual survey Hoyt & Co. conducts.

6   Tauber, Edward M. (1972), "Why Do People Shop?" *Journal of Marketing*, 36 (4), 46-49.

7   Carlson, Jay P., Leslie H. Vincent, David M. Hardesty, and William O. Bearden (2009), "Objective and Subjective Knowledge Relationships: A Quantitative Analysis of Consumer Research Findings," *Journal of Consumer Research*, 35 (5), 864-876.

8   Yalch, Richard F. and Eric R. Spangenberg (2000), "The Effects of Music in a Retail Setting on Real and Perceived Shopping Times," *Journal of Business Research*, 49 (2), 139-147.

9   Kaltcheva, Velitchka D. and Barton A. Weitz (2006), "When Should a Retailer Create an Exciting Store Environment?" *Journal of Marketing*, 70 (1), 107–118.

2

Who Is the Shopper Anyway?

Understanding the shopper is the *core* of shopper marketing. Understanding what is necessary for brands and retailers to do to attract a shopper and then to trigger purchase is its essence. There is a school of thought that says that shopper marketing should focus on the category because that is the only area of common interest between retailers and brands. We disagree. Our belief is that the *shopper* is the primary area of common interest between retailers and brands. Shopper marketing is about establishing connections with that shopper—both rational and emotional. We have seen folks wearing T-shirts, lying on beach towels, and playing with toys bearing the logos of Coke or Pepsi or Red Bull. Have you seen anyone in a T-shirt trumpeting the "Carbonated Soft Drinks" category? Many people have developed a tacit emotional connection with Charmin or Cottonelle. Do you have an emotional connection with the toilet tissue category? When shopper marketing is about the shopper, it is far bigger than a single category. It can be used cross-category to grow the shopper's basket size or broaden the average number of categories shopped. It can be used to build the retailer's brand as well as category sales. When shopper marketing is about the category, its focus is on the relationship brands and retailers have with each other. When shopper marketing is about the shopper, it's about building the relationship that both retailer and brand have with that shopper. Our belief is that *that* is where the focus belongs—let's make sure we keep the shopper as the centerpiece of shopper marketing.

So, who is the *shopper*? The shopper is a consumer with a predisposition to buy. He is in what we call *shopper mode*.

He is the person you want to buy your products, the person who will choose your brand over competition, the person who will determine whether you are providing value relevant to his needs at a given point in time. The shopper is not just the person at the cash register in the store. The shopper is also the person clipping coupons, doing research, checking the pantry, making a list. The shopper may go to a store or shop online. He may be browsing or in a rush, buying products for the household or for himself or for others, stocking up or picking up just one item. What distinguishes a shopper is the thought process.

While the consumer and shopper may be the same person, what influences the shopper is different from what influences the consumer. The consumer, thumbing through a magazine or watching TV, sees a product and, if it piques her interest, may listen or read enough about the product to create a desire. The product is then in her consideration set. When the consumer morphs into shopper mode, more concrete and practical considerations take over: Does this store carry that product? Where is it in the store? How much does it cost? Do I really need this right now? The *shopper* makes the decision among multiple products in the consideration set—or none at all.

Again, the consumer and shopper are often the same person but with different thought processes: The distinctions move beyond the definitions of consuming versus purchasing and into how we market to them. As marketers, we tend to focus more on influencing *attitude* in the consumer and on influencing *behavior* in the shopper. How we influence *attitude* is more through advertising/word of mouth and product performance, and the consumer is presented the benefits of one brand. For shoppers, we influence behavior more through stimuli across the path to purchase including in-store stimuli and a positive value equation. In this process, it is important to understand that the shopper views our brand as one of many in her consideration set. We can, for example, create the desire for Campbell's Soup as a lunch alternative with a beautiful ad, but when the shopper is in the store, other products and even other categories are competing for that shopper's lunch.

It's because of these differences—and how easily the wavering hand of a shopper can be drawn to another brand—that we need to understand our brands' consumers as shoppers, as shown in Figure 2-1.

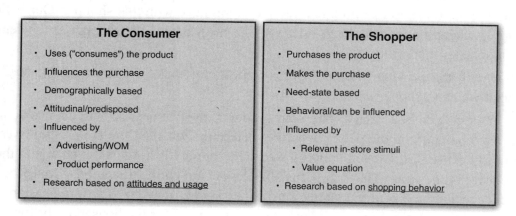

The Consumer
- Uses ("consumes") the product
- Influences the purchase
- Demographically based
- Attitudinal/predisposed
- Influenced by
  - Advertising/WOM
  - Product performance
- Research based on <u>attitudes and usage</u>

The Shopper
- Purchases the product
- Makes the purchase
- Need-state based
- Behavioral/can be influenced
- Influenced by
  - Relevant in-store stimuli
  - Value equation
- Research based on <u>shopping behavior</u>

Figure 2-1 *Consumer versus shopper.*

Learning about the Shopper

If there is one area within marketing where a great deal of scholastic and practitioner research has been done, it is in the area of consumer behavior. Many years of extremely rigorous research from every angle imaginable using every method available has revealed useful insights to all aspects of consumers, from product conceptualization through purchase, use, and disposal. We have sophisticated consumer decision-making models that accurately depict processes for all sorts of people. Segmentation, attitude, emotional, and many other models have become advanced. Some of this research has focused on shopping behavior specifically. For example, Paco Underhill's work *Why We Buy* is one of many books well known by both academics and practitioners for detailed anthropologically driven observational work in stores. Similarly, Herb Sorensen has spent more than 40 years studying shopping behavior. Spread throughout the top journals in marketing, such as *The Journal of Consumer Research*, *The Journal of Marketing*, and *The Journal of Marketing Research,* as well as other research books and textbooks, there is a wealth of knowledge on how and why consumers and shoppers do what they do.

So then why is shopper insight work gaining so much attention these days? Why is this area of research seen as so crucial to effective shopper marketing? Why are firms pursuing every piece of knowledge they can get their hands on related to shoppers? There are likely a number of reasons. Part of this interest is due to our natural curiosity into our own human behavior. Another reason is that much of what we know does not get disseminated to the practitioner community as effectively as it could. A third is likely that marketers feel that if they just knew a little bit more or something different about shoppers—something their competitors do not know—they could gain an edge in attracting them to their brands. While all are valid, the third reason gets closest to what we think is driving this renewed interest in consumer behavior with a specific emphasis on shopping behavior. At the most fundamental level, the shoppers we are most frequently trying to attract are hard to reach and persuade today. Contrast developed regions of the world—especially highly urbanized marketing meccas like New York, Tokyo, Paris, and Munich—to regions of the world where simple bare necessities are in short supply. Merely making products available at an affordable price allows them to fly off the shelf. In fact, Walmart has had significant success internationally now that it has realized this basic fact. By providing good quality products at reasonable prices to regions of the world where this is relatively uncommon, Walmart has created value for society, itself, and its vendors.

In developed regions, it takes far more to attract shoppers. Shopper marketing's rapid acceptance and growth is testament to this reality. As different as the developed regions of the world where shopper marketing is taking hold may be, they are all hypercompetitive. Consumers have an abundance of choices, so much so that some research has found that too much choice backfires, making us merely stick with what we know or ignore the category altogether. This is known as the *paradox of choice*. There are far more—we count at least 11—specific reasons why firms are so interested in shopper marketing and, by extension, shopping behavior.

1. **Population fragmentation**—Consumers can now hang out with people just like them no matter how "unique" they seem to be in their interests and behavior. Consumers spend the majority of their time in their social specialized groups both physically and virtually/digitally, making them hard to reach as one large group with one primary message. Furthermore, people often do not view themselves as part of a "marketable group" but as individuals who are looking for products "just for them."

2. **Media fragmentation**—There are so many ways to communicate a branding message today that merely relying on a single medium in several mainstream outlets and similar tactics are no longer effective enough.

3. **Consumer multitasking**—Read any book on the millennial generation, also known as generation Y, or even iY, and you will quickly see their expertise as multitaskers. Even though research says that multitasking is actually not possible; that is, focusing on two things simultaneously, we tend to claim that this is what consumers are doing. In actuality, they are shifting their focus from one task to the next very, very quickly. We all do it. The bottom line is that we spend less time processing information, and often that information we do focus on we do not want to be marketing-related. The one time we do spend more time, relatively speaking, on marketing messaging is when? When we are in a shopping mode! That's why marketers now want to promote to consumers while they are shopping rather than at other times. Why? Because it is more effective then, plain and simple.

4. **Retailer consolidation**—Over the last few decades in the United States and elsewhere in regions such as Western Europe, Australia, and Japan, retailers have gone through significant consolidation. Retailing is tough business. The larger chains keep getting larger and more efficient while the small independent stores find themselves unable to compete on costs. Kroger, for example, operates under 15 supermarket banners, two price warehouse store banners, one multidepartment store banner, four marketplace banners, six convenience store banners, four jewelry store banners, and three services banners.[1] Most of this came about through acquisition. These larger retailers and their stores have become viable as media in and of themselves.

5. **Retailer-defined shopper segmentation**—Manufacturers have long segmented their end-use customers; that is, consumers. Although many still rely on basic demographic information such as age, gender, ZIP Code, and socio-economic status, most have included behavioral and attitudinal variables as well. What's changed is that now retailers as well are segmenting their shoppers in more sophisticated ways, partly due to hiring leading marketing managers from manufacturers. Some retailer segmentation models look like manufacturer models. The more advanced ones include shopping behavior as key components to their segments while most manufacturer consumer segments do not. This all means that manufacturers now must deeply understand how their retail customers segment their shoppers and vice versa. Then they must get these models in alignment. The overlap between who the manufacturer targets; that is, the core target consumer, and who the retailer targets; that is, the heavy loyal shopper, can be referred to as the *mutual target shopper*.

6. **Retailer branding**—Retailers have become adept at marketing themselves and taking positions in the marketplace that have direct and specific appeal to different consumer segments; for example, Costco versus Walmart versus Target. A key part of this is retail store brands. Retailers now recognize that their store can be a brand like Apple or Nike, where the sum of the parts clearly stands for something and differentiates them in the eyes of the shopper. This is an important concept to understand because a key component of effective shopper marketing is the ability to synergize both retailer and brand equities toward the objective of attracting new shoppers and then encouraging these shoppers to buy more in the store.

7. **The need to differentiate**—Following on the previous point, the marketplace of brands and retailers is so cluttered, even with consolidation, that every firm must find a way to differentiate from its competitors. Shopper marketing is a way of doing that, and shopper insights help provide ideas on ways this might be done.

8. **Constant demand for higher ROI**—The continuous push to demonstrate higher returns on marketing investments as well as costs incurred as a result of marketing decisions, for example, packaging, distribution, inventory, is forcing manufacturers and retailers to be more effective at creating superior shopping experiences, which requires deeper insights to shoppers.

9. **Escalating advertising costs**—If traditional advertising is less effective than it has been in the past it is also more expensive to use to reach a fragmented audience. The rates have increased but so have the collective costs of using so many media forms to reach the same size audience that could be reached in the past. Shopper marketing offers the potential for more effective use of advertising funds but requires different insights and communications vehicles to capture and hold the shopper along the path to purchase.

10. **Advertising oversaturation**—Related to point 9 is the overcrowded space of advertising. The clutter is significant, driving consumers to tune it out. Communicating with and to consumers when they are in shopper mode, especially in the store, makes the message more relevant and therefore is perceived to be more effective.

11. **In-store decision making**—A significant percentage of purchase decisions, whether category, product, or brand, are made in the store. Numbers range from 60% to 75% depending on the consumer goods category.[2] Regardless of where you come down on the debate over the method for defining in-store decision making, the point is that many shopper decisions can be influenced while in the store. And make note that this "store" can be an online retail environment as well. This makes shopper marketing attractive and puts a premium on developing insights to how shoppers are influenced while in the store.

The Home Depot Example

In the mid-2000s, The Home Depot realized that, despite doing extensive homework, it did not truly understand its own shoppers as well as it should. The company knew the core demographics such as age, income, family status, education levels, employment status, kids versus no-kids, and so on. It had information on household penetration; trip frequencies; average transaction sizes; percent purchased on deal; loyalty versus Lowe's, Ace, and others; and number of channels shopped on average. Some could argue that this was far more than many retailers know about their customers. But management at The Home Depot was not satisfied.

The Home Depot worked with suppliers and an agency to conduct additional primary research. The company discovered that although it knew a lot about the statistics of shoppers (and nonshoppers), it knew very little about the mindsets of these shoppers once they decided to take on a DIY (do it yourself) project. What The Home Depot found is that virtually all DIY shoppers could be divided into two segments based on their mindsets or *need states*:

- **Planners**—Like to take on the big home improvement jobs and proactively seek help in learning everything before starting.
- **Taskers**—Have a problem—to repair or maintain—and want to find the product fast. They are unlikely to read or take direction. Their objective is to get back on the couch as fast as possible.

Although The Home Depot is considered one of the best in the business at providing know-how (through its associates), the company was not well organized or focused to service the respective needs of these two different groups and, specifically, how these two segments shopped specific stores. Once company executives dug deeply into the shopping behavior of these two segments they were more able to meet their specific needs for speed and information in store. Here is what they did:

- Provided store maps at the front of the store
- Improved signage, especially for aisles
- Installed interactive kiosks
- Staffed more associates at peak times
- Insisted that associates stay in their aisles
- Provided "how to" pamphlets near appropriate products
- Tapped suppliers for more instructional videos
- Changed clinic hours to accommodate two wage-earner families
- Changed store layouts so all were consistent
- Eliminated obstructions to aisle traffic and signage
- Reconfigured stores and added buying aids specific to the needs of planners and taskers

They developed unique services specifically for planners, such as interactive kiosks where one could understand what materials and tools would be needed for a specific project, how-to demonstrations, and a help desk. For taskers, they installed a greeter at the entrance to direct the shopper to the specific location of what he needed, shelved products commonly needed for a task together—for example, pipe, pipe cleaner, and glue—and ensured knowledgeable associates were in the aisle to help. These changes improved the shopping experiences for both key The Home Depot segments. Traditional segmentation and consumer research might not have revealed the unique insights to The Home Depot specific shoppers. Today, walk into The Home Depot nearest you, and like in many retailers, you will notice more sophisticated digital devices designed to assist shoppers in their decision making. These devices also drive shoppers to The Home Depot's website to place orders while at the store, especially items not available in store, and have those items delivered to shoppers' homes or local stores. All of this is designed to help shoppers have better shopping experiences by solving their shopping and consumption problems.

Shopper marketing is based on the premise that the minute your target consumer gets into her car to go shopping, or notices she needs or wants a product wherever she is, she shifts temporarily into a mindset that traditional demographic approaches do not anticipate or encompass. This mindset is driven by various need states that influence what she will buy, where she will buy it, and why. Need states provide a new and convenient way to segment shoppers because they cut across all demographic lines and provide both retailers and manufacturers with immediately actionable ways to satisfy the mutual shopper. Like with The Home Depot, the whole purpose of shopper marketing is to identify those need states that key retailers are best configured to service and do everything possible to make it easy for the mutual target shopper to find and buy specific manufacturer brands at specific partner retailer outlets.

Moments of Truth and Path to Purchase

A. G. Lafley of Procter & Gamble is widely cited for coining the phrase first moment of truth (FMOT) to describe the importance of when a shopper is standing in front of a product in the aisle ready to make a purchase. Lafley noted that *before consumers can consume our products…they have to choose our products off the shelf.* Thus, the first moment of truth is when marketers truly know whether all of their marketing dollars have been put to good use. If the first moment of truth occurs when a shopper chooses a brand over another brand at the shelf, the second moment of truth is when the consumer opens the package and tastes, uses, and consumes the product. In the digital world, FMOT may be when the shopper selects a brand off Amazon.com or any retail website. But that point of selection is where the rubber touches the road. Jim Lecinski's (of Google) book *ZMOT—Zero Moment of Truth* reflects on the place where shopping starts, emphasizing that it's often in the digital space, researching products. But recognize that the idea of a moment of truth suggests it is a time when we know whether our investments have worked.

As an example of how shopper marketing can impact the first moment of truth, let's look at the Mr. Clean Magic Eraser introduction. The launch was supported by nearly $18 million in multimedia, including television, print, sampling, couponing, and public relations. Despite this—initially—the launch did not meet objectives. Why? Because once the shopper got to the shelf the product appeared to be very expensive compared to other products and alternatives because the brand neglected to put the number of uses per eraser clearly on the package. Consequently, the shopper jumped to the conclusion of "one eraser, one usage" when the reality was one eraser, five or more uses. Key learning: The brand may have understood the demographics and psychographics of the Mr. Clean Magic Eraser consumer segment but completely missed what this consumer needed to make a decision as a shopper. By the way, once the brand understood this, it rapidly moved to clarify the number of uses on the package, thereby redefining the value proposition for the shopper. The restage was a brilliant success.

One of the lessons of this example is that shopper research is different from consumer research. Shopper research involves knowing how, where, when, and why shoppers think and act as they do all along the path to purchase.

Figure 2-2 depicts a simple, linear, and yet powerful image of the path to purchase. The path to purchase is a term used in industry to reflect the notion of a consumer shifting into one of several shopping modes and continuing along a journey that eventually leads to a purchase. It begins with a predisposition to buy a product or category and culminates at the point of sale (POS). In truth, there are really two paths to purchase. The first is the decision process the consumer/shopper goes through when making purchase decisions. This "path" is confusing and anything but linear because it attempts to map the thought process of the human brain. Shoppers are barraged by and seek out many sources of information as they jump into and out of shopping mode throughout the day and week on their way to stores or websites. And they reflect on their purchases long after money has changed hands. The second path, which is depicted in Figure 2-2, may be viewed by some as oversimplistic but is the path that leading marketers and retailers use to organize their marketing efforts and identify key strategic communication points that will most effectively influence the consumer/shopper in each particular segment of this path.

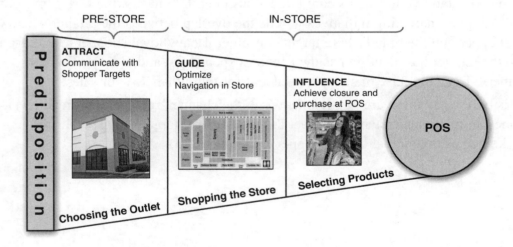

Figure 2-2 *Path to purchase.*

Who Is the Mutual Target Shopper?

So far, we've been talking mostly about the brand's consumer as shopper—or the brand's core target consumer. The core target consumers are those folks whom the brands have identified as having the highest potential to grow their brands. These comprise the nucleus of the brands' key consumers. Brands often segment these into different "buckets" for targeting purposes.

But something interesting happens to the shopper when she chooses *where* to shop. That decision triggers how much and what categories she is likely to buy, the time she allocates to the task, and how she determines value on that particular shopping trip. For example, a shopper choosing to shop at a convenience store or foodcourt is—at least subconsciously—placing time at a higher value than price. A shopper choosing to drive to a Walmart or Costco expects to spend more time but get great values. According to A. C. Nielsen, 73% of US shoppers shop five or more different stores every month. Where they shop reflects their expectations and attitudes at the moment. This means that your brand's core target consumer will be a little different in one store versus another. It is incumbent on the shopper marketer to understand the difference.

To do this, you need to understand who your retailer's shoppers are as much as you need to understand your brand's core target consumer. Ultimately, the target for your brand's shopper marketing initiatives will be the overlap between the retailer's heavy loyal shopper and the brand's core target consumer. Heavy loyal shoppers are those folks whom the retailer has identified as their highest spending—and most profitable—customers. Typically 33% of shoppers account for more than 75% of sales.

It is only when these are in alignment—on the channel, retailer, and brand level—that one can really understand and meet the needs of the target shopper. This target shopper is known as the mutual target shopper (see Figure 2-3).

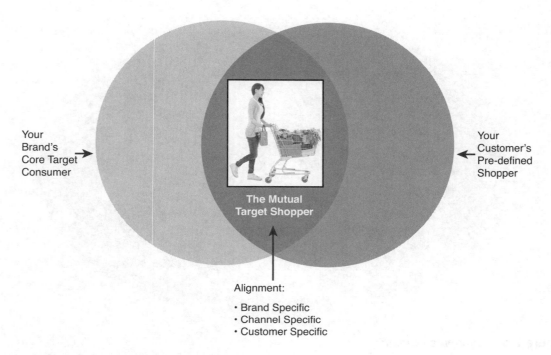

Your
Brand's
Core Target →
Consumer

The Mutual
Target Shopper

Your
← Customer's
Pre-defined
Shopper

Alignment:

• Brand Specific
• Channel Specific
• Customer Specific

Figure 2-3 *The mutual target shopper.*

Shopping Modes

One of the keys to winning at the point of sale is to understand the different reasons that shoppers shop different stores for the same brand. These are called shopping modes. Shopping modes have three distinct and different components: trip missions, trip mind-sets, and trip types, as illustrated in Figure 2-4.

Figure 2-4 *Shopping modes.*

A *trip mission* is what motivates your core target consumer to go shopping in the first place. Most trip missions are product focused. For example:

- To replenish items the shopper is low on or out of
- To satisfy an immediate hunger, thirst, or craving
- To stock up on a wide variety of grocery and household (HH) items for future use
- To take care of an immediate need for a specific item or items

Trip mindset or *need state* is the underlying attitude reflected in the shopper's mindset for the trip. Trip mindset is therefore attitudinally focused rather than product focused and is sometimes expressed as the reward the shopper seeks. For example:

- To get in and out of the store as quickly as possible
- To save as much money as possible
- To take good care of his family/household
- To feel like a smart shopper

Trip types are driven by both the trip mission and the trip mindset—"I'd like to do a full shop but only have time to pick up essentials" or "I just hate to shop!" Trip types are therefore a barometer for how much the shopper buys on a given trip and/or the time she is willing to invest in the trip. For example:

- Quick trip
- Fill-in trip
- Emergency trip
- Stock up trip

Importantly: We need to understand what informs the trip type, not just focus on the trip type itself.

These terms are most often used for grocery but actually apply to many product categories. The DIYer has quick fill-in needs for washers when he realizes his shop does not have any left and he needs them for a project. The clothing shopper has an emergency need when she spills a drink on her blouse right before an important business meeting. These descriptors, such as "quick" and "fill in," are mindsets shoppers adopt for specific trips.

If you think of all the reasons you and other consumers shop for groceries, you will quickly develop a list of 50 to 60 needs from standard pantry inventory replenishment to emotional relief from a romantic break-up and the mere social experience of it. We know because we ask our MBA students to do it all the time and research bears this out. The longer lists stimulate some interesting thoughts about retailing innovations. However, most firms seem to gravitate back toward the previous list.

The trip mindsets or need states for the shopping trip are primarily influenced by some combination of the following factors:

- Time
- Money
- Care for self
- Care for family/others

You can create a grid splitting time and money into dichotomies; that is, where time is an important factor, where time is unimportant, where money is an important factor, or where money is unimportant to the decision, and develop different shopper priorities from these four, as shown in Table 2-1.

Table 2-1 Key Shopper Factors

Time		Money	
Important	Unimportant	Important	Unimportant
Self		**Others**	
Important	Unimportant	Important	Unimportant

Some of these combinations correlate well with certain trip types. For example, convenience stores are designed precisely to serve shoppers who are time constrained. Most often they are also buying for themselves and although not willing to throw money away, willing to pay a bit more for the convenience. Most convenience store shoppers are not restocking inventory. Unless, that is, they live in densely populated urban centers in apartments with little storage capacity. In this case what one shopper may consider an amount equal to a quick trip another might consider inventory replenishment for their limited cabinet space. Additionally, that urban shopper may very well not be able to or be willing to travel great distances for groceries, preferring the "convenient" small footprint outlet on the city corner. Determining need states and then marketing toward them can be tricky. However, most successful retailers know their shoppers, why they come and how often, fairly well. For shopper marketing programs to be effective, manufacturers need to know this about their critical retail customers as well as the retailers do.

The Concept of Customer Value (Shopper and Retail Customers)

The call to create superior customer value has been loud and frequent over the last decade. But what does that really mean? As it turns out, we know a lot about what customer value means across numerous industries, and in this brief chapter we share that with you. We explain two distinctly different notions of customer value; one, the value of customers to an organization and two, the value customers want from interactions with products, services, retailers, and the like. We also describe how these concepts apply to the shopper marketing context.

Value of Customers to Organizations

We are not going to spend a great deal of time on this first notion, but it is critical that you understand the difference between the value of customers and the value customers want. The value of customers refers to a concept known as *Customer Lifetime Value* or *CLV*. This concept recognizes that not every customer is as valuable as the next to a retailer or a brand marketer. If we think of "customer" as meaning "shopper," not every shopper is of equal worth to the retailer. Even frequent shoppers may not be the most valuable. So what started out as straightforward calculations in the early days morphed into complex formulas that calculate the lifetime value in financial terms of the worth of a specific customer over the expected lifetime that she would remain a customer; that is, the net present value (all future dollars in today's dollar terms) of all of her transactions from now until she ceases to make purchases. In simple terms, think of it as

CLV = (avg price/product/trip) × (no. of products/trip) × (no. of trips/lifetime)

This logic would get you toward the revenue side. Reduce this value by the costs to serve (market to, deliver, and so on) this customer, and you could arrive at an expected profitability level for this customer. A significant body of research has made this basic calculation quite a bit more sophisticated, some might even say too complex. That being said, some firms have found that advanced approaches to calculating customer lifetime value are critical to their profitability.

In our context here, CLV can be calculated for individual shoppers, shopper segments, or any organizational customer, as in the CLV of certain retailers as viewed by brand marketers. Some retailers are more valuable than others to Procter & Gamble, right? And it's not simply the largest retailers. Sometimes the cost to serve is simply not worth it. The variables that come into play here are things like: Does the retailer comply with agreed upon in-store initiatives? Does the retailer pay in full and on time? Are the retailer fees for services in alignment with the service delivered?

Getting a handle on CLV has turned into a major focus for many firms inside and outside retailing and consumer goods. So when you use the term "customer value," some managers think you are talking about CLV. But you really may be talking about one of the more fun and interesting areas of customer value, and that's the psychology and social psychology of customers; that is, what's in their heads when they think about valuable products, services, and experiences. We cover that topic next.

What Customers Value

The area that has received far more research attention under the term customer value deals with what customers value from their interactions with products and services. We now have several decades of research here, some of which focuses on individual consumers and consumer segments while other focuses on what business customers value from their suppliers. Customer value here refers to what is in the customer's mind when she says something is valuable to her, or "worth it." We can look at this image of what it means to be valuable multiple ways and still be describing the same thing. It turns out that we can simplify most of these views into five ways of looking at value.

Value as a Trade-off

The first and most obvious way people look at value is in terms of a trade-off; that is, what I get for what I give up. Think in terms of more features at a lower price. If I add important features and keep the price the same, keep the features the same and reduce the price, or do both, I theoretically increase the value customers see in the product or service.

At the basic level, managers think about and promote features or quality for a given price. This is rather simplistic. At a more sophisticated level, what are promoted are benefits and sacrifices. These are the consequences of using the product features, not the features themselves. At the risk of being trite, customers want a 1.4 inch hole not a 1.4 inch drill bit. So if a shopper is able to obtain the groceries she wants and still have time to pick up her daughter from soccer practice (benefit) without much stress (minimal sacrifice), she may feel that the experience at that store was valuable or worth it. Attributes such as store layout, customer service, product placement, store environment, and pricing all contribute to delivering these benefits and sacrifices to her. This logic recognizes that she is really evaluating how stores and brands *help her* not the store and product attributes themselves. Attributes are merely means to an end.

Sacrifices are usually thought of as money, time, and effort or energy. The more money, time, and effort a person needs to put into acquiring or using the product, the more he expects to get out of it in terms of benefits. This is the conventional thinking anyway. It turns out that things have changed, and it is because of a concept now known as *co-creation of value*. But more on that in a minute.

So trade-off is the first way people think about value—what do I get for what I have to give up? This summation of what a shopper gets minus the sum of what she must sacrifice is depicted as follows:

$$(\Sigma \text{ what I get}) - (\Sigma \text{ what I give up}) = X$$

So ask yourself, what benefits does the shopper marketing program you are proposing bring to the shopper? What sacrifices does it remove? What sacrifices may it create? Ask the same questions of your retail customer. What benefits-sacrifice trade-offs is the retailer making as the retailer considers your proposal?

Comparative Value

Customers don't think of value in isolation. They think of value as being a better or worse value than other options they have. Knowing this, the savvy brand marketer drives retail customers and shoppers to make certain kinds of comparisons, as in with more expensive, higher quality brands. They don't want customers coming up with their own "wrong" comparisons for fear that the customer will conclude that the brand is not worth the costs given other options she has. Shoppers compare brands within categories, product categories, and stores based on which ones create greater value for them and their families. Retailers select vendors based on how much value they create for the retailers as compared to other vendors. Value perceptions are rarely formed in isolation. The conversation in our heads is "Is this worth what they are asking *given other options I have?*"

Value as a Hierarchy

One of the most powerful ways to understand what customers value is through a *means-end hierarchy*. Customers think about product attributes (features) in terms of the consequences they experience as a result of using those products. Attributes may have multiple consequences, some good and some bad. We call good consequences benefits and bad consequences sacrifices. These in turn lead to end states of existence. If we connect specific attributes with the consequences they help create and the end states they lead to we have a value hierarchy that resembles a series of ladders.

At the general level, the value hierarchy looks like Figure 2-5.

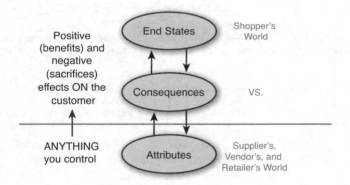

Figure 2-5   *Generic customer value hierarchy.*

Below the horizontal line are all the attributes a marketer can control. The brand features, the store attributes, training of store associates, and so on are controllable. What happens *to* shoppers are consequences above the line. When you create these by talking in an open-ended way with business customers such as retailers as they think about their vendors, they look more like Figure 2-6 and Figure 2-7.

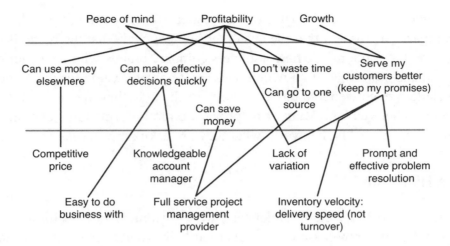

Figure 2-6 *Retailer value hierarchy: benefits from working with manufacturer.*

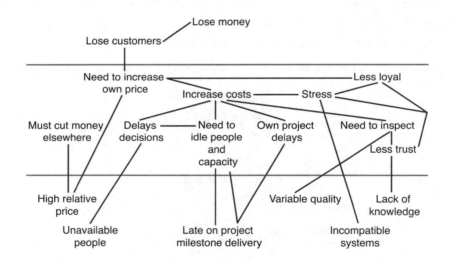

Figure 2-7 *Retailer value hierarchy: sacrifices from working with manufacturer.*

Knowing how customers connect attributes of brands or retail stores with consequences they experience is vitally important, as is knowing how retail customers think about working with their brand manufacturers.

We have found through many projects with many firms across industries that most businesses spend far too little time really listening to their customers. They listen for what they want to hear. When they ask questions, they defend and sell in their conversations; they don't openly listen with genuine curiosity about customers' worlds. The masters, the ones who seem to be loved by their customers, spend enough time genuinely listening that they "hear" things their competitors miss. Armed with a knowledge of the value hierarchy model, these masters connect specific things they can control (attributes) with the consequences they create for customers (benefits and sacrifices) in great detail enabling them to innovate in surprisingly effective ways. It cannot be overemphasized that the importance of value hierarchies lies not just in the words but more importantly, in the direct linkages—the lines—between specific attributes and specific consequences.

A savvy shopper marketer can use this exercise to identify shopping sacrifices his brand and program could eliminate and benefits desired by shoppers that his brand and program could help create for shoppers. Some shopping sacrifices can be referred to as *purchase barriers*, which we discuss in greater detail in Chapter 6, "Strategic Planning."

Value as an Interaction between Product, Values, and Use Situation

Shoppers don't think of products in isolation, and retailers don't think of their business relationships in isolation. They think of what products, services, and relationships offer in context. The context includes the shopper's or buyer's values and use situation. This means that consumers change what they value from brands and retailers depending on their values, much like the value hierarchy stipulates, but also depending on their situation. In shopper marketing terms, what we refer to as need state or shopping mode; for example, convenience, inventory replenishment, emergency trip (as in for a sick child), and so on, is merely a specific way of describing use situation. Concerning retailers as customers of brand manufacturers, what they value from their vendors can change depending on different use situations such as changing strategic positioning, distribution disruptions, or seasonality. These and other changes typically mean that retailers value different products and services from vendors differently.

If we conceptualize shoppers using the Venn diagram shown in Figure 2-8, shoppers evaluate products and services by comparing brands, product categories, and/or stores on a myriad of attributes. Different product categories may solve the same problem (for example, serve as a dessert for a dinner). For example, different retailers may be seen as more or less valuable simply based on their location. How the shopper makes these evaluations is linked to his use situation—for example, how quickly he needs a solution, how much money he has budgeted for this purchase. But his judgment will also be affected by the extent to which he values time, frugality (saving money), hedonics (having fun), being seen as a caring provider, or any other core value.

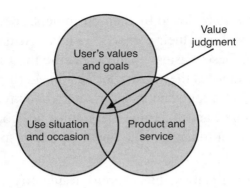

Figure 2-8 *Product, values, use situation Venn diagram.*

Research has shown that people hold a fairly well-defined set of core values. They're known as instrumental and terminal values. Instrumental values refer to modes of behavior and include values such as honesty, sincerity, ambition, independence, obedience, imaginativeness, and courageousness. Instrumental values are nearly permanent and thus difficult to change.

Terminal values are those things we can work toward. They are desirable states of existence. Like instrumental values, they are the kinds of concepts found at the top of customer value hierarchies. Terminal values as reflected in the Rokeach Values Survey include true friendship, mature love, self-respect, happiness, inner harmony, equality, freedom, pleasure, wisdom, salvation, family security, a sense of accomplishment, world beauty, and exciting life.

So why would a shopper marketer care about instrumental and terminal values? Some of the best marketing programs tap into this understanding of core values. Programs such as Box Tops for Education (General Mills), Susan G. Komen for the Cure (breast cancer awareness), and many other cause-related programs tap into instrumental and terminal values. Tapping into concepts such as love, sincerity, and ambition all can resonate with a wide segment of shoppers—as long as it does so with honesty and sincerity!

Value as Hedonic

Customers look for brand and retailing experiences that are, well, experiential! They want to enjoy these interactions. Now on a relative scale, shopping for groceries is more of a chore to endure than an exciting adventure to look forward to for many Americans. However, one particular brand with which we worked discovered that its target Latino shoppers indeed relished grocery shopping and often made it a family event. Some retailing experiences are set up to be highly hedonic, while others are not. The Disney Store, Bath and Body Works, and Teavana can all be viewed as hedonic retailers. For certain shopper segments, The Home Depot, Victoria's Secret, and Best Buy can as well. The flagship Burberry store in London is a highly hedonic experience. But regardless of the context, all else being equal, shoppers and business buyers alike prefer enjoyable, experiential interactions over dull, boring, and routine ones.

So the question becomes, as a shopper marketer, how well do you understand the shopping experiences your shoppers would relish and flock toward? Is it a flash mob, an outdoor concert event, or an interactive and education solution center in the store? Figure out how to make your programs a bit more experiential, and you will be on the right path toward creating value with your shoppers.

Value Is Dynamic

So those are the five ways research has shown customers of all types, consumers, shoppers, and business customers such as retailers, think of "value." To summarize they are

- Value as a trade-off
- Value as comparative
- Value as a hierarchy
- Value as an interaction between products, services, and use situations
- Value as hedonic

If this weren't enough to get your arms around, realize that customers' value perceptions change all the time. Some parts of what they value are relatively stable, such as shoppers wanting to find the products they want at a fair price. But at the level where businesses must operate; that is, in the details, things are in constant flux. Think of it as in Figure 2-9, where shoppers are evaluating the value of searching for products, the value of the shopping experience itself in store, and the value of consuming or using the product, which all in turn affect the next shopping experience in a continuous cycle. Within each of these phases, shoppers are constantly asking themselves "Is this worth it?" As such, the better term is customer *valuing* not simply customer value.

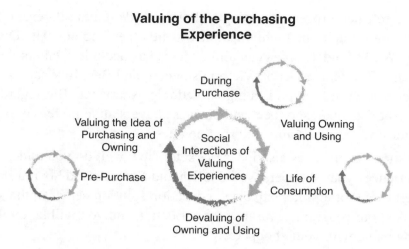

Valuing of the Purchasing Experience

During Purchase

Valuing the Idea of Purchasing and Owning

Social Interactions of Valuing Experiences

Valuing Owning and Using

Pre-Purchase

Life of Consumption

Devaluing of Owning and Using

Figure 2-9 *Customer valuing.*[3]

A far too often overlooked, ignored, or not even contemplated question is "How are my specific shoppers' value perceptions changing?" Far too many retailers and brands are still asking the basic question of "What do my shoppers value?" What we wind up with is a battle of market segmentation models, with each segment describing either simplistically, different demographic segments, or more sophisticatedly, different behavioral and attitudinal segments. But these still all ignore the way shoppers *change* what they value. With the data and tools we have available today, this is nothing short of shocking. If I accept that customer loyalty is important, that retaining a current customer is far less expensive than trying to acquire a new one, and that shoppers change what they value over time as their family, educational, financial, and living situations change, then doesn't it seem logical to try to keep up with or even anticipate those changes, which invariably affect what these shoppers value from my brand and my store? It seems so to us, but not evidently to most stores and brands. They seem to assume that as shoppers change what they value—that is, they leave a market segment—they will either migrate into another segment we also serve, or others migrating in will balance those leaving. That's not managing customer loyalty at all. That's just foolishness.

Interesting Findings from Research

Concerning shopper behavior, we know quite a lot. We provide a few interesting examples here.

1. Category characteristics, such as purchase frequency and displays, and customer characteristics, such as household size and gender, affect in-store decision making. Moreover, although the analysis reveals that the baseline probability of an unplanned purchase is 46%, the contextual factors can drive this probability as high as 93%. The results support the predictions that list use, more frequent trips, limiting the aisles visited, limiting time spent in the store, and paying by cash are effective strategies for decreasing the likelihood of making unplanned purchases.[4]

2. Checkout purchases are commonly influenced by store-visit frequencies. Not all checkout purchases can casually be referred to as impulsive because what items shoppers select at checkouts indicate conscious concern with making efficient use of their shopping time.[5]

3. Recent research suggests that consumers have in-store slack for grocery trips—that is, they leave room in their mental budgets to make unplanned purchases; savings (promotions) on planned items lead to stockpiling by higher-income shoppers when the savings occur before the in-store slack has been depleted but lead to increased purchase of unplanned items when they occur after in-store slack is depleted. The results also show that promotions on unplanned grocery items generate incremental spending at the basket level, which increases with income but only when the item is purchased after the in-store slack is exceeded.[6]

4. Consumers are constantly valuing throughout a shopping, purchasing, consuming, and devaluing process.[7]

5. Some shoppers create memories through highly experiential and enjoyable shopping contexts when they engage in shopper competitions like Filene's Running of the Brides event for discounted wedding gowns or Black Friday events.[8]

6. Consumers' shopping and storage decisions are distorted by inaccurate estimates of their average inventory and actual inventory levels. They overestimate low levels of inventory and underestimate high levels. These *beliefs* drive purchase, not actual inventory levels.[9]

7. Research in the United Kingdom suggests that ethical and social responsibility claims by retailers and manufacturers are important for some shoppers and even remain paramount for some, but these issues are taken into account while also considering traditional service, product quality, and promotions. These issues are usually important while on main and stock-up trips.[10]

8. Sold-out products seem to sometimes increase the sale of related items. This could be because it increases shoppers' sense of urgency and the perceived attractiveness of similar products.[11]

9. Some shoppers pay attention to their moods often but do not understand them while others do not often pay attention to their moods but understand them when they do. Moods and mood regulation by shoppers affect the kind of shopping

experience shoppers seek out, such as exploratory shopping experiences or utilitarian experiences. Shopper segmentation models are starting to take this kind of insight into account.[12]

10. "Priming" shoppers, as in making them aware of certain brands, impacts their behavior. For example, shoppers shown the Apple logo behave more creatively in experiments than do those shown the IBM logo.[13] (Sorry, IBM, we still like your company.)

11. Physical design of stores, the service environment, and customer care can influence shoppers' likelihood of exhibiting dysfunctional and disruptive behavior.[14]

12. Shoppers at malls have been studied to understand the behavioral segments they exhibit. Some research suggests that there are "mall enthusiasts" (high purchasing, high usage of services), "traditionalists" (unlikely to browse, eat, or use services), "grazers" (pass time by eating and browsing), and "minimalists" (low participation in anything), and that they're motivated by aesthetics, escape, exploration, knowledge, and social benefits.[15]

13. The most successful retailers stage experiences for their shoppers rather than simply deliver goods and services. Shoppers shop at their favorite retailers for experiential stimulation, bargain hunting, image-maintenance, and pampering to name a few. Loyal shoppers can be categorized as one of three types of shoppers: goal-oriented, bargain hunters, sociable. They each evaluate service experiences differently.[16]

14. Shoppers often don't pay attention to the first few feet of the store because they are literally slowing down and moving through a "decompression zone." They also don't like to be "bumped" by other shoppers and will change their shopping behavior when they are.[17]

15. Shoppers usually work a grocery store in a "U" pattern around the store perimeter with partial excursions into aisles to get needed products.[18]

16. Possessing processes for understanding at a deep level what customers value and how those value perceptions change and then leveraging that knowledge in brand management, manufacturer-retailer relationships, is a major source of competitive advantage.[19]

We could go on, but the point is that scholars know a lot about minute details concerning shopper behavior, attitudes, thought processes, emotions, social interactions, use of technology, and consumption. Many industry organizations also generate research results such as POPAI's (Point of Purchase Advertising International) 2012 Shopper Engagement Study, which, among other findings, suggests grocery shoppers can be classified as one of four types: time stressed, explorer, trip planner, and bargain hunter, with the explorer being the most profitable of all and in some grocery retail outlets, the only profitable one.[20] As a manager responsible for some part of shopper marketing, you absolutely need to get your hands on the relevant data, be it in the academic literature or an industry report. This may help you avoid reinventing the wheel by conducting primary research that is unnecessary. Then again you might want to replicate a study if you think your specific shoppers are unique in some way and the available research fails to address those shopper segments.

Endnotes

1   http://www.thekrogerco.com/. Kroger banners as of this writing: Kroger, Ralphs, King Soopers, City Market, Dillons, Smith's, Fry's, QFC, Baker's, Owen's, JayC, Hilander, Gorbes, Pay Less, Scott's, Kroger Fresh Fare, Food4Less, Foods Co, Fred Meyer, Fry's Marketplace, Smith's Marketplace, Kroger Marketplace, Dillons Marketplace, Turkey Hill, Kwik Shop, Loaf 'N Jug, QuickStop, TomThumb, Smith's Express, Fred Meyer Jewelers, Littman Jewelers, Barclay Jewelers, Fox's Jewelers, Kroger Personal Finance, The Little Clinic, Wireless.

2   POPAI (2012), *2012 Shopper Engagement Study: Media Topline Report.* Chicago, IL: Point of Purhcase Advertising International.

3   From Flint, D. J. (2006), "Innovation, Symbolic Interaction and Customer Valuing: Thoughts Stemming from a Service-Dominant Logic of Marketing," *Marketing Theory*, 6, 349-362.

4   Inman, J. Jeffrey, Russell S. Winer, and Rosellina Ferraro (2009), "The Interplay Among Category Characteristics, Customer Characteristics, and Customer Activities on In-Store Decision Making," *Journal of Marketing*, 73 (5), 19-29.

5   Miranda, Mario J. (2008), "Determinants of Shoppers' Checkout Behaviour at Supermarkets," *Journal of Targeting, Measurement and Analysis for Marketing*, 16 (4), 312–321.

6   Stilley, Karen M., J. Jeffrey Inman, and Kirk L.Wakefield (2010), "Spending on the Fly: Mental Budgets, Promotions, and Spending Behavior," *Journal of Marketing*, 74 (3), 34–47.

7   Flint, D. J. (2006), "Innovation, Symbolic Interaction and Customer Valuing: Thoughts Stemming from a Service-Dominant Logic of Marketing." *Marketing Theory*, 6, 349-362.

8   Satinover, Bridget and Daniel J. Flint, (2010), "That Item Is Mine! Consumer Competitiveness and Need for Control: A Study of Online Auction Bidding," *International Journal of Electronic Marketing and Retailing*, Vol. 3, No. 3, 261-292.

9   Chandon, Pierre, and John S. Wansink (2006), "How Biased Household Inventory Estimates Distort Shopping and Storage Decisions," *Journal of Marketing*, 70 (4), (Oct), 118-135.

10 Megicks, Phil, Memery Juliet, and Jasmine Williams (2008), "Influences on Ethical and Socially Responsible Shopping: Evidence from the UK Grocery Sector," *Journal of Marketing Management*, 24 (5-6), 637-659.

11 Xin, Ge, Paul R. Messinger, and Jin Li (2009), "Influence of Soldout Products on Consumer Choice," *Journal of Retailing*, 85 (3), 274-287.

12 Arnold, Mark J. and Kristy E. Reynolds (2009), "Affect and Retail Shopping Behavior: Understanding the Role of Mood Regulation and Regulatory Focus," *Journal of Retailing*, 85 (3), 308-320.

13 Fitzsimons, Grainne M., Tanya L. Chartrand, and Gavan J. Fitzsimons (2008), "Automatic Effects of Brand Exposure on Motivated Behavior: How Apple Makes you 'Think Different,'" *Journal of Consumer Research*, 35 (June), 21-35.

14 Reynolds, Kate L. and Lloyd C. Harris (2009), "Dysfunctional Customer Behavior Severity: An Empirical Examination," *Journal of Retailing*, 85 (3), 321-335.

15 Bloch, Peter H., Nancy M. Ridgway, and Scott A. Dawson (1994), "The Shopping Mall as Consumer Habitat," *Journal of Retailing*, 70 (1), 23-42.

16 McCabe, Deborah Brown, Mark S. Rosenbaum, and Jennifer Yurchisin (2007), "Perceived Service Quality and Shopping Motivations: A Dynamic Relationship," *Services Marketing Quarterly*, 29 (1), 1-21.

17 Underhill, Paco (2000), *Why We Buy: The Science of Shopping*, New York: Simon & Schuster.

18 Sorensen, H. (2009), *Inside the Mind of the Shopper*: *The Science of Retailing*, Upper Saddle River, NJ: Wharton School Publishing.

19 Woodruff, R. and S. Gardial (1996), *Know Your Customer: New Approaches to Understanding Customer Value and Satisfaction*, Cambridge, MA: Blackwell Business.

20 POPAI (2012), *2012 Shopper Engagement Study: Media Topline Report*, Chicago, IL: Point of Purhcase Advertising International.

3

How Retailers Work

If collaboration is a key principle of shopper marketing and mutually balanced benefit for brand, retailer, and shoppers is a key objective, then we need to make sure we understand our retailers as well as our shoppers. While both retailers and manufacturers share the same goal of selling more to shoppers, collaboration isn't easy:

- Priorities and performance measures require intense negotiation:
    - Brand equity versus store equity
    - Brand share versus category share
    - Brand margin versus category margin
    - Brand ROI versus category ROI
    - Brand's consumer versus retailer's customer
    - Brands versus store brands
- Roles and responsibilities need definition
    - "Who does what" expectations
    - Cost allocation—dollars/labor expectations

Successful collaboration requires knowing 1) what is important to retailers and why, 2) what objectives they have and what constraints limit their options, 3) who the key organizational players are and the role they play, 4) the tools available to advance shopper marketing initiatives and, finally, 5) the metrics by which they are measured.

The Realities of Retail

Three defining realities of retail underlie all retailer decisions:

1. Retailers operate on razor thin profits.
2. Retailer pricing is virtually capped by competition.
3. Retailers own the "real estate" of the store.

How do these impact one's shopper marketing collaborations? Let's take a look.

Retailers Operate on Razor Thin Profits

Retail is notorious for its low percentage profits. Department stores such as Macy's or Kohl's come in around 4%, mass merchandisers such as Walmart or Target and drug stores come in at the mid 3% range, consumer electronics stores at around 3%, clubs less than 2%, and supermarkets generally deliver less than 1.5% profit. In most brick-and-mortar retail, labor costs represent about 50% of operating costs. There is not a lot of room for frills or mistakes.

What this means as you collaborate:

- Initiatives are expected to deliver a revenue stream. A key sell-in point is to identify projected financial benefit of an initiative to the retailer.
- This revenue stream is generally expected to be *in addition to* existing trade promotion monies.
- Most direct costs of an initiative are expected to be covered by the manufacturer. The retailer generally provides *in kind* resources such as display space or promotional support in their own vehicles.
- There is a certain level of *quid pro quo* between the manufacturer buying into retailer-developed initiatives and the retailer accepting an initiative that is primarily brand-developed.
- Brand-developed initiatives must use minimal store labor or budget to purchase this labor from third-party brokers or merchandisers. One should not expect free labor from the retailer for most initiatives.

As you calculate the financial benefit of an initiative, you should understand a bit of retailer math. Today, most retailers use *margin* as the rule of thumb for pricing and profit calculations. Margin is the percentage profit on the *retail* price. If an item costs $1.00 and retails for $1.50, the margin is expressed as $0.50 profit on (divided by) the $1.50 price or a 33.3% margin. Margin is often confused with *mark-up*. Mark-up is the percentage profit on *cost*. In the same example, the mark-up would be a $0.50 profit on (divided by) the cost of $1.00 or a 50% mark-up.

Retailer Pricing Is Virtually Capped by Competition

The retail world went through a revolution in the 1990s as product availability exploded. In developed markets, retail channel assortment distinctions all but disappeared as drug stores carried food, food stores carried drugs, and Walmart carried everything. The result was a retail universe where different retail business models were competing with each other on the same products. For example, an Every Day Low Price (EDLP) broad line retailer like Walmart with a highly efficient cost structure could sell the same products for about 7 cents on the dollar less than the typical supermarket. On a $5,000 annual food expenditure, that translated to a $350 a year difference to the shopper. And shoppers noticed. Retailers initially reacted by cutting margins to lower prices, but it didn't take long to realize this was an exercise with a very bad end. Before long, leading retailers looked at ways to reduce their operating costs. The art of modern retailing is to constantly increase dollar sales on the demand side while at the same time reducing both cost of goods and operating expenses on the supply side. Accomplishing this is a huge juggling act, as depicted in Figure 3-1.

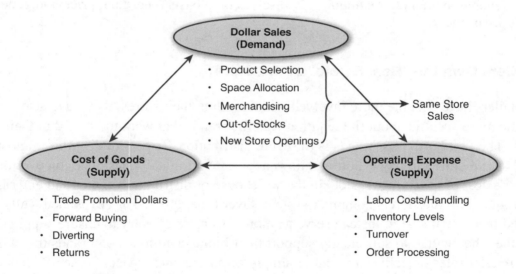

Figure 3-1   *Retail supply and demand.*

Today, we are experiencing a second retail revolution—one that pits an even more efficient business model against traditional retail—and that is e-commerce, epitomized by Amazon. Goldman Sachs estimates that 2015 will be the year that growth in e-commerce dollars exceeds traditional retail dollar growth—with no abatement in sight.

As digital-native millennials continue to establish households, e-commerce and price competition will only continue to grow. One can't roll back the smartphone.

As a result, many brick-and-mortar retailers today have established themselves in e-commerce and are taking an omni-channel approach that synergizes the benefits of both in-store and online. They are using online efficiencies to balance in-store costs to achieve more competitive pricing. They are using retail stores as an efficient delivery mechanism as shoppers order online and pick up at the store. They are reducing in-store inventories by having slow-turning SKUs (stock keeping units) available via online ordering rather than taking up in-store shelf space.

The implications for shopper marketing are

- The need to compete with online retailers places a premium on making the shopping experience a compelling differentiator.
- Communications with shoppers need to span all relevant media—reaching out to shoppers wherever they are with a compelling reason to shop at your retailer for your brand.
- Anticipate and drive more innovation, personalization, and customization that enable retailers to distinguish themselves on a basis other than price and generic assortment.

Retailers Own the "Real Estate" of the Store

As retailers have become more involved with branding their stores, they have also become more specific about the requirements for brands that want to be sold in their stores. The first hurdle for brands is to secure distribution. To accomplish this, almost all brands are required to pay a slotting allowance—a fee originally designed to cover the retailer's cost of assigning a "slot" in the warehouse or distribution center and entering the product into the store's computer system. Over time, this fee has expanded well beyond that actual cost to instead serve as more of a price of entry to ensure suppliers have the wherewithal to sufficiently support their brands and focus on brands that will meet retailer sales objectives instead of simply acquiring shelf space. Some retailers do not charge slotting per se but rather ask that suppliers use equivalent funding to promote the brands in the retailer stores.

Once the brand is in the store, category management takes over. This is a process that works to ensure that the most productive SKUs fill the shelves in relationship to their shopper demand. Metrics include dollars per foot and profit per foot relative to other products in a category and space is allocated to categories in a similar fashion. Space in the stores is truly viewed as real estate, and selection of product is driven as much (or more) by profitability as by consumer demand.

How brands promote their product is also heavily determined by the retailer. Trade promotion monies are most frequently based on an accrual contract wherein retailers "earn" dollars, primarily based on volume sold. Retailers can then use these monies for in-store volume-building activities like feature, display, and temporary price reductions. However, most retailers do not invest all of these monies into these types of activities and instead elect to divert some of these funds to profit enhancement. In fact, these funds are so important that some publicly traded retailers report them as a line item on their profit and loss statements, deriving more than 100 percent of their net profits from supplier trade promotion. Retailers also set the protocols for marketing and merchandising within the stores and in store-developed vehicles like websites and flyers.

How shopper marketing is impacted:

- Many retailers have enacted "clean store" policies that heavily control (if they allow at all) manufacturer-to-shopper communication vehicles (primarily point-of-sale materials and/or shippers) in the store.
- Many retailers push for fewer, bigger, better promotional events that encourage multiple brand/multiple manufacturer initiatives that they believe create a greater impact with the shopper. Some of these are retailer-developed, some are supplier-developed.
- All shopper marketing initiatives need retailer approval. These approvals may include the retailer's marketing department or operations, but almost always include the retail category manager.

Retail Objectives

Retailers broadly have two sets of objectives—financial and marketing. These objectives are synergistic in that meeting marketing objectives positively impacts the ability to meet financial objectives and vice versa. However, meeting financial objectives often takes precedence over initiatives to meet consumer demand because the retailer's very survival depends on it. As mentioned before, retailers do not have much room in their P&L (Profit & Loss) for mistakes. Some of the most common financial objectives can be categorized in terms of their impact on productivity, inventory, or operating profit.

Building Productivity (Driving Sales)

Retailers do many things to increase sales. Some of them include techniques designed to increase the frequency at which shoppers visit the store, the size of shopping baskets (number of goods purchased in each shopping trip), and profitability of each trip (affecting the assortment of goods in each basket). This is often referred to as *trip capture*. Retailers in the age of shopper marketing are trying to make their store a destination location. Rather than simply knowing that a particular brand is available at almost any grocer or consumer electronics store, retailers want shoppers to think of *their* brand of retail establishment as *the only or best place* to get that brand. Shopper marketing helps them do this through seasonal intensity, adding ancillary services, creating in-store events, and providing clarity of focus so consumers know exactly what the retailer stands for and what the shopping experience will be like *at that particular store*. Retailers have become brand managers themselves, where the brand being managed is the store.

Inventory

Retailers are in the real estate and asset management business. One key focal point for them is inventory management—maximizing the return on the available space. Inventory management is based on product assortment, which delivers the most return based on the combination of item cost, item profitability, and how quickly the item sells. Of particular interest is inventory turns. If an item with a profit of 20 cents "turns" one time per year, the retailer earns 20 cents on that item. If that same product turns five times per year, the retailer earns a dollar on that item. This is a key reason why the elimination of slow-moving SKUs (known as SKU rationalization) is so critical to retailer profitability. Retailers focus on turning their inventory more often through numerous supply chain optimization processes. Forecasting and S&OP (sales and operations planning) processes help here. This has to do with balancing enough inventory to avoid running out of stock without carrying too much. Most retailers do not have a great deal of storage space in their facilities.

Thus, inventory is often held offsite in distribution centers (DCs) and delivered on as close to a just-in-time basis as possible. This process is called flat-line inventory management or continuous replenishment and is depicted in Figure 3-2.

Managing inventory at a precise level requires detailed measurement systems at the SKU level. In the world of shopper marketing, products may become more customized for specific retailers. If so, the brand marketer needs to balance its own cost of carrying more SKUs against the benefit of customization. But to the retailer that carries one customized SKU instead of one generic SKU, the retailer's SKU count remains the same. More caution is needed when SKUs are time/event constrained; for example, custom product sold only during Halloween, breast cancer awareness month, or the Super Bowl.

In this case, products that aren't sold by the end of the event must be sold at deep discounts, redistributed, or discarded/returned. These all affect inventory turns and management. Thus, SKU rationalization is always an issue these days for retailers and brand marketers.

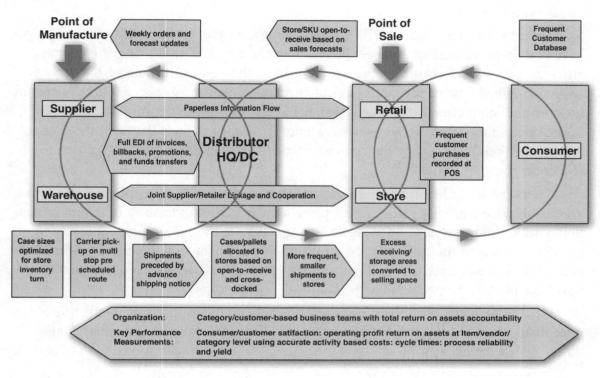

Figure 3-2 *The continuous replenishment process.*

Additionally, retailers manage inventory through terms they negotiate with vendors (brand marketers). Although there is no standard across all of retail, it is common for payment for goods to be due within a certain number of days of shipment (30/60/90 days) with a discount for paying early—for example, 2% discount if paid within 10 days, net due in 30. If payment does not occur until products are purchased by shoppers (scan and pay), then inventory is essentially on consignment. This means that the retailer holds and controls the inventory, but title (and costs) remains on the vendor's books. Vendors do not like this because this increases their costs and reduces their flexibility since they cannot reroute inventory to other locations where it might be needed more. Retailers may also demand price reductions within their terms or special inventory management support services that help them address their unique issues.

Operating Profit

Retailers keep a close eye on their operating expenses. Several ways they do this is by reducing in-store labor, shifting work centers, and becoming more efficient in operational execution.

In-store technology has increased significantly over the last ten years. These changes have both improved the shopping experience and helped make store operations more efficient. Self-scan checkouts, although requiring a little bit of learning on the part of shoppers, effectively reduce labor costs at checkout. Other in-store technology is making it easier and more effective to change pricing at the shelf, promote specials, and drive traffic through the store. Some in-store technology—such as carts that alert the shopper to promoted products as they traverse the aisles—serves marketing rather than cost-reduction goals.

In addition to these three major financial levers, retailers analyze their pricing strategies using price elasticity studies, their promotion strategies to identify optimum promotional price and frequency and evaluate how much trade promotion funding is passed through to the consumer versus used for profit enhancement—all to deliver profitability under 5%. The diligence required is daunting, especially when one considers that this rigor can apply to 50,000 separate SKUs.

Whereas financial objectives focus most heavily on the supply side, marketing objectives focus more heavily on generating demand. There are three primary marketing objectives for retail:

1. **Increase customer count**—In other words, find new customers to come into one's store. This is sometimes referred to as *building traffic*.
2. **Increase trip frequency**—This simply means having one's customers come into one's store more often.
3. **Increase transaction size**—This means getting one's shoppers to spend more on each trip, also referred to as *growing basket size*.

These are the 3Ts of retail marketing: traffic, trips, and transactions.

These retail objectives align quite well with the classic marketing objectives of trial, continuity, and volume with which retailers' manufacturing counterparts are probably more familiar.

As retail competition has ramped up, retailers have moved to differentiate their stores to appeal to specific demographic or psychographic targets. With this have come two additional objectives: 4) To build overall brand equity for the store, and 5) To appeal to and grow sales and trip frequency among specific target segments.

The issue that retail marketers have encountered in executing against these last two objectives traces back to the retail financials: This is a business with very thin profit margins, so there is little room for expensive brand-building advertising campaigns or loyalty premiums. Further, although many retailers broke new ground by investing in segmentation studies of their shoppers, few were able to translate this into the store-level assortment and pricing decisions they envisioned because the logistics involved were not economically viable. You see how some retailers found a way to achieve this when we discuss retailer tools later in this chapter.

The Retail Organization—Who's Involved?

There are, in most cases, three main retailer groups with whom one interacts when planning and developing shopper marketing initiatives: merchandising, marketing, and operations. Like many sizable organizations, there can be internal battles for dominance: Marketing is more focused on shopper connection; merchandising is more focused on revenue generation. Conflicts occur.

The traditional approach to merchandising might look like the following:

- Traditionally the alpha dog—merchandising has always run the show.
- Responsible for buying and merchandising products.
- Rewarded on category sales, growth, meeting or exceeding the procurement budget (dollars from manufacturers).
- Category managers within the merchandising group are a great source for understanding category objectives and obtaining data on one's brands' performance in that retailer.

Whereas, marketing can by viewed in this way:

- The new dog in town—big retailers have hired a lot of high profile retail "outsiders," especially from the supplier community to staff jobs in their marketing departments as they ascribe greater importance to this function. This has created some degree of turf protection and tension between merchandising and marketing.
- Responsible for understanding the shopper, developing programs to attract new shoppers, and build loyalty with existing shoppers.
- Rewarded on growing total store sales, traffic, customer loyalty.
- The marketing group is a great source for understanding corporate/total store objectives and growth strategies.

Finally, operations can be viewed as follows:

- The old bulldog—watching merchandising and marketing fight it out. Practical with a streak of independence.
- Rewarded on efficient delivery to stores, efficient store operations.
- Operations is your source for making operations things happen at the store level.

A note of caution: In most manufacturer organizations, sales "owns" the relationship with the retailer. Shopper marketers need to work with the sales key account manager to establish ground rules on direct communications between shopper marketing and retailer personnel.

There are three tiers of collaboration between retailers and manufacturers. These extend across the entire retailer/supplier relationship, not just shopper marketing alone:

- Partners:
    - Generally limited to four to five manufacturers with each key retailer because this level of intense, often top-to-top, collaboration is too time-consuming for more.
    - Most commonly manufacturers with a broad line of strong products in many categories.
    - Have the resources, knowledge base, and objectivity to make a difference for the retailer.
    - Work on total store initiatives together but also participate in category leader and category-seller initiatives.
- Category leaders:
    - The top one or two in the category.
    - Have the consumer pull to drive traffic.
    - Primarily drive *category* initiatives where brand(s) benefit or *brand* initiatives where the category benefits.
- Category-seller relationships:
    - Shopper marketing initiatives skew more to participants in retailer-driven marketing programs.
    - Tend to evaluate programs more heavily on potential volume gains than shopper connection with brand.

Retailer Tools to Advance Shopper Marketing Initiatives

In developing shopper marketing initiatives, brands and their agencies often use a build, borrow, or buy strategy. By this we mean that they choose the most efficient method to achieve the initiative goal given available options. For example, on a particular initiative, a brand might choose to *build* a microsite supporting the initiative, *borrow* the brand's TV ad and edit for in-store video or screen shots for POS materials, and *buy* certain retailer marketing options such as retailer website space, in-store sampling, or display. Consequently, it is important to understand what tools are available in specific retailers—and to understand that retail marketing tools are not limited to in-store only but, for most retailers, span the path to purchase, as shown in Table 3-1.

Table 3-1 Path to Purchase Media

Pre-Store Media (Examples)	In-Store Media (Examples)
TV/cable	In-store TV, radio
Radio	Signage
Print	• Print
Billboards	• Digital
Internet/mobile	Displays
• Websites	Sampling/demonstrations
• Blogs	Interactive
• Coupons	Packaging
• Applications	Solution centers
Direct mail	In-store events
Professional selling	Customer service/sales

Shopper marketers need to know which tools are tactical (profitable volume), which are strategic (contribute to equity build/retailer differentiation), and how to leverage trade, consumer, and co-marketing programs for maximum impact and retailer acceptance.

Solution Centers

Solution centers refer to areas within the store where bundles of products and/or services solve a particular shopper problem. An example is a meal-type solution center, such as healthy breakfasts, or combining movies and chips for "family fun night" at home, as in the Frito-Lay-Red Box-Kroger initiatives. These solution centers have been fundamentally manufacturer-driven. They frequently satisfy consumers' need for fast, easy, and convenient; for example, shelf stable, microwavable. (Did you know that 70% of all new food items are now targeted for fast, easy, and convenient?) Manufacturers are working with other manufacturers to bundle related products into solutions packages. Retailers are grouping related items on end-aisles to provide solutions. They are providing secondary locations for products often linked in the minds of shoppers—for example, Pepperidge Farm goldfish in the baby aisle, or tartar sauce hanging on the door of frozen fish. Solution centers are ideal vehicles for making it easy for the shopper to find and buy one's products.

Watchout

If one is buying into a retailer's solution center, have a clear understanding of what brands will be used to constitute the solution. Solution brands should be complementary, not competitive.

Some solutions are service solutions. Many are retailer-driven as a key means of differentiation. They provide core services under one roof and as a result add value and convenience to the shopping experience—and valuable revenue for the retailer. Examples might be

- Optical shops
- Coffee shops or buffets
- Banking services
- Film processing
- Internet access
- Gasoline
- Gift card centers

Many of the alliances that drive these service solution centers have yet to be explored from an empirical sense; that is, what makes a good partnership for service solutions?

Under what conditions do service solutions work? All of these solution center ideas, be they product or service, offer CPG manufacturers greatly expanded opportunities to cross-merchandise and tie-in.

Loyalty Programs

Loyalty or frequent shopper programs, FSPs, offer one of the most powerful "services" retailers have incorporated into their mix. Their ubiquity (most shoppers carry frequent shopper cards for multiple stores) has caused them to be viewed by shoppers as little more than a discount card, but for retailers, frequent shopper cards provide an invaluable tool. Together with brand analytics, through the use of firms such as dunnhumby or

LMG, the data provided by FSPs is a gold mine of opportunity for ways to better understand and serve loyal shoppers.

Retailers generally have the following strategic objectives for their frequent shopper programs:

- Develop store loyalty and retailer brand equity.
- Develop understanding of individual consumer behavior.
- Develop understanding of individual consumer profitability.
- Define categories from the consumer viewpoint.
- Determine the role of categories in individual stores.
- Evaluate the impact of alternative pricing and promotional approaches.
- Concentrate on the most valuable and loyal consumer groups.
- Identify the best metrics to evaluate store and category performance.

They also have tactical objectives for their frequent shopper programs, which include

- Provide discounts to key consumers.
- Distribute offers to influence consumer buying of key products.
- Target promotions aimed at specific behavior such as increased frequency, pantry loading, or brand switching.
- Measure the impact of changes in assortments, pricing, or merchandising.
- Qualified lists for target marketing by manufacturers.
- Develop themed vendor participation promotions.
- Cross-promotion of complementary products.
- Minimize cherry picking.
- Minimize or even eliminate coupon handling.

These days, retailers and brand manufacturers are collaborating far more than they did ten years ago around data collection and analysis. The strategic basis for this collaboration as it pertains to FSPs includes

- Enhanced knowledge of individual consumer behavior.
- Improved category leadership initiatives.
- Optimize supply chain efficiency.
- Collaborative loyalty efforts with retailers.
- Maximize promotional efficiency by consumer targeting.
- Redefine product and category roles.
- Establish sustainable competitive advantage through knowledge leadership.

Likewise, the tactical reasoning behind manufacturer and retailer collaboration on FSPs is to

- Develop store assortments through analysis of consumers.
- Develop merchandising approaches and/or cross-promotions to provide key consumers with solutions.
- Develop targeted advertising and promotions.
- Implement product development initiatives by store, based on purchase potential.
- Test price elasticity to find optimal price points.
- Develop shopper marketing programs aimed at prime user groups.

Ironically, the store-level targeting, which proved too costly to implement when retailers began identifying shopper segments, has morphed into a far more efficient one-on-one marketing through frequent shopper programs. These frequent shopper programs offer manufacturers an opportunity to target heavy users and convert nonusers because the data are available to identify and target these shoppers. For example, we know that approximately 16% of households consume 83% of total yogurt category sales (see Figure 3-3). Instead of spending one's $100K budget against all shoppers, targeted promotions to this 16% can be much more impactful.

Key Performance Measurements: Consumer/customer satisfaction; operating profit return on assets at item/vendor/category level using accurate activity-based costs; cycle times; process reliability and yield

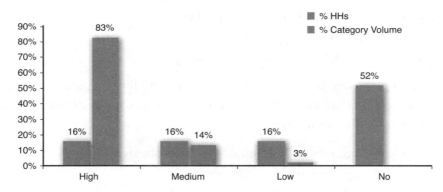

Figure 3-3 *Concentration of volume to households.*

Some data analysis firms like dunnhumby take FSP data a step further. They have developed algorithms through market basket analysis that allow a retailer to predict which shoppers buy products offered in their stores someplace else. Retailers are then able to offer high value incentives to the shopper to buy those specific products in their store.

It is important to know that manufacturers have no access to the actual names from retailers' FSPs due to privacy laws. The retailer and its database contractors are the only parties that may access this information for FSP targeting. Retailers who have FSPs do, however, share *generalized* data about a participating brand's shoppers based on FSP data.

In addition to FSPs alone, retailers have other tools upon which they rely often, some of which rely on FSP databases.

Direct Mail

Firms like Valassis, Catalina, dunnhumby (Kroger), and more emerging like them have access to proprietary retailer FSP and mailing list databases. Much like retailers use database information for in-store targeting, firms like these analyze shopper purchase behavior and target specific household consumption patterns in specific store location areas via direct mail. This enables manufacturers to do targeted co-branded (retailer-supplier) mailed or downloadable coupon offers that shoppers can redeem at the cash register when they scan their loyalty cards. Direct mail sampling personalizes communications to current, new, or competitive-user households. Customized advertisements and offers based on life stage events—for example, new residents, new parents, new home-owners—are possible. Retailers and manufacturers can segment heavy users from occasional shoppers and cherry pickers. Manufacturers can now make programs turnkey-executable. Direct mail has essentially become much more targeted and as such, potentially useful by recipients.

Community Outreach

Another vehicle being used by retailers is community outreach. Although this has been done for years, now it is being done in collaboration with major brands in a more sophisticated and strategic manner.

These out-of-store local community events sponsored by local retailers, divisions of national retailers, or brand-retailer partnerships, help to differentiate and build a retailer's "personality." They are often funded incrementally by manufacturers in high BDI (Brand Development Index)/CDI (Category Development Index) areas. The funds come directly from brands or shopper marketing and *not* out of trade promotion funds. These can be positioned as an "auction"—where only so many sponsorships are available and one bids to become the vendor for a particular category. These events offer the opportunity to sample, coupon, or demo onsite. They generally tie back to in-store displays, features, and signage, and if so, this in-store activity is usually included in the price.

Omni-Channel Retailing

As competition grows—particularly from e-commerce—retailers are increasingly adopting an omni-channel strategy. As discussed earlier, this is a strategy to synergize the strengths of online, brick-and-mortar, and sometimes catalog, phone, or other channels to provide the shopper with the easiest and/or most affordable way to purchase the products they need. In addition, the inventory management and ordering processes are coordinated. Marketing communications are integrated, and one form drives traffic toward the other. Smart manufacturer marketers are following this trend closely as opportunities arise to tie-in with omni-channel retailers for both greater communication reach and product assortment.

Learning to work with e-commerce and omni-channel retailers is critical. As GenY establishes households and GenX moves into their prime spending years, e-commerce is becoming an important channel to a great number of categories. GenY currently shops online at an average of 14.8% versus the total population's average of 9.4%. When GenY consumers, many of whom are still living at home, start buying categories typical of household establishment such as hand and power tools, baby supplies, and household cleaning products at the rate at which GenX currently buys, online spending is anticipated to increase by an average of 26%.[1]

What are the benefits to e-commerce?

- For retailers:
    - Increased Return on Net Assets (RONA)
    - Improved asset utilization
    - Improved competitiveness
    - Online/offline synergies
- For manufacturers:
    - Potentially more productive trade spending
    - Test bed for new product concepts, packaging improvements, and pricing
    - Partnership equity—embedded presence on all fronts

A great many retail tools can be used for building both brand equity and profitable sales for one's brands. There are also several manufacturer funding streams with which to purchase these, such as trade promotion funds, co-marketing/co-advertising funds, and shopper marketing funds. While some retailers and manufacturers are pooling funds from different sources to develop big shopper marketing initiatives, the same result can often be accomplished by coordinating spending from different streams to cover different parts of the initiative.

Here are some examples of initiatives that cross traditional spending buckets:

- Otis Spunkmeyer Cookies pays Costco for Costco's demo company to sample fresh-baked product in store.
- Colgate pays Stop & Shop to hand out manufacturer coupons for its toothpaste in store.
- Evian pays for brand-bannered coolers in Target.
- Bristol Myers pays A&P to run its broadcast radio spot on A&P's in-store radio.
- Unilever pays the coupon and mailing costs for Kroger to direct mail a coupon for Lever 2000 Soap to frequent shopper card holders who have purchased Dial Soap in the last three months.
- P&G produces and pays for a TV spot that features an independent restaurant chef discussing why he uses Tide and why he shops at Sam's Club.
- Coke pays Safeway to monitor consumer purchases of Coke products over a four-week period and issue a mail-in coupon at the register for a free Harry Potter kit to consumers who purchase Coke products during that period.
- A baked-beans manufacturer, a sausage manufacturer, and a soft drink manufacturer supply product and pay the HEB grocer to be sponsors of HEB's food table at a community jazz concert in Austin where their products are served.

Retailer Metrics

As should be clear by this chapter, successful retail is a balancing act between the supply and demand sides—between generating revenue and managing costs. The key metric for this balancing act is RONA. RONA drives everything. The calculation for RONA is easy—a retailer's operating profit divided by the retailer's total assets. As illustrated in Figure 3-4, this one calculation captures all the key levers that make retail work.

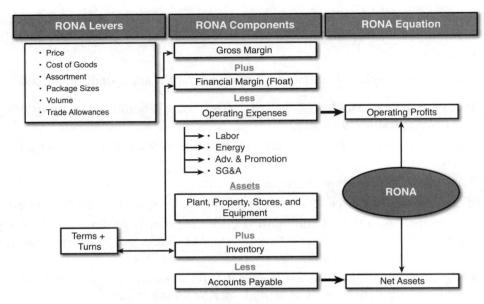

Figure 3-4 *Derivation of Return on Net Assets (RONA).*

Table 3-2 lists some historical comparisons of three retailers in terms of RONA to bring this into perspective. This captures a time when Walmart was heavily investing in supercenters (hence, expending a lot of working capital) and Kmart was filing for bankruptcy.

Table 3-2   RONA for Three Retailers

	Walmart	Target Corporation	Kmart
Gross margin as % of reported revenue	22.2%	33.4%	14.6%
Operating expenses as % of reported revenue	16.6%	25.9%	23.6%
Operating margin	5.5%	7.4%	-8.9%
Working capital as % of reported revenue	-1.5%	10.0%	12.9%
Net fixed assets as % of reported revenue	18.5%	14.8%	14.7%
Net assets as % of reported revenue	17.1%	24.8%	27.6%
RONA	32.4%	30.0%	-32.3%

To expand on the components of Table 3-2:

- Working Capital/Sales = (Current Assets – Current Liabilities)/Sales
- Net Fixed Assets/Sales = Total Assets – Current Assets – LT Debt – LT Capital
- Investment Capital/Sales = WC/Sales + Net Fixed Assets/Sales
- RONA = Operating Income/Investment Capital

It is in the context of improving RONA that the following metrics have become the language of modern day retailing:

- Same store sales versus year ago
- Sales per square foot
- Gross profit per square foot
- Gross margin as a % of sales
- Space to sales ratio
- Operating profit as a % of sales
- Gross inventory as a % of sales

For RONA productivity, the devil is in the details. What seem like small things create an impact when applied to 50,000 or 100,000 SKUs:

- Product selection and assortment:
    - High ticket, high profit, high turn items.
    - Improve variety, eliminate duplication.
- Shelf space and position (sales per sq. foot):
    - Micromanage every inch to maximize best combination of high turn, high profit SKUs.
    - Done via space management software, which facilitates modeling.
- Increase transaction size:
    - Stimulate impulse sales via displays of basic elastic consumables.
    - Trade customers up to larger quantities, bigger sizes of same items (24-pack versus 6-pack).
- Build volume by securing new customers:
    - Feature high penetration, high usage, low-cost SKUs as loss leaders (milk, bread).
    - Target staples regarded as providence of other trade channels (health and beauty aids (HBA), prescriptions, lawn furniture, etc.).
    - Ensure top quality shopping experience first time out.
- Minimize/eliminate out-of-stocks:
    - Especially on featured SKUs.
    - Trick is to keep inventories low at the same time.
- Promotion:
    - What retailers promote and how they promote it is the single most powerful tool for increasing same store sales.

In addition, there are things that retailers do that can seem "unfair" to the supplier community that works with them, but become more understandable when viewed in the context of retailer financials and RONA. For example:

Consolidation:

- Reduce operating expenses.
- Develop economies of scale.
- Gain leverage against suppliers.

Make money on the buy:

- Get as much up front as possible.
- Make every activity a profit center.
- Set up competition among suppliers.

Transfer costs to suppliers:

- Distribution, freight, and labor.
- Terms that allow the retailer to sell before paying for product.
- Have suppliers do business analyses.

Supplier rationalization:

- Limit to the "best" (20/80).
- New products, consistent innovation.
- Proprietary, well-known brand names (or unique items).
- Leading edge on service—meaning:
    - 100% order completeness.
    - 48-72 hour turnaround time.
    - In-store detailing.
    - Semi-annual category reviews.
- Ability/willingness to pay.
- Supply private label as well as branded (ship on same truck).

The net result is that retailers would rather deal with four suppliers who do 80% of the category than 20 who do 100%. It winds up being more efficient, requiring less time, and meaning less hassle.

The Takeaway

There is an inherent structural conflict between retailers and manufacturers. Most are not "partners" as many in the industry have attempted to depict the relationship. There are, however, certain areas of common interest that do serve as the basis for collaboration. One of the single most important benefits of shopper marketing is that, by focusing on how best to satisfy the needs of the mutual shopper, it has elevated this collaboration to an entirely different and refreshing plateau. Now much of the conversation focuses on strategic issues such as how best to leverage common equities, which, in turn, provides a framework in which both parties can flourish.

Interesting Findings from Research

1. Store knowledge and time available for shopping have an impact on such shopping behaviors as failure to make intended purchases, unplanned buying, brand and product class switching, and purchase volume deliberation.[2]

2. Ambient and social elements in the store environment provide cues that consumers use for their quality inferences. Store environment, merchandise quality, and service quality lead to perceptions of store image rather than exist as components of store image (as they are typically treated in the store image literature).[3]

3. Brighter lighting influenced shoppers to examine and handle more merchandise, though sales were not influenced.[4]

4. Shoppers taking major trips (versus a fill-in trip) were more prone to shop in a free-form layout, whereas those taking fill-in trips tended to prefer a grid layout. Grid layouts allow for more efficient shopping and are less appropriate for browsing than free-form layouts. Consumers with a specific goal shop more and spend more time in a grid layout of the store, whereas consumers with a loose plan spend more time and money within a free-form layout.[5]

5. Despite a growing array of nonstore shopping alternatives, consumers do a large portion of their shopping by visiting brick-and-mortar stores. Relatively few consumers shop to mingle with other shoppers. Instead, consumers tend to be drawn to shopping's more private pleasures, particularly the enjoyment of bargain hunting.[6]

6. Most shoppers appear to travel select aisles—rarely in the dominant-thought up and down pattern; extensive aisle travel occurs mostly in the way of short excursions into and out of the aisle again, rather than traversing the entire aisle.[7]

7. As consumers spend more time in the store, they become more purposeful—they are less likely to spend time on exploration and more likely to shop/buy. Consistent with "licensing" behavior, after purchasing virtue categories, consumers are more likely to shop at locations that carry vice categories. The presence of other shoppers attracts consumers toward a store zone but reduces consumers' tendency to shop there.[8]

Endnotes

1 Kantar Retail ShopperScape, industry report, July 2011.

2 Park, C. Whan, Easwar S. Iyer, and Daniel C. Smith (1989), "The Effects of Situational Factors on In-Store Grocery Shopping Behavior: The Role of Store Environment and Time Available for Shopping," *Journal of Consumer Research*, 15 (4), 422-433.

3 Julie, Dhruv Grewal, and A. Parasuraman (1994), "The Influence of Store Environment on Quality Inferences and Store Image," *Journal of the Academy of Marketing Science*, 22 (4), 328-339.

4 Areni, Charles S. and David Kim (1994), "The Influence of In-Store Lighting on Consumers' Examination of Merchandise in a Wine Store," *International Journal of Research in Marketing*, 11 (2), 117-125.

5 Massara, Francesco and Giovanni Pelloso (2006), "Investigating Consumer-Environment Interaction Through Image Modeling Technologies," *Int. Rev. of Retail, Distribution and Consumer Research*, 16 (5), 519-531.

6 Cox, Anthony D., Dena Cox, and Ronald D. Anderson (2005), "Reassessing the Pleasures of Store Shopping," *Journal of Business Research*, 58 (3), 250-259.

7 Larson, Jeffrey S., Eric T. Bradlow, and Peter S. Fader (2005), "An Exploratory Look at Supermarket Shopping Paths," *International Journal of Research in Marketing*, 22, 395-414.

8 Hui, Sam K., Eric T. Bradlow, and Peter S. Fader (2009), "Testing Behavioral Hypotheses Using an Integrated Model of Grocery Store Shopping Path and Purchase Behavior," *Journal of Consumer Research*, 36 (3), 478-493.

4

How Consumer Goods Manufacturers Work

We have spent some time discussing how retailers work. Now let's shift to the other critical player in shopper marketing, the consumer goods firms that are referred to interchangeably in the industry as *manufacturers*, *brand marketers*, *vendors*, *suppliers*, *CPG (consumer packaged goods) companies*, and *FMCG (fast moving consumer goods) firms* in Europe. These represent the firms that want to sell brands in retailers. We use the term *manufacturers* predominantly just for consistency.

Shopper marketing is a discipline driven largely by manufacturers. It is a way, as we have said, for manufacturers to work in more strategic ways with retailers to close the deal at the first moment of truth (at the shelf purchase decision), to help retailers differentiate themselves more powerfully, and to do this by helping retailers improve the shopping experience for shoppers. The problem is, as good as this idea is, there is a fair amount of history in the way manufacturers have traditionally operated (and thought) as well as how they have interacted with retailers (partially discussed in Chapter 3, "How Retailers Work") that can sometimes create tension between manufacturers and retailers that can get in the way of shopper marketing fully realizing its potential.

We begin by providing an overview of how manufacturers traditionally have operated and have been structured. We then take you into a discussion of how shopper marketing has been changing this. In the first part of this chapter, we address the manufacturer's marketing organization, the sales organization, typical budget allocations, attitudes toward private labels, category management, and the concept of partnering.

Fundamentals of Manufacturers' Marketing Organizations

The traditional consumer goods manufacturing company's organization for a long time has looked like Figure 4-1.

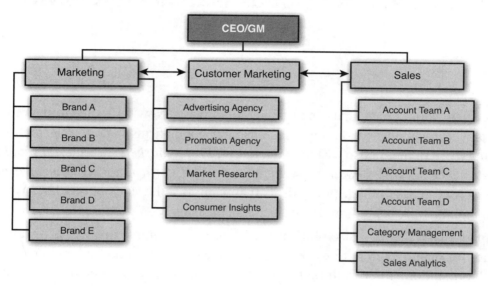

Figure 4-1 *Typical manufacturer demand-side organization chart.*

Within this traditional structure, marketing and sales are separate with distinctly different responsibilities. Marketing, for example, is considered strategic. It is the driver of the business, responsible for brand management, entrusted with discretionary budgets, and seen as the path to general management. Brand managers must have MBA degrees.

The Sales and Customer Business Development (or Customer Marketing) departments are sometimes considered more tactical. Sales teams are responsible for executing plans designed by marketing. They are considered great at social interaction and persuasion; that is, they are "people persons," and most are college educated, some with MBAs. However, not many MBA programs have historically encouraged their graduates to pursue sales careers, which is unfortunate. They do not generally have discretionary spending authority. They do have significant control over the relationship with key retailers or *banners* and have specific budgets they can spend on their accounts for specific purposes. Somewhat ironically these budgets—trade promotion budgets—account for the majority of total marketing dollars in many CPG companies.

Within the marketing department, brand management teams are charged with growing share, managing and improving brand equity, protecting the franchise, and meeting assigned volume, profit, and ROI objectives. The tools they have at their disposal include the advertising and promotion budget (A&P budget). They also have input into new product innovations, brand extensions, and line extensions. They fund market research, which may involve market demand assessments as well as consumer behavior/attitude research. These days a growing percentage of this research is focused on developing the findings on which shopper insights are based. Sometimes the research is a specific project, while at other times it involves pulling Nielsen, IRI, or retailer data and trying to generate insights from these that might be useful in their brand management activities. Marketing will use these insights sometimes to reposition a brand or completely reinvent it, as was the case when General Mills developed a Wheaties brand extension for men called Wheaties Fuel.

Brand Marketing Fundamentals

There are some basic tenets to brand marketing. First, each brand is viewed as its own business. For some firms, particularly large industrial firms such as GE, brands fall into what is known as a *branded house*. Here, every brand generally fits under the GE name. Most consumer goods firms do not operate this way. They are what are known as *houses of brands*. This means that they own many brands, each with its own identity. These brands can be bought and sold as standalone businesses. PepsiCo can decide whether to invest in, maintain, or divest any of its brands such as Quaker or Tropicana. In some cases, especially with what is known as "flanker" or "fighter" brands, the parent company does not want the general public to associate the brand with the parent company due to brand imagery baggage; that is, corporate imagery that does not entirely align with the identity of the brand. As such, each brand is an independent profit center, placing great pressure on brand management teams to perform—and potentially creating the opportunity for significant competition with other brands in the same company. This competition is especially evident when it comes to the dispensing of shared asset resources.

All budget money is derived from the brands. The marketing budget is simply the sum total of individual brand budgets. Management of the product portfolio; that is, portfolio marketing, must always be demographically and/or psychographically justified for each participant. How cleverly a brand allocates its A&P budget is the determinant of its success. Most brand budgets are 90% to 95% committed by the start of the manufacturer's fiscal year. There is not much flexibility or discretionary money left after that. Brand planning typically starts six to nine months in advance. So, if your initiative is not included in the original budget, it's tough to crack the ice.

CPG Advertising Agency

It is absolutely critical that you understand the role of advertising agencies in the brand manager's thinking and processes. Advertising agencies play many roles. In the world of shopper marketing, specialized agencies rule. It is not uncommon for a major brand initiative to involve three to five agencies at the same time. There may be a primary agency of record, but numerous others may be sought to contribute their unique talents to a project.

The primary advertising agency, ones like Ogilvy and Mather, Young and Rubicam, Saatchi and Saatchi, and so on, generally has well understood responsibilities to the brand management team. Typically, these responsibilities include

- Create demand—stimulate trial and awareness, household penetration, and share of mind (SOM).
- Develop an overall communications strategy.
- Develop a media strategy.
- Develop and execute media spending plans.
- Develop creative plans.
- Develop messaging content.
- Measure the impact of advertising programs.

Measurement, in particular, has been a contentious issue with brand teams for years. The universal problem facing most advertisers is tracing a direct cause and effect relationship between the advertisement and the purchase decision. Because so many factors can intervene, this is a difficult metric to measure accurately. Consequently, agencies have adopted a standard effectiveness planning/rating tool called gross rating points (GRPs). These GRPs estimate the number of people likely to see the advertisement (reach) and how often they will likely see it (frequency). Linking "eyeballs on target" to actual purchasing is a bit vague at best. As we discuss later, because shopper marketing initiatives often occur closer to the time of actual purchase, their impact has great measurement precision potential. An ancillary metric to GRPs, called TRPs or targeted rating points, measures reach and frequency of a specific target group (for example, the 18-29 age demographic).

When interfacing with the product marketer, agencies primarily deal with the VP of marketing, brand teams, and top management for annual reviews. Historically, retailers have not done much with advertising agencies. However, over the last decade they have done more in part because retailers have staffed their marketing departments with brand management experts from CPG firms with knowledge of what agencies can do for them. As a result, many retailers better understand the importance of building their own brand image.

One should realize that not all brands advertise. In fact, most don't. These brands survive on public relations, word of mouth, product placement, direct-to-consumer sales (for example, QVC), sponsorships, consumer promotions (free standing inserts (FSIs), direct mail, event marketing), trade promotion, or by filling a niche. These brands operate under the radar, but some do very well at this—for example, Fiji Water, WD-40.

The Promotion Agency

Whereas the role of advertising agencies is to create awareness and desire, the role of promotion agencies is to close the sale. Ideally, the strategies and tactics developed by both advertising and promotion agencies should be coordinated, but historically they have not been. Contrary to some opinions, promotion agencies are independent of advertising agencies—even if owned by the same conglomerate such as WPP or Omnicom.

Shopper marketing is beginning to change all this. Because shopper marketing focuses on capturing and sustaining the consumer's interest across the entire path to purchase, brand marketers are finding solid business reasons to coordinate the efforts of all the various service organizations they employ to "win" at the point of sale. The promotion agency plays a crucial role in this. In fact, to address the unique challenges of shopper marketing, many promotion agencies have repositioned themselves as shopper marketing agencies and, in this process, have extended the focus of their activities beyond in-store to include the pre-store segment of the path to purchase. What does all this mean?

Where promotion agencies used to be relegated to the sidelines of this business, shopper marketing has placed them at the front and center. A few agencies that excel in this space are Mars Advertising, JWT Ogilvy Action, Catapult Marketing, TracyLocke, Acosta Sales & Marketing (MatchPoint), Integer, Integrated Marketing Services, ARC Worldwide, and Saatchi & Saatchi X. But many more do excellent work for their clients. The primary objectives of these firms include developing programs, incentives, and/or events that motivate the target consumer to visit a specific retailer or make a specific trip to buy one's brands, buy one's brands once inside the store, and tie out-of-store brand messaging to in-store messaging; that is, to integrate marketing communication all along the path to purchase.

Historically, the promotion development process was typically driven by "The Big Idea." It was focused on out-of-the-blue creative, developed by truly brilliant minds with the objective of fielding an idea that was so cute or compelling that it would motivate the target consumer to buy one's brands. Unfortunately, this process worked well for the sponsoring brand but not for the retailer whose interest is in driving category sales as opposed to brand sales. As a result, retailers began to insist that manufacturer promotion efforts be grounded in fact-based criteria that would enhance the overall shopping experience not only for the sponsoring brand but for the category and shopper as well. This changed the dynamic. Now promotion recommendations have to be developed within a strategic framework that encompasses retailer and shopper objectives as well as brand objectives. While these may not be as cute and compelling as big ideas used to be in the past, they are significantly better at meeting the objectives of all stakeholders.

This has revolutionized the agency business. Agencies have responded to the demand for fact-based promotion development by hiring people with completely different skill sets and backgrounds than were formerly required. Now, leading shopper marketing agencies have elevated account management and insight development as well as planning to a level as or more important than creative development.

A key component of this is digital. Some shopper marketing agencies have created and staffed their own digital departments to fill in the digital requirements of shopper marketing initiatives that were too small to capture the attention of the corporate digital agency. This has expanded to providing full digital capabilities to clients without a separate digital agency.

So what do shopper marketing agencies actually do today? The HUB/Hoyt & Company Shopper Marketing Survey of December 2012 identifies the roles listed in Figure 4-2.

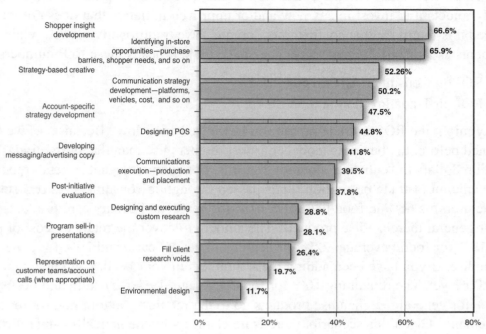

What role or functions do you think are most important for your agency to perform with respect to shopper marketing? (Check all that apply)

- Shopper insight development — 66.6%
- Identifying in-store opportunities—purchase barriers, shopper needs, and so on — 65.9%
- Strategy-based creative — 52.26%
- Communication strategy development—platforms, vehicles, cost, and so on — 50.2%
- Account-specific strategy development — 47.5%
- Designing POS — 44.8%
- Developing messaging/advertising copy — 41.8%
- Communications execution—production and placement — 39.5%
- Post-initiative evaluation — 37.8%
- Designing and executing custom research — 28.8%
- Program sell-in presentations — 28.1%
- Fill client research voids — 26.4%
- Representation on customer teams/account calls (when appropriate) — 19.7%
- Environmental design — 11.7%

Figure 4-2 *Shopper marketing agency roles.*

Typical CPG Budget Allocations

The typical CPG marketing budget is approximately 30% of gross sales. This is divided into specific allocations—advertising, consumer promotion, trade promotion, and shopper marketing. The amount allocated varies by type of business—for example, the retailer HBC spends a significantly greater proportion of its marketing dollar on advertising, less on trade than food manufacturers. For most manufacturers, the allocation to the trade budget is contractual: An agreement is in place that allows a certain amount of funding based on volume sold (usually on a case rate basis).

Typically, the advertising budget funds out-of-store media, both traditional (TV, radio, print) and digital as well as marketing research. The consumer promotion budget funds FSIs, on-pack and bonus pack promotions, consumer sweepstakes, and events. The shopper marketing budget funds shopper marketing initiatives directed at shoppers with a retail tie-in and, frequently, shopper research. The trade promotion budget funds monies given to the retailer for features, displays, and/or temporary price reductions.

Brands have long had a target of 2.5:1 as an expected ROI on consumer advertising investments (television/radio/print) and now digital (web/mobile phones). Brands are typically reluctant to invest in any new and/or unproven initiative that does not meet or exceed this return. In this context, most brands have traditionally viewed retail investments as a distasteful necessity. They have in their heads these ROI numbers:

- ROI on Consumer Advertising 2.5:1
- ROI on Trade Promotion 0.58 - 0.75:1

Why might the ROI on trade promotion be viewed as so low? Because, as we have mentioned before, the business models of most retailers use manufacturers' trade promotion dollars to "enhance" operating profits. For example, Kantar Retail reports that the amount of trade promotion funds passed through to consumers (as reported by manufacturers) is 66% in food/beverage, 61% for health and beauty care products, and 52% for general merchandise products. The amount to cover the retailer's cost of promotion is 19% for food/beverage, 22% for health and beauty care, and 26% for general merchandise. If you have been adding these numbers in your head, you know that we are not at 100% yet. The remaining 16% for food/beverage, 19% for health and beauty care, and 22% for general merchandise products go to the retailer's bottom line for revenue enhancement.[1] Given this scenario, there is no chance—mathematically—that investments in traditional trade promotion activities will ever consistently return more than 1:1 for manufacturers.

Retailer Attitudes Toward Manufacturer Trade Promotion Dollars

Retailers have developed a rather strong perspective and reliance on trade promotion dollars. For one, many seem to have the attitude that "all of this money is *mine*!" This belief, in some respects, is understandable since most manufacturers, in an effort to comply with federal laws like Robinson-Patman and Sarbanes-Oxley, have established accrual systems for "earning" trade promotion dollars based on volume sold and, occasionally, compliance with other manufacturer requests. Since they have "earned" the dollars, the belief is that they should be allowed to be spent as the retailer sees fit. Additionally, they seem to say that "There is never enough," according to a recent Kantar Survey. In most retailers' minds, $1.00 in trade promotion is worth more than the strongest consumer, shopper, or category-based selling story one can muster (Walmart and Costco notably excluded). For example, one of our clients invited a group of executives from a large and prominent retailer to join other retailers at a golf tournament at the client's expense. The retailer's response: "Thank you for your kind invitation but could you please just send us the money instead?" And yet another client received a bill from another retailer—literally out of the blue—charging them for "their share" of the cost of the new warehouse the retailer had just built.

While these examples may seem off the wall—and certainly are memorable to us—it is important to understand that in the minds of most retailers these requests are not outlandish but simply a way of leveling the playing field between manufacturers and retailers. This stems from the retailer's idea of partnering, which as one retailer described it to us is as follows: "If the supplier makes 8% on the bottom line and we make 2%, true partnering occurs when both of us make 5%—even if we have to take the difference from our suppliers."

This is not a joke and is the cause of most manufacturers' distress. As an example, we can look at trade promotion allowances' contribution to operating profits for Kroger and Safeway in Table 4-1. In both cases, manufacturer trade promotion allowances, identified in corporate annual reports as vendor allowances, *exceed their operating profit* by more than two times. When one's operating profits are totally dependent on manufacturer spending, the likelihood of this practice going away in the supermarket business model is nil.

Table 4-1   Trade Promotion Contribution to Profits

	Safeway 2012	Kroger 2012
Trade Promotion (TP) Dollars	$3.0B	$6.2B
Operating Profits (OP)	$1.1B	$2.6B
% TP/OP	273%	238%

As discussed in Chapter 3, monies that manufacturers pay to retailers fall into several groups. Slotting allowances are funds paid to be accepted into the store in the first place. Promotion allowances are funds paid to support one's brand—typically feature advertising, in-store display, or temporary price reduction. "Pay to stay" are funds paid to enhance the financial performance of a brand or SKU to the retailer so that it can meet the retailer's productivity requirements and avoid delisting. On average, trade promotion (TP) allowance contribution breaks down as shown in Table 4-2.

Table 4-2 Trade Promotion Allocation

Slotting	5%
Promotion allowance	75%
Pay to Stay	20%
Total	100%

Any manufacturer-sponsored in-store marketing initiative (like advertising, messaging, or in-store design) must be funded incrementally out of marketing dollars, not trade money. As stated by a senior Kroger leader to us at Hoyt & Co., "Despite our need to differentiate on a non-price basis, we will not spend one dime of our trade promotion money to do this unless the ROI can be convincingly proven to be higher."

As a result, there exists a permanent anxiety among retailers where they constantly wonder, "Are we leaving any money on the table?" Additionally, there is a lack of trust reflected in the attitude, "I just *know* that XYZ retailer is getting more than we are!"

In contrast, if one looks at A&P spending trends over the past 30 years, listed in Table 4-3, it is not difficult to understand why most CPG brand marketers feel that they have been bilked to death with regard to "black hole" trade spending.

Table 4-3 % CPG Manufacturer A&P Spending Trends: 1978-2011

	1978	1985	1997	2007	2011	% vs. 1978
Trade Promotion	33%	38%	53%	60%	58%	76%
Consumer Promotion	27%	27%	24%	14%	15%	(55%)
Advertising	40%	35%	23%	26%	27%	(67%)
TOTALS	100%	100%	100%	100%	100%	N/A
% A&P/Total Sales	13%	N/A	22%	29%	36%	277%
% Trade/Total Sales	4.3%	N/A	13%	17%	16%	372%

Sources: Carol Wright, Accenture, Cannondale Associates, 1997-2007; Kantar Retail, 2011; Reuben Donnelly, 1980-2002.

Exacerbating this is the fact that brand management has no control or say in how the roughly 60% trade promotion portion of their budgets is allocated or spent. This is entirely the province of the Sales department. Allocations are legally proscribed by Robinson-Patman, meaning that funds must be proportionately equal based on each retailer's share of total corporate volume. Within this, spending is contractually committed to focus on only three types of activities:

- Features (ROP—run of paper)
- Displays (or a combination of feature and display)
- Temporary price reductions (TPRs)

Temporary price reductions (TPRs) are used to close price gaps between national brands and private label brands, or other competitors' "value brands" (as private labels grow, so must this segment of TP spending). With the exception of sales training, there are *no* meaningful discretionary dollars available within manufacturer trade promotion budgets.

CPG Beliefs

Virtually all brand managers still (want to) believe that it is advertising, *not* in-store marketing, that builds demand. They feel that advertising brings new people into the franchise; in-store marketing appeals only to those who already shop a particular retailer. It is axiomatic among CPG brand managers that one cannot build share through all commodity volume (ACV), or cobbling together a bunch of retailers.

ACV works like this: ACV is the common denominator used to weight percentages to make them more meaningful to product manufacturers. For example, if a brand is being displayed in one of ten stores in a town during a given period, a straight percentage would report 10% distribution and 10% display activity. However, if that one store handles 90% of the sales in that town (all products, all commodity volume), then the correct numbers would be 90% ACV distribution and display. It is the percentage of exposure to consumers in a particular class of trade for specific products/SKUs during a given time period. It is not an index.

Leading CPG marketers generally will never view the retail store as an acceptable substitute for national advertising. While the retail store does appear to be emerging as a potential consumer communications channel, its viability in this regard is far from proven. To date, there are few if any industry-accepted measurement systems to enable manufacturers to benchmark in-store marketing effectiveness or ROI against other types of traditional marketing investments, despite the early initial attempts. As a result, expect brand marketers to push back strongly on additional retail investment unless the benefits are obvious and easily measurable.

There are traditional CPG attitudes toward retailers. But first, you should realize that there are two types of manufacturers: those with strong brand equities—P&G, Coca Cola, PepsiCo, Kellogg's, General Mills, and so on—and those who are trade dependent. There exists an axiom within CPG marketing: The stronger one's equity with consumers, the less trade dependent one becomes. For strong brand equity companies, no single retailer is all that important because they know that consumers will switch stores to find their brands. According to Symphony IRI, three-quarters of consumers shop in five or more channels and only 10% shop in one to three channels.[2] Walmart may be the sole exception because of the sheer volume at stake. For trade-dependent manufacturers, most feel that retailers will not de-list them because they don't want to lose trade promotion "pay-to-stay" dollars.

CPG Sales Department

The sales department of a manufacturer works separately from, but sometimes in coordination with, the marketing function. CPG sales departments are traditionally focused almost exclusively on meeting gross or net sales volume objectives—by brand, by account, and in total. For most, 15 to 20 accounts comprise 65%+ of the business. Most use cross-functional customer teams to call on these accounts at headquarters and food brokers who service their needs at store level. Sales executives tend to think in terms of direct cause and effect, for example, "If I spend 'X', I need to get 'Y' in return," and this must be directly measurable.

Manufacturer sales departments have virtually no discretionary spending authority. The entire trade promotion (TP) budget is committed during annual account planning meetings, with funding usually being committed 15 to 18 months in advance of the activity. To fund *ad hoc* opportunities, the customer team must go back to the brand groups who have either already committed themselves or lack the retail understanding (or interest) to make an informed decision. For most CPG sales organizations, getting one's program proposal accepted by a retailer is always a hit or miss proposition. With approximately 2,500 CPG manufacturers, all competing for the retailer's time and support, retailers will receive nearly 15,000 program proposals per quarter. If the customer team targets 15 to 20 retailers, success will be if 5 of the top 20 agree to cooperate on the initiatives proposed.

Execution for CPG manufacturers always refers to ACV (all commodity volume) penetration rather than store count. For example, if out of 1,400 stores, the top 20% (280) account for 70% of a retailer's business, then the manufacturer's objective is to hit the top 280, not 1,400. If successful, the initiative represents only 20% of stores but 70% of retailer's volume.

The reality is that because of intense competition, for most manufacturers just getting one's proposal accepted is viewed as a significant accomplishment. In this environment, manufacturers tend to "sell what sells" or "fish where the fish are" regardless of any consumer or shopper rationale that might support a better idea.

They will confine proposals to programs that are easy to understand and simple to execute at no cost to the retailer and avoid complicated ideas that require more than a sentence to explain and whose benefits to all parties aren't obvious on the face of it.

Sales and Views on Category Management

Category management, first introduced into retailing in large part due to the efforts by Dr. Brian Harris of The Partnering Group in the 1990s, is essentially a way for retailers to run each category as a separate business unit and shift much of the category planning and execution to suppliers; that is, manufacturers. Virtually every retailer, especially grocery retailers, operates through category management principles.

Category management is a retailer-driven initiative designed to market individual categories as a mini-business. Although retailer-driven, manufacturers shoulder the responsibility for all category analytics and recommendations. The CatMan function, as it is known in the industry, usually resides in the sales department and is viewed by marketing as having no strategic value. Category management provides sales executives with a jumping-off point to establish above-buyer relationships; that is, focus the dialog on categories versus individual brands. Importantly, one reason for widespread adoption by virtually all CPG manufacturers is *retailer insistence that all program recommendations be presented within a category management framework*. Unfortunately, because shopper marketing has the word "shopper" in its name, many companies jump to the conclusion that it is the next logical phase in the evolution of category management and position it as an extension of category management in their organizations. Shopper marketing, however, is much more about marketing than retail in that it necessitates total cross-functional commitment and coordination as well as requiring skill sets and resources of which category management and sales are only a part. In fact, as companies gain more experience with shopper marketing and understand its strategic potential, many have repositioned it from sales to either marketing or general management and have made category management a subset of shopper marketing. Nevertheless, this does not make category management unimportant or take away from its impact.

So how do category management programs get implemented? Over the years, category management has been truncated, but it is perhaps easiest to understand by looking at the traditional nine steps:

1. **Industry/channel assessment**—A broad review of the competitive environment, assessing the retailer's strengths and weaknesses versus competition.
2. **Category definition**—What range of products should be encompassed by the category? What products will be compared to evaluate the category?
3. **Role assignment**—What role do you expect the category to play in relation to the store? Sample roles include destination, routine, occasional/seasonal, and convenience, and these roles impact space, assortment, promotion, and pricing decisions.
4. **Category assessment**—How well are the category, segments, and individual products within the category performing?
5. **Scorecard**—The retailer develops a scorecard identifying key measures on which the category, its suppliers, and their products will be rated.
6. **Strategy development**—How will different predefined strategies be deployed against different segments of the category to achieve category objectives? Which segments will be used as traffic generators, profit generators, image enhancers, and so on?
7. **Tactical development**—What tactics will be employed to achieve the desired strategic result? This includes product selection and assortment, pricing, planogramming (planning the layout of where items will be placed), and promotion.
8. **Plan implementation**—The execution of the tactics.
9. **Review**—The assessment of how well the plan achieved its scorecard objectives with recommendations for improvement.

As one can see, nowhere in this program is the focus on the shopper.

Sales and Partnering

Despite fundamental differences on things like trade promotion, private labels versus national brands, and even performance measurements, most retailers and manufacturers actually do collaborate with one another as opposed to "partner" with one another. In fact, the word "partnering" began as a manufacturer's term—never supported or endorsed by retailers. Our feedback from retailers is that because of these differences, use of the word "partnering" by manufacturers is inherently hypocritical. Nevertheless, retailers provide manufacturer "partners" with data, intelligence, access, and support that they do not provide to other run-of-the-mill suppliers. Like any business, because of time constraints, retailers can only afford to partner with a limited number of manufacturers (five to eight is typical) and therefore are careful in anointing the most favored. It is instructive to review retailers' criteria for partnering because manufacturers who meet these criteria are generally those most open to new ideas. Following is an amalgamation of different criteria we have seen.

Retailer criteria for selecting a manufacturer "partner":

- Size and importance of supplier's categories to overall store sales
- Supplier's overall importance to retailer as a company
- Supplier's strength in category (#1 or #2 is advantageous but not a must)
- Potential contribution to category/departmental and/or total store growth
- Value of insights, intellectual capital contribution beyond distribution value of one's product lines
- Technological expertise and willingness to share/apply
- Innovation, energy, attitude, and responsiveness of supplier as a company ("Does the supplier understand our issues and opportunities and help us address these?")
- Consistency in meeting/exceeding retailer financial objectives and scorecard metrics
- Supplier's ability to execute at store level
- Whether the supplier has the size, strength, and willingness to be objective/unselfish in developing category and/or total store program recommendations

How Shopper Marketing Is Changing Traditional Approaches

Shopper marketing's impact on CPG marketing and sales organizations has been fundamental and significant. When shopper marketing is planned and implemented in the manner originally intended, it requires cross-functional integration between brand marketing and sales. The cornerstone of this is the shopper marketing department whose representatives are both brand-facing and customer-facing. These people ensure that brand strategies and objectives are reflected in the programs developed to satisfy shopper needs in individual retailers. Figure 4-3 illustrates how this interface works.

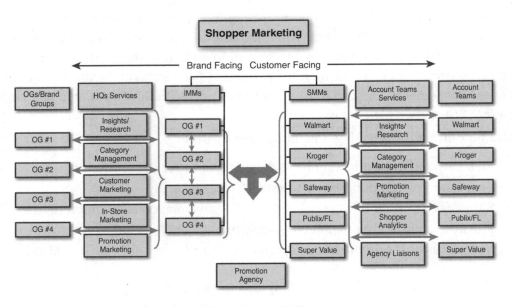

Figure 4-3 *The modern shopper marketing organization.*

So how does this organization differ from the traditional CPG organization illustrated at the beginning of this chapter in Figure 4-1?

- Brand groups are reprogrammed for 360° marketing, which nets down to budgeting for shoppers and key retailers in annual brand plans.
- Brand managers and marketing directors are furloughed to customer teams on a two-year rotating basis to provide onsite marketing input to customer development plans.
- *All* shopper initiatives become strategically based as opposed to driven by "The Big Idea."
- A separate shopper marketing function/department is formed that acts as driver and watchdog in coordinating all the corporate resources necessary to planning and implementing shopper-based initiatives.

How this translates to retail is in the composition of the customer or account teams. For those retailers with whom ROI justifies it, a shopper marketer (and occasionally a shopper insights specialist and/or an account manager from the shopper marketing agency) is added to the account teams. An account team for a large manufacturer generally consists of a team leader (sales), key account managers (sales) for different brands or divisions that are being sold, a business development or trade marketing function, and a category management function in addition to shopper marketing. Some manufacturers also add a finance function to the team. A key responsibility of the team leader is to develop the annual account plan. This account plan is based on input from key account managers, business development/trade marketing, category management, and shopper marketing representatives on the account team and is coordinated to maximize the impact of all initiatives (both sales and shopper marketing) in the account.

The net result is that in a shopper marketing-focused organization, all resources of the customer or account (sales) teams are coordinated and dedicated to the objective of winning at the point of sale in their retailer.

Beyond the customer teams, these same objectives and focus are integrated through-out the marketing, shopper marketing, and sales effort—all in alignment—through retail-ers and, ultimately, to the target shopper as illustrated in Figure 4-4. The messaging and research from marketing need to inform shopper marketing, which, in turn, needs to inform or align with sales decisions on category management and trade promotion. Marketing establishes objectives that shopper marketing and sales develop plans to meet. And the interaction goes both ways: Sales and shopper marketing inform marketing on opportunities to connect with shoppers in specific retailers. The effort is integrated—and often includes other functions within the company such as supply chain and IT. If this integration is in place, roles and responsibilities are clearly defined, and communication between and among these different functions is strong, one can have a strong and successful shopper marketing effort no matter where it reports. However one's shopper marketing effort lays out on an organization chart, the general idea is to structure to coordinate and vector all resources toward the objective of winning at the POS.

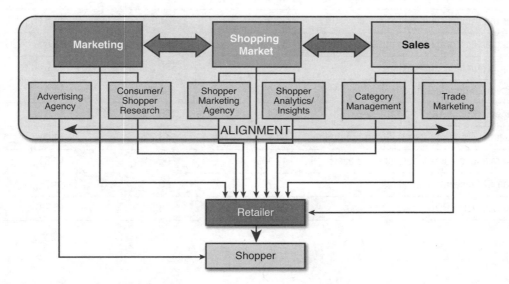

Figure 4-4 *Cross-functional alignment.*

Characteristics of a Best Practice Manufacturer's Shopper Marketing Organization

In the 2012 HUB Magazine/Hoyt & Company Shopper Marketing survey, respondents were asked to rate their own company's proficiency in planning and implementing shopper marketing strategies and initiatives. The options were Excellent, Very Good, Average, and Poor/Not so Good. The results listed in Table 4-4 reflect the responses of companies that consider their shopper marketing efforts Excellent—in other words, best practice. What are the most important criteria that set the "Excellents" apart?

- 100% of Excellents use a full path-to-purchase approach.
- 100% measure results on an account-specific basis.
- 93% have a dedicated budget for shopper marketing and two-thirds also have a dedicated budget for shopper research.
- 79% report to marketing or general management, and two-thirds of these have changed their reporting structure since inception.

Table 4-4 Key Criteria That Differentiate Shopper Marketing Best Practitioners

Measure	All Respondents	Excellents	Not So Good/Poor
5+ years in SM	38.1%	80.0%	20.0%
20+ people in department	21.2%	60.0%	4.0%
SM reports to marketing/general management	65.5%	78.6%	48.0%
Changed reporting structure	32.2%	66.7%	23.5%
Positioned as corporate cross-functional strategy	51.8%	53.3%	38.8%
Full path-to-purchase approach	58.9%	100.0%	42.9%
Established funding/dedicated budget	75.0%	93.3%	62.8%
SM budget is 7% of A&P	30.4%	46.7%	14.3%
10+ retailers with account-specific programming	24.9%	46.7%	14.0%
Measure results on an account-specific basis	42.1%	100.0%	17.6%
Dedicated SM research budget	53.7%	66.7%	34.7%
Measure long-term ROI	23.1%	53.3%	10.7%

Despite the years of developing shopper marketing expertise displayed by these best practitioners, key problems are still exhibited by too many practitioners of the discipline. These problems are discussed in the following sections.

Lack of Top Management Understanding and Commitment

A lot of new companies come into shopper marketing every year. The percent of 2012 respondents new to shopper marketing in the past two years exceeds both 2010 and 2011, as shown in Table 4-5. While growth of the discipline is positive, often companies establish shopper marketing groups without much top-level understanding of what it is or the commitment it requires if it is to be done well. It is not uncommon for a retailer to ask the sales department to present the company's shopper marketing programs or to buy into the retailer's shopper marketing programs. Sales, in an attempt to be responsive to that retailer, quickly determine that they need to "get into" shopper marketing without a complete understanding of what this involves. Ironically, even a bad shopper marketing program can show improved results over trade promotion alone, so they think they have accomplished something without understanding what the true potential of shopper marketing might be for their brands and company.

Table 4-5 Experience with Shopper Marketing

Years in Shopper Marketing	2009	2010	2011	2012
1-2 years	34.3%	27.0%	24.0%	27.2%
3-4 years	21.3%	26.5%	25.6%	26.9%
5+ years	28.7%	34.5%	45.5%	38.1%
Not involved	15.7%	12.0%	5.0%	7.7%

Lack of Preparation, Process, and Procedural Know-How

When, as in the previous example, shopper marketing departments are authorized with no prior planning and no idea of who or what is involved, nothing of significance changes except titles and nomenclature; for example, category director becomes shopper director, and the word "shopper" is substituted for the word "consumer" in all marketing communications. As one retailer put it, "The same person is performing the same activities as before with only a title change."[3]

Lack of Collaboration and Integration across Multifunctional Organizations

In many cases, marketing divorces itself from the process because it views anything having to do with the word "shopper" as tactical. Firms that "get" shopper marketing see it as anything but simply tactical. In our minds and the minds of top leaders at major Fortune 100 manufacturers and some leading retailers, for example, Kroger, Safeway, and Best Buy, shopper marketing is a key strategic approach to survival and growth. But in the cases where firms see shopper marketing as tactical, even sales does little more than pay lip service to it because sales is incented to meet GSV (gross sales value) objectives, not "build equity" through what it perceives as nonimpactful activities such as in-store messaging. What they miss is the fact that shopper marketing ties some of the most powerful messaging—that is, in-store—with out-of-store—or pre-store—messaging through the entire path to purchase.

It is actually amazing that brands have done so well over the past 40 years *despite* having so little tie-in or integration between out-of-store and in-store marketing communications. Shopper marketing is so intuitive that it begs the question: "Why didn't we think of this before?!"

One answer to this is the advertising agency that for a long time—and we might say justifiably—viewed direct-to-consumer advertising as the only meaningful way to communicate with target consumers. All other forms of communications were viewed as secondary or supplemental. However, retailer consolidation changed this game: Currently, more people visit Walmart in a month than see prime-time ads on the three major television networks combined. The advent of digital technology and digital devices compounded this: Now consumers could be "touched" through more than a TV set and, in fact, turned to the Internet, mobile, television, and social networking's word-of-mouth to inform their purchase decisions. In addition to this, retail stores became communications vehicles in themselves. For whatever reason, most advertising agencies have been slow to recognize these changes and therefore have been reluctant to cooperate with the many other service providers now required to communicate effectively with the target shopper across the path to purchase continuum.

Lack of Funding

Of the 101 manufacturers who participated in the 2008 Deloitte/GMA Shopper Marketing study, 53% reported that all of their shopper marketing programs were developed on an *ad hoc* basis—in other words, without budgeted funding. While the

2012 HUB/Hoyt study shows improvement—now only 30% operate without a shopper marketing budget (see Table 4-6)—this remains a huge deterrent to shopper marketing success. As mentioned before, marketing funds are committed in advance, and expecting brand teams to fund shopper marketing initiatives opportunistically is unrealistic.

Table 4-6 Shopper Marketing Budgets as a Percent of Total Marketing Budget—2012

Percent Marketing Budget	All	Excellents	Not So Goods
1-3%	17.2%	6.7%	24.5%
4-6%	22.8%	20.0%	16.3%
7-9%	11.4%	20.0%	4.1%
10%+	19.0%	26.7%	10.2%
No budget	29.7%	26.7%	44.9%

The bottom line is that when shopper marketing is marketing-driven it gets funded—and funding is significantly more robust than when shopper marketing is viewed as a function of category management or sales.

Shopper marketing programs that are positioned as cross-functional have significantly more latitude and discretion with respect to the types of shopper-based initiatives that are funded from the shopper marketing budget. Note in Table 4-7 that the cross-functional funding for different types of shopper-based initiatives is significantly greater than the funding from CatMan-based programs in every instance. With respect to this, it is important to note that when these types of events are funded by the shopper marketing department (as opposed to CatMan or sales), the shopper marketing department has significantly greater control over both the construct and execution of the program. On the other hand, it should be acknowledged that in most companies, the category management department—or sales department, for that matter—simply does not have the perspective, skills, or authority to make funding decisions on most of the program initiatives listed in Table 4-7 (syndicated shelf-talkers excepted). In other words, the demands of being Best Practice in a path-to-purchase-driven marketing environment are gradually but inevitably outstripping the capacity of CatMan-based organizations to effectively address them.

Table 4-7 Marketing- Versus Sales-Driven Shopper Marketing Program Funding

Programming funded from shopper marketing budget	All	Marketing-Driven			Sales-Driven			
		Excellents	Cross-Functional	3 years +	Not So Goods	CatMan/ Sales	New
Retailer web ads	29.9%	46.2%	36.4%	34.6%	17.9%	22.8%	22.4%
In-store digital	52.3%	61.5%	61.5%	57.5%	28.6%	43.1%	47.8%
Shopper promotions	46.7%	61.5%	54.0%	49.2%	37.2%	38.7%	46.7%
Syndicated shelf-talkers, coupons, POS	28.7%	27.3%	31.1%	29.6%	15.9%	26.9%	32.9%
Retailer targeting programs (JustforU, dunnhumby)	42.3%	50.0%	50.0%	48.8%	24.4%	35.9%	30.3%

The next four chapters walk you through the details of a four-stage shopper marketing management process that represents the kind of processes that lead to great success stories like these. Although not every company follows the same process, the one we share with you here resembles the general idea followed by those that are most successful. We suggest you adapt this process to suit your own strategies, objectives, and organizational culture.

Interesting Findings from Research

1. Store brands and national brand promotions attract consumers with distinctly different psychographic profiles; differences constitute well-defined and identifiable consumer segments and allow avoidance of head-to-head competition between retailers and manufacturers.[4]

2. Private label brand purchases in a category increase when consumers perceive reduced consequences of making a mistake in brand choice in that category, and when that category has more "search" than "experience" characteristics.[5]

3. Shoppers judge a national brand and a store brand to be of equal quality in an aesthetically pleasing store, but judge the national brand to be of higher quality in an aesthetically unpleasing store. Hence characteristics of an unpleasant store environment might be transferred by consumers onto store brands.[6] (Note that this is an old study but may still be true.)

4. Using techniques developed by the authors, a brand manager can track brand equity using store-level data, gain insights into the drivers of the brand's equity, and manage these drivers to achieve brand equity targets.[7]

5. A measure exists to determine the importance of brands, brand relevance in category (BRiC), that has been tested with 5,777 consumers across 20 product categories and 5 countries.[8]

6. The average image price premium for national brands over private label has been estimated at 26%.[9] (This is an example of the kind of research that must be validated within your own category and updated frequently.)

7. Retail chain loyalty first increases with private label share, but the effect turns negative at private label shares around 35% to 40%. Beyond that, the effect can be negative, so retailers must have a good balance of national and store brands to optimize store traffic, sales, and loyalty.[10]

8. A change in objective brand quality is not fully reflected in customer perceptions of quality until after about six years on average. Across categories, the range is three to nine years. In the first year, only about 20% of the total effect is realized. High-reputation brands enjoy an advantage when competing on quality because consumers update their favorable perceptions more quickly.[11]

Endnotes

1   Kantar Retail, Retail Trade Promotion Study, 2012.

2   SymphonyIRI Consumer Network, 52 weeks ending 4/15/2012.

3   Deloitte, "Delivering the Promise of Shopper Marketing," 2008.

4   Ailawadi, Kusum L., Scott A. Neslin, and Karen Gedenk (2001), "Pursuing the Value-Conscious Consumer: Store Brands Versus National Brand Promotions," *Journal of Marketing*, 65 (January), 71-89.

5   Batra Rajeev and Indrajit Sinha (2000), "Consumer-Level Factors Moderating the Success of Private Label Brands," *Journal of Retailing*, 76 (2), 175-191.

6   Richardson, Paul, Arun K. Jain, and Alan Dick (1996), "The influence of store aesthetics on evaluation of private label brands," *Journal of Product & Brand Management*, 5 (1), 19-28.

7   Sriram, S., Subramanian Balachander, and Manohar U. Kalwani (2007), "Monitoring the Dynamics of Brand Equity Using Store-Level Data," *Journal of Marketing*, 71, 61-78.

8   Fischer, Marc, Franziska Volckner, and Henrik Sattler (2010), "How Important Are Brands? A Cross-Category, Cross-Country Study," *Journal of Marketing Research*, 47 (5), 823-839.

9   Sethuraman, Raj (2000), "What Makes Consumers Pay More for National Brands Than for Store Brands: Image or Quality?" Cambridge, Mass.: Marketing Science Institute Report No. 00-110.

10 Ailawai, Kusum L., Koen Pauwels, and Jan-Benedict E.M. Steenkamp (2008), "Private-Label Use and Store Loyalty," *Journal of Marketing*, 72 (6), 19-30.

11 Mitra, Debanjan, and Peter N. Golder (2006), "How Does Objective Quality Affect Perceived Quality? Short-Term Effects, Long-Term Effects, and Asymmetries," *Marketing Science*, 25 (3), 230-247.

5

Opportunity Identification

Given the foundation provided in the background of shopper marketing, who shoppers are, and how retailers and manufacturers operate, you are now ready to dig into the four-stage process of shopper marketing management. The first stage is opportunity identification and the one we cover in this chapter. All four are shown in Figure 5-1.

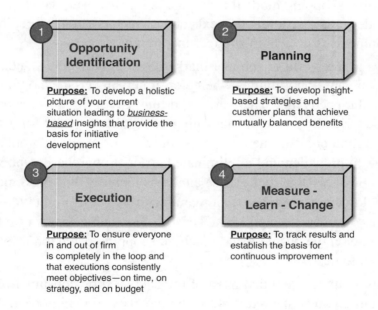

Figure 5-1 *Four phases of the shopper marketing process.*

The difference between best-in-class shopper initiatives and best-in-class promotion initiatives is that with best-in-class shopper initiatives, business-based insights drive the agenda, whereas with best-in-class promotion initiatives, the creative drives the agenda.

Translated into practical terms, this means that shopper initiatives are not about the "Big Idea" but about what strategies and executions address mutual problems and opportunities for both brands and key retail customers. In addition, because the scope of these problems and opportunities is almost always broader than activating purchase at the point-of-sale, shopper marketing is not just about promotion but encompasses the full range of considerations and tools necessary to *market* one's brands across the full path to purchase.

As we explained earlier, shopper marketing is greater than the sum of its parts. It is not traditional marketing and merchandising "stuck together." In shopper marketing, insights are focused on consumers *when they are in shopper mode*. This point cannot be emphasized enough. The same person, that is, consumer, behaves, thinks, and feels differently depending on the shopper mode she is in. Certain retailers are set up to focus on her needs when she is in a specific mode—for example, Walgreens when she is concerned about convenience and pharmaceuticals—so a retailer can often anticipate, at least generally, what shopping mode the shopper is in. However, recognizing that different shopping modes create different contexts and as such create the need for different shopping environments is critical in shopper marketing.

Opportunities in the world of shopper marketing are not simply standard business opportunities. There are opportunities where consumers in certain shopping modes are not having particular needs met. There are opportunities for brands to address packaging that is not shopper-friendly or create messaging that makes it easier for a shopper to feel she is making the right choice. There are opportunities for manufacturers and retailers, working together, to grow demand or eliminate barriers to purchase. Opportunities are revealed through business analytics. These analytics include SKU movement data, for example, what sold where and when, that manufacturers get from retailer transaction databases, such as Walmart's Retail Link. They also include analysis of many other forms of data, some on the business and much on shopping behavior, as revealed through numerous methodologies.

It is important to understand that most of the data used by consumer packaged goods (CPG) and consumer goods marketers are a commodity and readily available to anyone who chooses to purchase them. The data that differentiates the "best from the rest" is proprietary—defined as the result of special research conducted to uncover a particular point that will not be addressed by syndicated studies.

The other factor that separates the best from the rest is how one absorbs and processes the available data to derive meaningful and actionable insights. While we are on this subject, let us reiterate what we mean by an *insight*. An insight is a conclusion based on a finding or findings, not the finding or fact itself. For example, "The sky is blue and the sun is shining" are findings. "It probably won't rain today" is the conclusion or insight.

This is an important differentiation because most confuse the two. *Prioritized* business-based insights are the optimum end-result of the opportunity identification step.

This step should culminate in a list of prioritized insights that evolve naturally from the research one does in working one's way through the opportunity identification process. Obviously, the more thorough and exacting your research in this step is, the better the quality and depth of your insights will be.

Best practice companies suggest that the opportunity identification step be done annually on a zero knowledge basis—that is, rigorously completed from top to bottom regardless of what one might think he already knows about his situation, brands, consumers, customers, shoppers, and so on. This is to ensure that no stone is left unturned and that prior impressions or biases do not get in the way of developing fresh insights that incorporate year-upon-year market changes or shifts in consumer/shopper attitudes. It is obvious, for example, that because of the economic changes that occurred through 2007 to 2010, what the shopper thinks and feels today is significantly different from what he thought just two years ago. Conducting a fresh opportunity identification analysis is the only way to ferret out these details and ensure that one's shopper initiatives are currently relevant.

Opportunity Identification Process

The opportunity identification process involves a situation assessment, followed by an identification of whom one wants to target, and then culminating with specific insights relevant to that target group of shoppers, as illustrated in Figure 5-2.

Figure 5-2 *Generating insights.*

Five key areas must be diagnosed to develop a holistic picture of your current situation, which include socioeconomic trends, brand understanding, consumer understanding, customer understanding, and shopper understanding (see Figure 5-3).

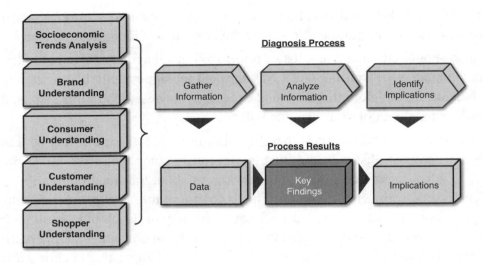

Figure 5-3   *Understanding the market.*

Socioeconomic Trends Analysis

In looking for socioeconomic trends, focus on macro consumer trends that influence or can influence the trajectory of the business. Key analyses may include

- Population trends
- Aging trends
- Economic trends
- Social trends
- Retail trends
- Ethnic trends
- Health trends
- Eating trends
- Shopping trends
- Technological trends
- Competitive trends

Sources of information for this assessment include trade publications, industry conferences and newsletters, mainstream press, Internet, your key customers, current almanac, local chamber of commerce, USDA, and your company's proprietary shopper insights.

You will use this for

- Identifying trends that can be leveraged to grow the business and potential ways to leverage them
- Identifying trends that could hurt the growth of the business and how to mitigate their impact
- Providing a top down framework for the development of your shopper strategy

How are trends influencing your consumers today? What opportunities do you see for your brands given your knowledge about how socioeconomic trends are affecting the following areas?

- Change in impulse versus planned purchase ratios (are shoppers making more lists—and sticking to them?)
- Eat-at-home versus away-from-home meal occasions
- Private label inroads
- Private label pricing spreads
- Unemployment—geographic pockets
- Consumer confidence/retreat to essentials
- Payday-to-payday spending patterns—which brands/categories? Which retailers?
- Resurgence in value brands
- Increased retailer pressures on price points/demand for additional price subsidies
- Impact on basket/transaction sizes
- Retailer changes in positioning/merchandising strategies
- Supermarket versus supercenter versus club trip frequencies
- Impending inflation

Brand Understanding

This section focuses on developing an in-depth understanding of your key brands' fundamentals. If you are a manufacturer, we mean your brands. If you are a retailer, we mean either the critical brands you rely on or your own private label brands. It all applies. Focus on those aspects that are relevant in planning and implementing your shopper initiatives.

You may want to gather information by working down a checklist like this:

- Brand positioning (value/middle/premium)
- Brand dynamics—elastic/merchandising responsive or need based
- Brand usage cycles/purchase frequencies

- Core equities—POPs (Points of Parity) and PODs (Points of Differentiation) to highlight in in-store marketing and messaging
- Position in market and growth trends—channels/key customers versus national
- Short- and long-term objectives—by trade class and channel, if available
- Pricing, messaging, and promotion strategies (for alignment with in-store initiatives)
- Market advertising and promotion support schedule (to vector resources)
- HH (household) penetration, CDIs (Category Development Index), and BDIs (Brand Development Index)—in-market versus national (for efficient targeting)
- Key brand/SKU distribution voids
- Market basket analysis—impact on basket sizes (for initiative development)
- Seasonality (for timing)
- Performance in your key customers—strengths, weaknesses, and opportunities/gaps

Sources of data for this kind of research include CAPs (customer assistance programs or corrective action plans), annual brand plans (ABPs), and brand team-provided CTC profile (core target consumer profiles).

You use this information for

- Foundational knowledge you will use in virtually *all* shopper marketing-based activities
- Leveraging your equities to guide and influence along the path to purchase
- Making informed in-store marketing and messaging choices
- Portfolio marketing—grouping like brands with lead brands

The Brand Equity Pyramid

For many manufacturers, shopper marketing is now marketing. Unlike traditional marketing, however, the objective of shopper marketing is to capture and sustain the target consumer's attention and interest throughout the entire path to purchase—as some put it "from couch to shelf." The principal way that best practice marketers do this is by leveraging their equities via messaging at strategic points along the path. The key to this is to know what equities are most relevant to one's target consumers as they morph into a shopper mindset. Fortunately, there is a structured way to address this issue known as the *brand equity pyramid*. This enables one to identify and catalog the core equities of one's brands relative to competition and is illustrated in Figure 5-4.

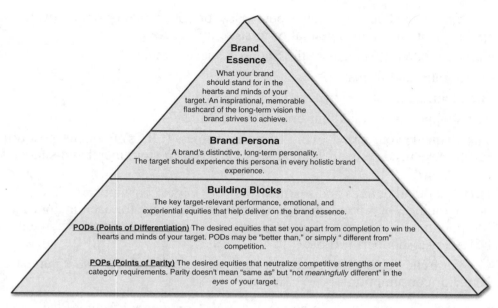

Figure 5-4 *The brand equity pyramid.*

Consumer Understanding

Consumer behavior has been a central part of scholastic marketing research for many decades. This research draws a great deal on the disciplines of psychology, social psychology, sociology, anthropology, behavioral economics, and neurology to name a few. Researchers rely on many methods, from observation, to one-on-one depth interviews, group interviews, participation, surveys, experiments, and mathematical modeling to better understand consumer behavior. To do this well requires an understanding of philosophy of science as well since there are many ways of "knowing." We offer some interesting pieces of knowledge we have on consumer behavior as it relates to shopper marketing in our "Interesting Findings from Research" sections of each chapter. But what you need to know at this point are two things. First, most brand managers and now many retailer marketers are very well versed in what we know about consumer behavior. Thus, we do not feel a need to cover a lot of that here. Here we are focused on a management process for understanding consumers. Second, there is a distinct pattern to the kinds of consumer understanding shopper marketers want. The basic objective here is to determine who the consumer is for your brands and understand why she loves these brands. Again it may help to follow a checklist of questions or categories of information you will need:

- Percent planned versus impulse purchases for your brand or brand loyalty indices (predisposition versus potential of in-store influence)
- Purchase intent (to calculate the Shopper Success Index)
- Usage rates and forms
- Brand attitudes
- The shopper needs that your brands best fulfill
- The channels your brands' core target consumers (CTCs) frequent most often to fulfill these needs (channel/brand alignment, for in-store merchandising and messaging)
- How the brand defines and segments its core target consumers (CTCs)— demographics, psychographics, and shopping behavior for each major segment— for potential alignment with your customers' predefined shopper segments or heavy loyal shoppers (HLSs)
- Current trends/competitive activities that would affect *this brand's* purchase behavior/consumption

Sources of this information can be brand teams, Commercial Action Plans, and Annual Brand Plans. Brands should provide brand CTC profiles and update annually.

You use this information for understanding consumers' predisposition to buy versus in-store potential to influence the purchase of your brands, determining how best to leverage shopper needs by channel and customer, and understanding your key brands' CTCs by segment. You need this for alignment with your key retailers' predefined shopper segments or heavy loyal shoppers (HLSs).

Customer Understanding

"Customer" here refers to the retailer, that is, the manufacturer's customer, not the "consumer" or the "shopper." Customer understanding should be sufficiently deep to identify issues and opportunities that *only* your brands can effectively address.

The checklist that helps you think through what you know about your retail customer follows:

- How do your key customers position themselves against their key competitors ("Shop smart. Live better" versus "Ingredients for life," etc.)—*their* key equities/Points of Differentiation (PODs)?
- What are your customer's business objectives—overall and by department/ category?

- What strategies do your retail customers utilize to execute against these objectives—for example, themes/platforms and/or shopper segmentations—and to what extent do they actually execute against these segmentations?
- What technology is employed by your customers—digital signage, in-store TV/radio, direct mail coupons, use of customer demographics and profiles, self-service technology, as in coupon dispensers, self-checkouts, and so on, and what are the costs of using each?
- What are your customers' promotion merchandising protocols? What are the "dos and don'ts" of what is acceptable versus what isn't?
- How do your customers segment their shoppers—the demographic, psychographic, and behavioral composition of each segment—for alignment with your brands' CTC segments?
- What shopper needs/trip missions are your customers best configured to fulfill—for in-store merchandising and messaging executions?
- What are the current customer issues and opportunities relative to one's brands/categories?

Sources of information here might be customer teams, category management, retailer 10Ks/annual reports, industry conferences (for example, Kantar Research), trade press, and collaboration with relevant customer departments and executives.

You use this information for identifying customer issues and opportunities that are "ownable" by your brands, developing *relevant* shopper-based strategies and initiatives that provide *balanced mutual benefits,* and as a basis for higher level collaboration and customer penetration.

Shopper Understanding

The next step beyond customer understanding is to focus on the shopper. Shopper understanding should "get under the numbers" and focus on how your brands' CTCs behave as shoppers of your key customers. The checklist we offer for helping you think through this analysis includes

- Shopper needs/trip missions—what are they and how can you best address these needs? This seems to be best done via brand-sponsored proprietary research on a customer-specific basis.
- Where are key shopper decision points for your brands? Does your brand need to be on the shopper's list? Does the category or the occasion when the shopper uses your brand—for example, lunch—need to be on the list? If your brand is primarily impulse-driven, what are key locations or messaging that trigger purchase?

- The purchase barriers—what are they for your CTCs and your customers' HLSs? What needs to be addressed to ensure that nothing gets in the way of your winning at the POS? (We cover purchase barriers later in this chapter.)
- How do your key brands' shoppers typically navigate the store? What are the optimum locations for media/POP placement to guide and influence shoppers along the path?
- Shopper Success Index results—calculate the simple single number equation for evaluating the effectiveness of your previous year's shopper initiatives.
- What is the overall health of your brands at the POS? Determine this by performing an in-store brand health assessment.
- Research opportunities—what would you like to know but don't and how might this *significantly* benefit both your brands and your key customers?

Sources for this information include brand teams, customer teams, category management, shopper insights, store checks, and collaboration with relevant customer executives.

You use this for understanding how to best message the path to purchase, leverage the in-store environment to win at the POS, identify in-store problems and opportunities relating to your key brands, and establish a basis for meaningful collaboration.

Shopper Success Index—SSI

The Shopper Success Index (SSI) is a diagnostic tool that enables you to assess whether the shopper's predisposition to buy a brand and the brand's in-store performance are in balance. By recalibrating the index on a semi-annual or annual basis, you can decide where to put emphasis for each brand in each of your key customers for the following year. The SSI is calculated by determining the ratio of on-the-shelf market share to claimed purchase intent among consumers when not in the store. The calculation is shown in Figure 5-5.

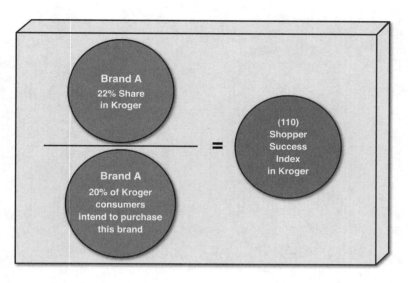

Figure 5-5   *Shopper Success Index.*

Using SSI in your Key Customers

As a rule of thumb, if the SSI is between 80 and 120, your shopper marketing initiatives for your brand in this customer are meeting expectations. The optimum value is 100. If the SSI is over 120, the brand is either too retailer-dependent and/or lacks sufficient predisposition to buy (equity/awareness outside the store). To clarify, a higher SSI means that share in the store is *higher than what would be expected* given consumers' (relatively low) predisposition to buy. Specifically, shoppers are not aware enough and excited enough about the brand outside the store ahead of time to produce a higher score in the denominator.

If the SSI is under 80, the predisposition to buy is there, but the brand is not performing to potential in this retailer. Specifically, whatever is happening in the store is not translating into enough share inside the store to make the equation balanced.

Once again, over 120 as shown in Figure 5-6, the brand is too trade dependent or lacks sufficient predisposition to buy (equity/awareness).

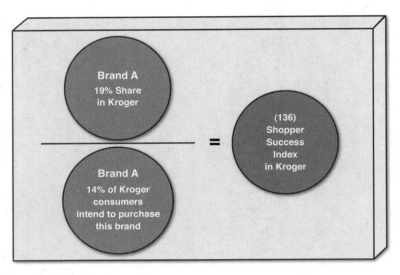

Figure 5-6 *SSI over indexing example.*

If SSI is under 80, as shown in Figure 5-7, consumers are predisposed to buy, but the brand is not winning at the POS.

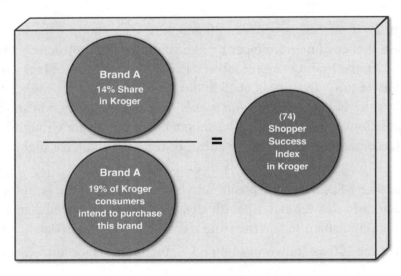

Figure 5-7 *SSI under indexing example.*

To obtain the information to calculate SSI, one can use the following sources. For in-store/category share, use data from one's category management group, Nielsen/IRI, or customer-provided POS data. For purchase intent, one can use Nielsen/IRI Household (HH) Panel Data (easiest) or proprietary customer-specific research. To then calculate SSI, simply divide one's brand share in retailer by purchase intent of retailer's customers specifically (ideally) or in-market. This can be done nationally or regionally. Update the calculation semi-annually or annually.

Situation Assessment Summary: Listing the Key Implications

Look across the full diagnosis of trends, consumer, customer, and shopper assessments looking for opportunities. Search for *patterns* in the marketplace and at your key customers. Connect the elements. Ask yourself, what are the major factors impacting your market? What opportunities do these lead to for your brands? Are there brand opportunities within *your key customers*? Remember, shopper marketing is about leveraging brand equity all the way through the path to purchase to the point of sale, which means within specific retailers. What works with one retailer may not work with another. Replication of an idea with a second retailer who directly competes with the first *is not shopper marketing!* This is because you would not be helping your retail customers differentiate themselves from *their* competitors. Implications for your brand emerge out of the research conducted, such as trend analyses, as suggested in Figure 5-8.

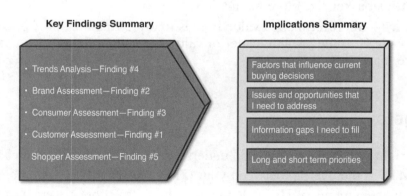

Key Findings Summary

- Trends Analysis—Finding #4
- Brand Assessment—Finding #2
- Consumer Assessment—Finding #3
- Customer Assessment—Finding #1
- Shopper Assessment—Finding #5

Implications Summary

- Factors that influence current buying decisions
- Issues and opportunities that I need to address
- Information gaps I need to fill
- Long and short term priorities

Figure 5-8   *Implications summary.*

So, getting back to interpreting your assessments, what does it look like? Figure 5-9 shows an example. Using the information depicted in Figure 5-9, we can offer some implications.

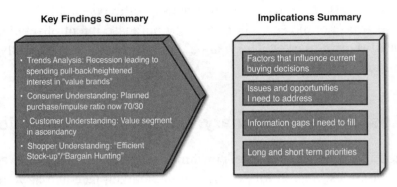

Figure 5-9 *Implications summary example.*

Interpretation (These Are Hypothetical)

- **Influencing buying decisions**—Recession benefiting our "value" brands.
- **Issues/opportunities**—Shift in planned/impulse ratios places premium on winning at POS.
- **Information gaps**—How money concerns have changed shopping behavior—needs/trips/basket size/store navigation?
- **Priorities**—Short term: Use value brands to draft laggards, portfolio approach. Long term: Become growth leader in value segment/collaborate on value image in-store marketing opportunities.

Right Targets

Targeting the right shoppers demands an understanding of the mutual target shopper (MTS). The MTS is the overlap between your CTCs and your key customer's (that is, retailer's) shopper segments or HLSs. Knowing who these shoppers are and why they choose or don't choose your brands is essential to developing *relevant* strategies and efficient initiatives (see Figure 5-10).

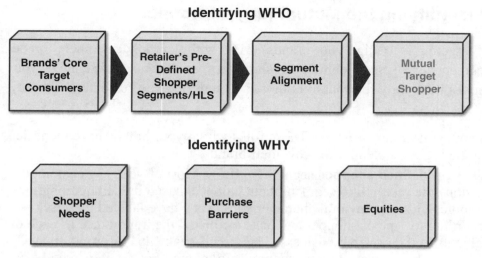

Identifying WHO

Brands' Core Target Consumers → Retailer's Pre-Defined Shopper Segments/HLS → Segment Alignment → Mutual Target Shopper

Identifying WHY

Shopper Needs   Purchase Barriers   Equities

Figure 5-10 *The who and the why.*

Targeting involves defining right target choices and making them actionable. It requires an understanding of both the consumer and shopper. Although these are often the same person, a consumer's mindset may shift once she gets into a shopper mode. Therefore, knowing how shoppers think helps you shape your brand and category marketing strategies and plans. Brands and initiatives should be tailored to break through the clutter and delight shoppers while winning with your key customers. To meet this challenge, it is important to understand your target shopper and her desires, wants, and aspirations. This means immersing yourself in your target shopper's life and seeing the world as she sees it. This enables you to discover insights about how she shops and about her desired shopping experience.

Understanding your CTC encompasses more than his demographics, psychographics, and attitudes. We need to understand how your CTC shops and who and what influences his purchase decisions, when, and how. To do this, we need to consider his shopping needs and purchase barriers—that is, barriers the shopper confronts. You need to learn how to leverage your equities to guide and influence the shopper along the path to purchase and to "stop/hold/close" along this path to ensure that your brands become the brands of choice at the POS.

The process and business rationale for a) targeting (identifying the mutual target shopper), b) leveraging shopper needs, c) overcoming purchase barriers, and d) leveraging your equities along the path to purchase are detailed in this book. What follows is a summary of the key steps involved in this process.

Remember: *If you don't understand how your CTC shops, you don't understand your CTC!*

Process for Identifying the Mutual Target Shopper

The objective of targeting is to align your brands' CTCs with your key customers' predefined shopper segments or HLSs to identify the *mutual target shopper*. This enables you to develop initiatives inherently relevant to both your brands and key customers. The key elements are

- **Brand's core target consumers**—Those folks whom your brands have identified as having the highest potential to grow their brands.
- **Customer's predefined shopper segments/HLS**—Most of your key customers have also done the research to segment their shoppers based on demographic, psychographic, and/or behavioral characteristics. They have labeled these segments according to type of shopper and have estimated the importance of each of these segments to their overall business. They freely make this information available to their suppliers because they encourage alignment. For retailers who have not segmented their shoppers, the default is to align with their heavy loyal shoppers for whom similar information is available.
- **Segment alignment**—HLSs or heavy loyal shoppers are those folks whom your retailers have identified as their highest spending, and most profitable, customers. According to IRI, 33% of shoppers account for over 75% of sales in all channels except Grocery (where 33% do 59% of sales). Every retailer with a frequent shopper card knows exactly who its heavy shoppers are.
- **Mutual target shopper**—This is the overlap between your brands' core target consumers and your customer's predefined shopper segments or heavy loyal shoppers. While this is never a precise alignment, you should strive to make it as close as possible.

Understanding Why Shoppers Buy or Do Not Buy Your Brands

A key part of understanding your target shopper is to understand why she goes shopping in the first place (shopper needs/trip missions) and why she does or does not buy your brands once in the store (purchase barriers). Equally important is the ability to leverage your core brand equities via marketing and messaging along the path to purchase so that your brands become the brands of choice at the POS. These three subjects are summarized here:

- Shopper needs influence why your CTCs shop where they shop, what they do once inside the store, and why they buy what they buy. At a basic level, shoppers are often time constrained (or unconstrained), money constrained (or unconstrained), shopping for themselves or shopping for others (only or as well). By developing a solid understanding of what shopper needs your brands best fulfill, and the channels or formats your CTCs shop most often to fulfill these needs, you can develop shopper-based initiatives that are relevant to the mutual shopper.

- A purchase barrier is an element of the product offering or retail environment that prevents a shopper from buying your brands. There are two types of purchase barriers:

  - **Deselection barriers**—Barriers that cause a brand to be ruled out on a cursory overview of the category
  - **Selection barriers**—Barriers that prevent a brand from being chosen upon closer inspection

  The order of priority is to address deselection barriers first, and then selection barriers. Overcoming purchase barriers is a top priority.

- Equities are what your brands stand for in the hearts and minds of your core target consumers (or what they want them to stand for). To leverage your equities along the path to purchase, you want to guide and influence the shopper's journey with reminders of how great your brands are, what they can do to make her life easier, and how they can help fulfill her *immediate shopping needs*. A key component of leveraging your equities is relevant and effective in-store messaging.

The outcome of all this work should be a mutual target shopper profile (MTS profile) as laid out in Table 5-1.

Table 5-1 Shopper Profile/Implications Template

Shopper Profile	Planning Implications
Who	• Brand bundling choices
• Demographics/psychographics?	• Cross-merchandising
• What are his/her intellectual needs?	• Messaging choices
• What are his/her emotional needs?	• Imagery choices
• What's on his/her mind?	• Equity choices
• How does he/she define value?	• Value positioning
What	• Messaging choices
• What's the purpose of the shopping trip?	• Equity choices
• What hurdles does the shopper have in purchasing our brands?	• Packaging
Where	• Messaging choices
• Why does he/she shop at this retailer?	• Display placement
• What parts of the store does he/she shop?	• Our firm's value to customer
• How important is he/she to this retailer?	
• Where else does he/she shop?	

When

- When does he/she shop?
- How often does he/she shop?
- How often does he/she buy our categories?
- What other categories does he/she buy?

- Timing (frequency/demos, etc.)
- Offer requirement (size/units)
- Our brand bundling choices
- Cross-merchandising
- Display location

Why

- Does he/she like shopping?
- For whom is he/she shopping?
- With whom is he/she shopping?

- Messaging choices
- Shopper-based design

How

- Does he/she shop for everything the same way?
- For how long does he/she shop?
- For how long does he/she shop the category?
- Is he/she shopping from a list?
- Is he/she shopping within a specific budget?
- What can he/she afford?
- How does he/she make purchase decisions?
- How does he/she get to the store?

- POS impact
- Messaging placement
- Display location
- Our brand bundling choices
- Cross-merchandising
- Value positioning
- Equity choices
- Product size requirements

Right Insights

Now that you have done a situation assessment and zeroed-in on the right targets, the last step in the opportunity identification process is to develop the right insights. Right insights are derived from our knowledge of our brands, consumers, customers, and shoppers to drive initiatives that achieve one or more of the six primary shopper marketing objectives.

Where do insights come from? Insights evolve or "pop out" naturally from your research in the situation assessment and right target steps (the "Ahas!"). They are not forced but come to you as you work your way through these steps. Most of the best inductive, theory-building scholastic research also lets insights (also known as interpretations) emerge. They come from being steeped in the data, not from giving them a cursory glance. Immersion is the key. You are looking for those nuggets of gold that your competitors did not take the time to dig for. These provide the basis for relevant opportunity identification and strategy development. The key elements of an insight-generation process are

- Information
- Integration
- Immersion
- Implications
- Insights

The more thorough your research, the fresher and more compelling your insights will be. Use what you have learned to form a holistic picture of the mutual shopper and why he buys or doesn't buy your brands in your customer. Think carefully about predispositions, shopper needs, purchase barriers, brand and customer equities, equities that you can leverage along the path, and so on. Step inside your shopper's life to understand how he thinks (intellectual needs) and feels (emotional needs; "affect" in psychology). Which barriers and shopper needs predominate at the present time? Think through the decision process from the shopper's point of view and determine what will best overcome barriers and/or meet his needs. Make sure these are actionable and lend themselves to executions that address specific objectives (for example, highlighting equities, overcoming purchase barriers, and/or leveraging shopper needs and opportunities).

Prioritizing Insights and Opportunities

Insights are not findings or facts but *conclusions* you draw about your findings or facts. For example, what would you *conclude* about the following? Focus not just on the individual questions but the big picture. Connect the dots:

- Who are your key brands' CTCs? What is important to them? What sets them apart—differentiating characteristics that you can leverage?
- Why does she shop in your customer? What shopper needs does your customer best fulfill?
- How is this relevant to your CTCs? How would you leverage this in in-store marketing or messaging?
- How does your CTC shop your customer (frequency, transaction size, categories shopped, navigation, and so on)?
- What purchase barriers do you need to overcome?
- What is the impact of the current socioeconomic pressures on your CTC's shopping behavior?
- Customer's objectives, priorities, equities, platforms, and protocols?
- Segmentation alignment—your brands' CTCs with your customer's predefined segments or HLSs?

- How are your brands performing in your customer versus category, market and national?
- Overall effectiveness of previous year's shopper marketing initiatives (SSI)?
- Role of our brands/categories in addressing key shopper issues/capitalizing on opportunities?

At the conclusion of this step, you may have developed six or seven insights coming out of the preceding subjects that could be used as the basis for shopper-centric strategy or initiative development. Translate these insights into opportunities that you know on judgment are actionable within the protocols and capabilities of your particular customer. Use the Opportunity Evaluation Worksheet in Table 5-2 to "rank" each opportunity according to the criteria on the worksheet. You may also want to develop your own criteria to add to this list. But the ones we offer here are important. Then transfer your scores for each opportunity to the Opportunity Ranking Worksheet in Table 5-3. This gives you a prioritized list of opportunities on which to focus. Finally, conduct an initiative value assessment to prescreen the potential of your brands to address the opportunities you identify.

The Opportunity Evaluation Worksheet helps you prioritize the opportunities that seem worthy of pursuit. It gives a bit of discipline to what otherwise could be a subjective process. Rank each opportunity on a scale of 5 (High) to 1 (Low) based on your judgment of how well the opportunity meets the following criteria. Then transfer scores to the Opportunity Ranking Worksheet.

Table 5-2   Opportunity Evaluation Worksheet

Is Opportunity Ownable?	Is Opportunity Sustainable?	Addresses Key Brand Objectives?	Addresses Key Customer Objectives?	Addresses Mutual Shopper Objectives?
Can we "own" this opportunity in this retailer? Do we bring unique equities that other brands cannot replace (e.g., category leadership position, scale, contractual assets, etc.)? Can this retailer hijack this opportunity and easily do it on its own? Can we bake-in elements that require our involvement for success?	Is this opportunity ongoing? Or can this opportunity be repeated over time, (e.g., annual event)? Can this opportunity be refreshed over time? Can this opportunity be expanded over time?	Financial objectives—volume and profit? Awareness/trial? Loyalty? Specific target? Enhances relationship with CTC?	Financial objectives—volume and margin? + Transaction size? + Traffic? + Loyalty/Frequency? Enhances relationship with HLS? Provides source of differentiation? Makes it easy to find and buy? Leverages retailer equities?	Saves time? Saves money? Solves a problem? Improves shopping experience?
Ex: 2 Points	2 Points	4 Points	3 Points	4 Points

When you use this to determine the priorities for your initiatives, focus only on those that will deliver the most important balanced mutual benefits (see Table 5-3).

Table 5-3 Opportunity Ranking Worksheet

Opportunity	Ownable?	Sustainable?	Brand Win?	Retailer Win?	Shopper Win?	Score
Ex. Expand underdeveloped baking category	2	2	4	3	4	15

Initiative Value Assessment

The initiative value assessment (IVA) is a rubric. This means that it not only offers scores on criteria but explains in detail what each score for each criterion means. It is used to score the value a particular shopper marketing initiative brings to the retailer. Use the IVA to gauge the potential of the opportunities you identify to gain customers' acceptance. This is not a tool to gauge the value of an initiative to your brand or your company. Adjust priorities as necessary.

The IVA focuses on five key customer needs, each weighted based on importance. Note that these weighting assignments are customer-specific and should be reallocated according to your assessment of how important each of these five factors is to your particular customer. The following weights and the weights on the IVA template itself are therefore hypothetical:

- **Customer profitability (20%)**—Initiatives that build overall customer category margin and cash profit with above-category average and sustainable margins receive greater than average sales fundamentals support.
- **Category growth (25%)**—Customers consistently respond favorably to fresh ideas that add new category volume.
- **SKU productivity (30%)**—Initiatives need SKU-level volume projections sufficient to earn and maintain retail distribution.
- **Shoppability (10%)**—The combination of packaging, in-store design, and POS/shelf/case efforts needs to sufficiently communicate product concept and consumer benefits.
- **Customer simplicity/efficiency (15%)**—Turnkey executions that leverage existing customer capabilities and timings receive stronger support than ideas requiring new capabilities.

As you will see, the IVA provides a range of qualitative descriptions for each of the five criteria, allowing your initiative development team to rate each initiative on a scale of 5 (high) to 1 (low). To arrive at a final determination of the overall potential value of your initiative to your customer, multiply the scores you give to each category by the weighted value you assign to each.

Insight Examples

Insights do not need to be complicated, but they do need to be business-based. We share here some sample insights that have driven successful shopper initiatives.

- Pet food purchased at farm and feed stores is a destination, yet many farm and feed shoppers shop other channels for pet food. The sporting goods category in these stores is a major adjacency and major source of business. In-store marketing and messaging needs to relate to the strong bond between the owner and his sporting dog (mutual and unconditional love, respect, devotion, pride, satisfaction, and trust).
- Mom could understand her baby better and become her own "expert" if she could see the world through her baby's eyes.
- Aware that breakfast is important but time limited in the morning, breakfast varies according to time and choices easily available.
- Health and Beauty Care (HBC) in a supermarket doesn't engender the "emotional connection" necessary to have successful HBC merchandising because of commodity approach and poor departmental ambience, for example, linoleum floors.
- Shoppers are skeptical that a full-size, quality mop could come in a box this size.
- The 18 to 24 year old male sees the local convenience store as his refrigerator.

Methodologies for Developing Insights

Although this book is not intended to serve as a market research methods text, we do want to offer a few comments on research methods being employed in industry so that you are aware of your options. The market research and specifically shopper insights community is extensive and highly skilled. You should be aware of

- The methods available
- The kinds of questions each method is best suited to answer
- Sources of expertise for planning and executing the research

Because so much of shopper marketing rests on solid insights, the old adage of garbage in garbage out has never been more appropriate.

Inductive Methods

Some methods are best used to "build theory" or in practitioner terms, develop frameworks and hypotheses. They are used to break your mind from conventional thinking, to look deeply into a "phenomenon" such as a particular shopper segment's shopping experiences. Several approaches are used in industry and academia to develop theory:

- **In-depth interviews**—In-depth interviews are conversations conducted by a skilled researcher to elicit complex nuances of individuals' experiences, perceptions, attitudes, motivations, and emotions. They can be conducted many different ways, but this is a case where not just anything goes. These conversations are guided by one or more theoretical lenses. For example, you may be interested in the "meaning" of a shopping experience. Conversely, you may be interested in the shopping process. Looking for social processes is different from looking at psychological meaning. Analyzing this form of data involves transcribing interviews verbatim and conducting extensive *interpretation* of what was said not simply repeating what was said. The skills required here involve not only conversational abilities but a solid understanding of psychology, social psychology, and sociology.
- **Ethnographies**—Ethnographic research emerged out of anthropology. This method involves not only interviews, but also detailed observation and the collection of artifacts, or evidence of the culture of the people being examined. This method is used to understand cultures—groups of people. If you are interested in the norms of behavior and the generally accepted attitudes of a group, you may want to use ethnographies.
- **Shop alongs**—Following along with a shopper either literally or virtually with digital equipment is common in this industry. It is one way researchers have tried to dig deeply into shopper processes as well as their thoughts and emotions as

they actually shop. Often shoppers are asked to "think out loud" into a recorder or to a researcher. It turns out that after a short period of time, most people ignore the intrusion of other researchers or data collection equipment such as cameras and quickly return to their normal shopping behavior.

All these more qualitative methods of induction work well but are limited by what people can and are willing to articulate. Additionally, we know that people often (a) do not do what they say they do, (b) do not accurately recall what they actually did, and (c) do develop reasons for why they did what they did that may not be accurate despite their best efforts at trying to be accurate. We as humans are not very good at tapping into our own motivations, especially for habitual shopping behaviors. For these reasons, many researchers prefer more observational methods. But remember, *all* of these methods should be used in combination to develop the most holistic image of your shoppers. Some of the observation methods being used include

- **Eye tracking**—Eye tracking is used to see where shoppers actually look and how long they focus on specific aspects of packaging, signage, displays, or even other people. We have discovered that humans are prone to notice other humans. How shoppers react to other shoppers or sales associates is as critical to your shopper insights as how they react to marketing media.

- **Video tracking**—Cameras tell you a lot. Watching what people actually do as they shop has long been an effective way to generate insights to behavior. This method is used to observe what aisles shoppers use, the routes they use to shop, how long they stay in certain parts of the store, and the level of interaction they have with products, displays, and people. An enormous amount can be learned from shopper and consumer observation. The limitation here is that observation tells us nothing about motivation, specifically why shoppers are doing what they are doing or what they are thinking and feeling at the time. For example, standing in front of a display may not be—and is often not—a good thing. It may very well mean that the shopper is utterly confused.

There are many other ways we gain insights that help us build frameworks and develop hypotheses. Some border between inductive and deductive tools:

- **Data mining**—The science of finding patterns in large datasets reveals aspects of shopping behavior that we would not generally hypothesize up front, or *a priori*. Data mining is often used to examine transaction (checkout) data and loyalty card data.

- **Neurology**—Neurology is a field, but it relies on various methods for applying this discipline to marketing such as EEG and MRI equipment that help us "see" what parts of the brain are actually activated based on environmental stimuli. This means we can notice if our brand messaging is making shoppers work too hard or if it elicits positive feelings. The former is bad and the latter is good.

- **Behavioral economics**—Like neurology, behavioral economics is a discipline, but it brings with it an approach to developing shopper insights. Much of the work in this area focuses on iterative testing of ideas in an experimental sense, but it has also been used to generate unexpected insights.

Deductive Methods

Then there are the methods we use to test hypotheses and theories. These methods are deductive methods and usually more quantitative in nature. Behavior economically inspired iterative experiments would fit here as well. But the tried-and-true traditional methods involve the following:

- **Surveys**—We are all used to completing surveys. Industry to be honest has rarely tapped the full potential of survey use. Far too often what is measured are simply frequency counts or basic attitudes. In academia, surveys are used to test theories. This is done by using multiple questions to measure specific constructs, think in terms of specific beliefs, feelings, judgments, and behaviors. Sophisticated statistical analyses developed in the field of psychology and applied in marketing for consumer and shopper behavior research can test hypotheses around motivations of behavior we observe. These motivations or drivers of behavior match up quite nicely with what you in practice will call shopper insights. That said, surveys of shoppers' attitudes seem to be falling into the background. There is a risk that we will lose some insights if we eliminate them entirely.
- **Experiments**—The tried-and-true method of choice of deductive researchers is an experiment. Some are controlled and some are field. A controlled experiment has the potential to provide a precise answer to a specific question. Whereas most of the work in inductive research is exerted in analyzing the data once collected (it may take weeks or months to pore through and code video files and interview transcripts), the hard work in experiments and even surveys is up front in the design of the experiment or survey.
- **Mathematical modeling**—All of this research either builds or tests models. However, within the category of mathematical modeling we refer to researchers who, using mathematical estimates or databases of secondary data, construct equations that help predict market behaviors. The field of pricing is well known for this as is currently the field of ROI analysis. Marketing mix modeling helps us determine what marketing media is working to generate the outcomes we want. But it can also help us test hypotheses we have.

The idea in conducting research is to identify patterns, motivations, understanding of shoppers, and business operations that are *insightful,* not merely factual. The deeper and more meaningful your insights the more likely you will create successful shopper marketing programs.

Interesting Findings from Research

1. Category management (CM) never finds the optimal solution (in contrast to the theoretical model) and provides both less variety and higher prices than optimal. This study also demonstrates that profit loss due to CM can be significant.[1]

2. When retailers offer extensive product assortments, they may also be adding cognitive costs to consumers—costs that may diminish the assortment's attractiveness; shoppers find large assortments more favorable in high-risk purchases.[2]

3. Stating prepurchase expectations leads customers to focus on negative aspects of the shopping experience and perceive the same performance more negatively.[3]

4. This research is about drivers impacting the likelihood of adoption and time to adoption of a new loyalty card in a grocery retail context. Attitudinal drivers: customer commitment to store increases likelihood and speed of adoption; behavioral drivers: perceived complexity (of understanding functionality and usefulness of card) increases reluctance to adopt card; perceived risk (privacy loss) does not affect likelihood of adoption, but lengthens adoption time; sociodemographic drivers: customers living close to the store are more likely to adopt and adopt quicker; price/promotion-oriented customers tend to adopt the loyalty card before other adopters.[4]

5. Compensation for a service failure (a substandard service performance as a result of either the service provider or an external factor) enhances repurchase intentions only when the company is responsible for the failure and the failure occurs frequently. If the failure occurs infrequently or the company is not responsible, compensation does not affect repurchase intentions.[5]

Endnotes

1   Cachon, Gérard P. and, A. Gürhan Kök (2007), "Category Management and Coordination in Retail Assortment Planning in the Presence of Basket Shopping Consumers," *Management Science*, (Jun) Vol. 53 (6).

2   Boyd, Eric D. and Kenneth D. Bahn (2009), "When Do Large Product Assortments Benefit Consumers? An Information-Processing Perspective," *Journal of Retailing*, 85 (3), 288-297.

3   Ofir, Chezy and Itamar Simonson (2007), "The Effect of Stating Expectations on Customer Satisfaction and Shopping Experience," *Journal of Marketing Research*, 44 (1), 164-174.

4   Demoulin, Nathalie T. M. and Pietro Zidda (2009), "Drivers of Customers'
    Adoption and Adoption Timing of a New Loyalty Card in the Grocery Retail
    Market," *Journal of Retailing*, 85 (3), 391-405.

5   Grewal, Dhruv, Anne L. Roggeveen, and Michael Tsiros (2008), "The Effect of
    Compensation on Repurchase Intentions in Service Recover," *Journal of
    Retailing* 84 (4), 424-34.

6

Strategic Planning

The second step of our four-stage shopper marketing process is strategic planning (labeled in Figure 6-1 simply as "planning"). Planning involves three components: identifying the right strategies, implementing the right initiatives, and developing the customer plan.

Figure 6-1 *Planning phase.*

Right strategies are your plans for *how* you will capitalize on the opportunities you identified in the previous step. Strategies provide your shopper marketing agency with the platforms/framework for the initiatives and executions your agency will develop to achieve your objectives.

Initiatives are the tactics or executions that bring your brand equities to life. They are what the shopper will experience! The goal is to create a holistic brand experience that reaches the shopper at every contact point and influences her thoughts and actions toward your brand, category, or customer. Although initiatives are tactical, all shopper marketing initiatives should be developed with a strategic framework. Conversely, one must diligently try to avoid "one-offs" designed to satisfy the needs of a moment or placate a retailer's desire for a temporary volume bump to meet quarterly objectives. The way to achieve this is to create a shopper marketing customer plan that is approached strategically with a strong foundation in insights, purchase barriers, and equities.

The customer plan is focused on achieving the *strategic objectives* that you established based on your research in the opportunity identification step. It outlines the nature of—or objectives for—the *specific initiatives* you use to achieve your strategic objectives. Costs should be fully estimated and accompanied by performance metrics that are relevant to all stakeholders, that is, brands, sales, and customers. Remember that shopper marketing is a collaborative effort. Your initiatives are more likely to be approved if you give your retailer the opportunity to input the plan before finalizing.

Shopper marketing develops strategies, determines the nature of—or objectives for—initiatives, finalizes the customer plan, and then turns the plan over to a shopper marketing agency to develop specific executions that align with the strategies outlined in the plan. The process might be depicted as shown in Figure 6-2.

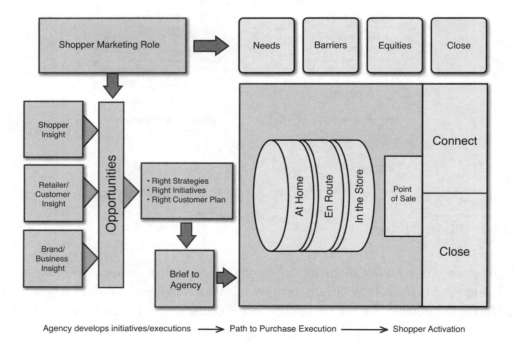

Figure 6-2   *The shopper marketing planning process.*

Right Strategies

What is meant by strategy in this shopper marketing context? A shopper marketing strategy can be viewed as a statement that describes the "how-to" for capitalizing on the prioritized opportunities you identified in the opportunity identification step.

The ideal strategy is a course of action based on your brands' and/or customers' intrinsic strengths that forces your competitors to react to you, rather than the other way around. Walmart's "Always Low Prices" is an example of a strategy that forced supermarkets to react to Walmart for nearly a decade. Your strategy should be broad enough to provide a framework for multiyear implementation yet specific enough to address issues of mutual interest. For example, "Overcoming all purchase barriers involving our health and wellness brands" to support Safeway's "Ingredients for Life" platform is broad enough to enable multifaceted executions over a period of years yet specific enough to be continually relevant to Safeway.

The tendency for many is to jump immediately from the opportunity identification step into thinking about the specific executions that enable them to capitalize on the opportunities or immediately "solve the problem." Agencies can be particularly susceptible to this. In the absence of a strategic framework, this results in a series of disconnected one-offs that have no long-term benefit for either your brands or your customers.

We provide examples of several strategy statements in this chapter. Again, strategies should not be confused with tactics or executions, which are the means to achieve a strategy. Tactics and executions by contrast are the specific activities that can be deployed, consistent with the stated strategy, to capitalize on prioritized opportunities and accomplish stated objectives.

An example might look like this:

Opportunity: Increase relevance with kids.

Strategy: Partner with hot kids properties.

Tactic: Utilize LeapFrog partnership on packaging, website, FSI creative, premiums.

Strategic platforms are often based on the research and specific insights and issues developed during the opportunity identification phase. In the following example, it was learned that the retailer was seeing trip erosion (primarily to the supercenter channel) among an important shopper segment—new moms. Further research uncovered that the erosion occurred when these new moms went back to work and their lives became a juggling act of work and home responsibilities. The objective was to win these new moms back. The strategy was to recognize the new mom's needs and help her address them.

Consequently, the strategic platform was based on the concepts of Daily-Delight-Development as shown in Figure 6-3.

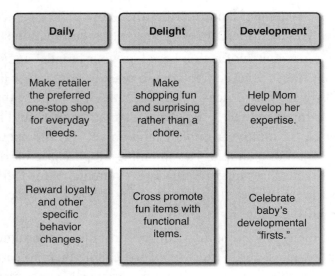

Figure 6-3   *Example strategic platform.*

Formulating a Strategy Statement

Your shopper marketing strategy choices should be broad enough to encompass all you intend to achieve but specific enough to keep your efforts focused. There should be a standard format to your strategy statements.

> **Sample format:** Our shopper marketing strategy with (customer) is to support her objective of (customer's objective) by (customer's strategy) (with target shopper) using (manufacturer's strengths). We expect this to benefit (manufacturer) by (desired benefits).

> **Example:** Our shopper marketing strategy with Safeway is to support their objective of expanding their customer base by making budget-convenience shoppers more valuable to Safeway using PepsiCo marketing expertise and our budget-convenience brands as drivers. We expect this to benefit PepsiCo by increasing customer penetration and gaining retail support for PepsiCo programs.

Planning

In the planning stage we use worksheets to document and guide us through our thinking. In the shopper marketing Strategy Development Worksheet in Table 6-1, you list your customer's objectives, strategies, and HLSs/target segments. Then list strengths and desired benefits for your key brands. Identify which customer objectives, strategies, and targets are most in alignment with your brands' strengths and desired benefits. You need to make explicit choices of strategies to pursue and *not* to pursue.

Table 6-1 Shopper Marketing Strategy Development Worksheet

Customer's Objectives	Customer's Strategies	Target (HLS/Segment)	Your Brand's Strengths	Benefit to Manufacturer

It helps to see a few examples. Here is an example of an over-the-counter brand doing an education/awareness program.

Strategy: Enhance brand's therapeutic image through shopper education by aligning with diabetes care opportunities in retailer.

Research findings that supported this initiative were that:

- There is a strong secondary disease connection (which this brand treats) among those with diabetes.
- Shoppers associate pharmacy with products that promote good health.
- Pharmacy is one of the most heavily visited areas in the store.
- Average waiting time is 10+ minutes.
- Mutual shopper tends to be older, more health conscious.
- Mutual shopper is receptive to reading and receiving health messages.

Shopper initiative/execution: Increase $ / trip of pharmacy shopper by communicating brand's unique benefits in the prescription area to motivate regimen change. Tactics:

- Pamphlet that informs about the connection with diabetes available in the wait area coupled with a product display.

- Floor graphic in the pharmacy area that highlights a salient "headline" about the connection.
- Brief infomercial on in-store TV over the pharmacy counter informing about the connection and how brand can help.

Another example of translating strategy to executions is shown by a cookie brand.

Research: Milk is one of the most frequently purchased items in a supermarket—often the purpose of fill-in trips—yet is often sold as a loss leader with the result that category profitability can be low.

Strategy: Increase basket size for retailer and purchase frequency for cookie brand by associating milk category and cookies in a supermarket.

Shopper initiative/execution: Create impulsive reminders of cookie brand during "fill in" shopping trips. Tactics:

- Shelf-talkers for cookies on milk case
- Shopping cart signage of milk with cookie
- Cookie shipper in the shape of a milk carton
- Disruptive cookie and milk signage with emotional connection messaging

Our third example is a premium-priced men's antiperspirant brand with high brand loyalty but little space on the shelf.

Research: Although brand has high loyalty, its loyal customers had difficulty finding the brand on the shelf in this drug chain. Customers sometimes switched brands—impacting brand sales—or, more frequently, went to another store to buy—impacting retailer sales. While this lack of shelf presence impacted sales, increased shelf space was not justified under category management metrics.

Strategy: Drive sales by guiding and influencing male shoppers to shelf location of the brand in drug chain.

Shopper initiative/execution: Connect with the "no nonsense" mutual target shopper using messages focused on his view of the shopping experience implying that needing guidance for shopping is a badge of manhood. Tactic:

- Use humorous but easily brand-identifiable shelf-talkers or floor graphics for navigation and to help brand stand out in the category.
- Reinforce the "manly" self-image of the target shopper.

Aligning Equities

An important part of strategy development is leveraging mutual equities (see Figure 6-4). Where do your brands and key customers align? Which of your customer's equities or platforms can your brands best support for mutual benefit?

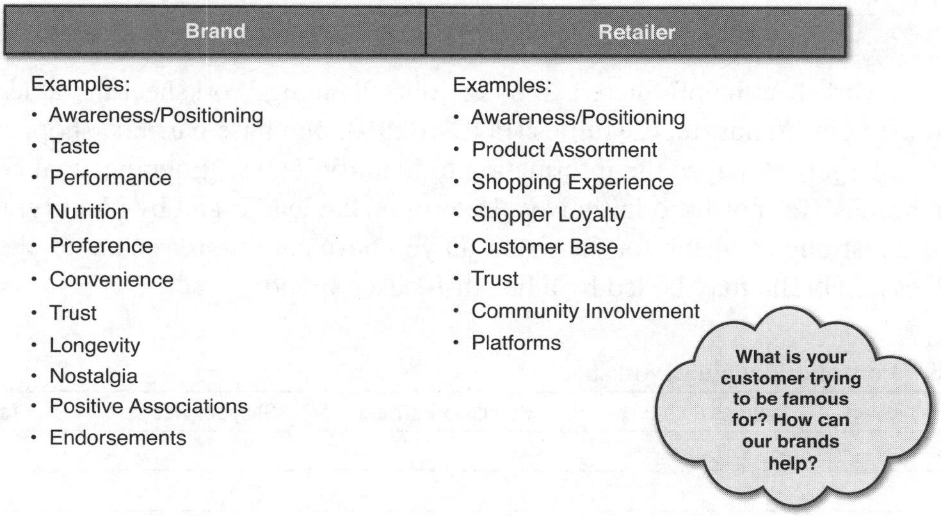

Brand	Retailer
Examples: • Awareness/Positioning • Taste • Performance • Nutrition • Preference • Convenience • Trust • Longevity • Nostalgia • Positive Associations • Endorsements	Examples: • Awareness/Positioning • Product Assortment • Shopping Experience • Shopper Loyalty • Customer Base • Trust • Community Involvement • Platforms

What is your customer trying to be famous for? How can our brands help?

Figure 6-4 *Aligning equities.*

Strategy Prioritization

Use the Shopper Success Index (SSI) to prioritize shopper-based strategies in specific customers. Remember that we stated your objective should be to maintain balance by managing the SSI to within the 80 to 120 range (optimum is 100). If SSI is over 120, then your brand lacks enough predisposition to buy (equity) and/or is too retailer-dependent. In this case, your strategy ought to be in line with building/rebuilding out of store brand equity and a desire to buy the brand. If SSI is under 80, the predisposition to buy is there, but the brand is not performing to potential in this retailer. In this case, your strategy would be to focus on overcoming purchase barriers at this retailer.

Portfolio Marketing

Some initiatives may involve a portfolio of brands, each with potentially different equities, barriers, shopper needs, shopper targets, and objectives. Shopper marketing shifts the ground rules for the basis of portfolio composition in key areas, listed in Table 6-2.

Table 6-2   Portfolio Marketing

From	To
Driven by creative	Driven by strategy
Product selection according to what fits the theme	Product selection based on common equities, shopper needs, and shopper targets
What retailer will promote	What's right for the shopper
Volume-focused	Marketing-focused

Another worksheet helpful here is the Portfolio Planning Worksheet in Table 6-3. Here you list your brands, their equities (PODs/POPs), purchase barriers, shopper needs, and shopper targets. Analyze the information to identify logical groupings that could form "umbrellas" for portfolio initiatives. Determine the lead brand by identifying which brand has the strongest match for the umbrella you have chosen, for example, the health and wellness umbrella may be led by a health-focused brand.

Table 6-3   Portfolio Planning Worksheet

Brands	Equities	Purchase Barriers	Shopper Needs	Targets

Right Initiatives

Now that you have determined your strategies, it is time to think about the nature and objectives of the initiatives you believe will best help you achieve your strategic goals. As noted at the beginning, shopper marketing is not just about promotion. This is why we use the word "initiatives" to describe the variety of actions you might take to address your shopper-based opportunities. When thinking about how you are going to capitalize on these opportunities, be aware that initiatives can include any of the following:

- A variety of activities to overcome purchase barriers or leverage shopper needs, for example, targeted messaging, strategic POP placement, category redesign, advertising, packaging and sampling, each used to address a specific shopper-based opportunity relating to better fulfilling needs or overcoming purchase barriers.

- Communications or messaging to leverage equities along the path to purchase and/or "Stop/Hold/Close" to create an immediate desire to buy.
- Packaging—one of the most important in-store marketing components for a brand and the only one over which the brand has complete control.
- In-store vehicles/POP—shopper marketing's challenge is to know what types of vehicles and in-store locations (hot spots) are most effective in reaching shoppers.
- Campaigns to reinforce customer differentiation objectives consist of any activity or set of activities unique to the retailer and your brands in which a common business opportunity, target group, and communication idea are developed to bring joint equities to life with the goal of increasing joint value.
- Environmental design in which a shopper's usage habits are identified and married with your shopper's desired shopping experience. The focus is on category reinvention or aisle/departmental redesign.

Shopper-Based Initiatives

We have emphasized the importance of developing initiatives within a strategic framework. This does not mean that every shopper-based initiative has to have a two to three year horizon to complete. While the *strategy* may be relevant for three years, the individual initiatives you develop to achieve the objectives of the strategy will be mostly short-term actions that deliver immediately measureable results. Because these actions are strategically based, the *cumulative* effect of each action should be to build toward achieving the long-term strategic objectives. Here is an example:

Brands: Brand Q Regular and Lower Calorie Frozen Dinners

Channel/customer: Supermarkets/Chain A

Insight/opportunity: Research indicates that around 4:00 p.m. the busy working single professional becomes concerned about what to buy for dinner that requires minimum preparation. (Singles do very few "stock-up" trips.) Nutrition is another concern. What he wants is a nutritious "Grab 'N Go" solution. Because of time pressures, supercenters and clubs are unlikely choices to fill this need.

Strategy: Capitalize on this consumer's predisposition to buy in supermarkets by making *Chain A* the store of choice for the single working professional. Use Brand Q dinners as the drivers and cross-merchandise to increase basket size and aisle penetration.

Initiative *objectives*: a) Make it easy for the target shopper to find and buy Brand Q in Chain A; b) structure POP and messaging to highlight "Grab 'N Go" convenience and brand nutritional benefits for the target shopper, and c) cross-promote to increase basket size/encourage aisle penetration.

Initiative *tactics*: (developed by Agency based on preceding objectives) Could be 25 to 30 separate initiatives across a three-year period that all build to the overall strategic objective of making Chain A *known* as the store of choice for busy single professionals and Brand Q as the dinners of choice in Chain A.

Barriers

Purchase barriers are elements of the shopping experience or in-store environment that prevent your brands from being purchased by your target consumer. They come in two varieties—deselection barriers and selection barriers (see Figure 6-5). In terms of priorities, deselection barriers need to be fixed first.

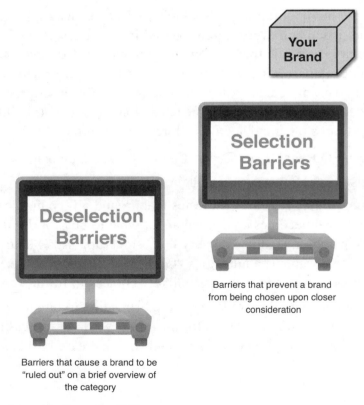

Figure 6-5 *Purchase barrier schematic.*

Deselection barriers are things that contribute to the target shopper dismissing the very idea of buying your brand (see Table 6-4). Remember, we are talking about the *target shopper* here. This is the person who the brand has determined is likely to be the source of growth for your brand. Overcoming deselection barriers is not an exercise in getting a single 50-year-old male to buy the baby food category. It is about understanding why someone who should be interested in your brand is just dismissing it.

Table 6-4 Deselection Barriers—Barriers That Cause a Brand to be Ruled out on a Cursory Review of the Category

Research Findings	Deselection Barrier	Potential Initiatives/Solutions
• "I couldn't find it on the shelf." • "I don't have the time to search."	Poor visibility	• Packaging that pops • Improved shelf position • Organizational fixturing • On-shelf merchandising
• "I've never heard of it."	Low brand awareness	• In-store advertising • Increased/improved messaging • Disruptive merchandising
• "I couldn't find it in the store." • "I don't go down that aisle."	Poor location	• Relevant adjacencies • Secondary permanent location • Relevant display placement
• "That's not for me!"	Perceived irrelevance	• Relevant messaging • Relevant imagery • Cross-merchandising
• "It's not on my list." • "It's nice but not necessary."	Lack of interest	• Relevant claims • Relevant equity choices • Disruptive merchandising • Cross-merchandising

Selection barriers are things that keep the target shopper, once in the category, from selecting your brand (see Table 6-5).

Table 6-5 Selection Barriers—Barriers That Prevent a Brand from Being Chosen upon Closer Consideration

Research Findings	Selection Barrier	Potential Initiatives/Solutions
• "I don't believe that." • "I don't believe it can do that." • "Yeah, right."	Unconvincing claim	• Demos • Sampling • Educational POS
• "It's not worth it."	Poor perceived value	• Relevant equity choices • In-store messaging
• "Will I really like this?" • "Will I really use this?" • "Will my kids like this?"	Confidence uncertainty	• Sampling • Relevant messaging • Relevant imagery • Usage suggestions/recipes • Cross-merchandising

Research Findings	Selection Barrier	Potential Initiatives/Solutions
• "I don't know what's right." • "I don't know what flavor to choose." • "Too many choices." • "Looking at that shelf makes me tired."	Choice confusion	• Package clarification • Review planogram hierarchy • Organization fixturing
• "I don't see much difference; why switch?"	Poor differentiation	• Equity choices • Package claims • Relevant messaging • Relevant imagery

One way to discover what barriers your mutual shoppers face is to complete the barrier audit worksheet shown in Table 6-6. Note that this requires not just evaluating the prestore environment but physically checking the status of your brands in a representative number of stores in different channels. When doing these, be on the alert for barriers common across multiple channels.

Table 6-6   Purchase Barrier Audit

Brand: _____ **Retailer:** _____ **Location:** _____ **Date/Time:** _____/_____

Purchase Barriers—Audit

Pre-Store	In-Store	In-Aisle
Do potential target shoppers know in what stores our product is available?	Is our product shelved in a logical location (where it is in the most stores)?	Does our product pop on the shelf?
In what channel/store would our target shopper normally shop for our product?	Is there signage in the store for our category?	Is our brand dwarfed by competition on the shelf?
Is the shopper using a list? Is our category on the list? Is our brand on the list?	Are there navigational signposts for our category (well-known brands that would trigger category recognition)?	Is a benefit highlighted that makes our product relevant to the target shopper?
Did the shopper check with family members for their needs or preferences?	Does our brand provide the navigational signpost?	Is there anything on package or POS that would make targets think our product is "not for them"?
Does the shopper have a budget for this trip?	Is our product in relevant secondary locations?	Does the section feel cluttered?
Did the shopper check retail flyers before shopping?	Are non-price messaging techniques being used in this store—e.g., cart signs, TV, radio, floor graphics?	Are there multiple forms or flavors of the product in the category?
Did the shopper check retailer website before shopping?	Does the shopper go down our aisle?	Are we providing the shopper with guidance on which to choose?
Did the shopper receive direct mail from either the retailer or our company before shopping?	Are there "hot spots" in the store where traffic is heavier? Are we visible from these hot spots?	Do we answer questions about usage or performance?
Does the shopper use coupons?	If we have displays, is there messaging beyond price on the display?	Are we highlighting a benefit that indicates why our product is a smart choice?

Pre-Store	In-Store	In-Aisle
Does the shopper use a retailer loyalty card?	Are we cross-merchandising with relevant products? Other corporate products?	Are we priced higher than competition?
If urban, how did the shopper get to the store?	Are we tied-in with relevant retailer programs or platforms?	If so, are we communicating why we are worth the higher price?

Once you have completed the purchase barrier audit, the next step is to address the problems identified by bringing these to the attention of those departments within your company that are best equipped to resolve them. Figure 6-6 illustrates the appropriate department in most companies.

Solution / Barrier	Pre-Store Media	Package Physical	Package Messaging	In-store Media/ Message	Shelf Presence	Sampling/ Product Engagement	Category Education	Brand Architecture (Price, SKUs, Equity)
Low Brand/Line-up Awareness	★★	★★	★	★	★★	★	★	★★
Poor Visibility		★★			★★			
Lack of Relevance/ Need		★★	★★	★★				★
Habit Change		★	★★	★★		★★	★★	
Unconvincing Benefit		★★	★★	★★		★★	★	
Choice Confusion		★★	★★	★	★	★		★
Usage Uncertainty	★	★★	★★			★★	★★	
Poor Value Perception	★	★★	★★	★			★	★★

★★ Important Tool ★ Additional Tool

Marketing | Shopper/Sales

Figure 6-6 *Purchase barrier responsibilities.*

Messaging

Integration of shopper marketing messaging across the entire path to purchase helps to reinforce your message in the mind of the shopper. Shopper marketing messaging—wherever it is along the path to purchase—focuses on helping the shopper make a decision to buy your brand. It tends to answer questions more than just create desire—things like where do I get it? How much does it cost? Does it come in gluten-free? What's the pixel count? How do I use this? Will my kids like it? Ultimately, it should reinforce your equities in the mind of the shopper—that is, why she loves your brand—and make the shopper feel like she is making a good decision when buying your product.

To achieve these objectives, your messaging needs to be available to the shopper at the time she needs it. The ubiquity of mobile technology has made this a requirement—and also so much easier. Spirits companies have embraced this with mobile apps with geolocation that can tell shoppers where the closest store—or best bar—is that carries their product. They also provide cocktail recipes, direct the shopper to nearby hotels, or provide the phone numbers of local cab companies.

Diageo and their Smirnoff brand integrate their message across the path to purchase by using the Virtual Bartender. The at-home message come across on a website that helps shoppers with drink recipes and party tips, including what products to buy for a well-stocked bar. The on-the-go smartphone message focuses on nightlife options in the shopper's market—again using the Virtual Bartender to help the shopper make decisions. The in-store messaging is a digital kiosk where the Virtual Bartender again appears to help the shopper pair wines and spirits with food choices (and not forget any necessary ingredients for cocktails) to help the shopper feel smart and efficient. The result: One consistent voice is there to help them.

While the out-of-store messaging in this example clearly focuses more on meeting shopper needs, the message environment is not significantly different from communicating with a consumer. It is important to note, however, that the needs of in-store messaging are different from most traditional marketing so we have dedicated a section to this.

In-Store Messaging

Effective in-store messaging is key to capitalizing on shopper needs, overcoming purchase barriers, and leveraging brand equities in-store. A strong in-store message is a claim, equity communication, or education or motivations message that gives the shopper the desire to immediately buy your product. While the content of an in-store message may be similar to traditional mass media, there are key differences in how you should talk to a shopper versus a consumer, given that his mindset is different when he is in the store.

An effective in-store message should:

- *Stop* shoppers! Shoppers are on the go, so you need to break through the clutter and grab their attention.
- *Hold* their attention. Shoppers are easily distracted, so you need to help them understand quickly what you are offering (that is, be simple).
- *Close* the sale! Shoppers have not decided yet, so you need to overcome purchase barriers and activate drivers that cause them to choose your product on this shopping trip. If the shopper does not close, your efforts have failed. An example of creating urgency: "Try it today!"

There are some basic rules for effective in-store messaging. First, it should empathize with your shoppers. It should reflect an understanding of the reality of the in-store environment. It should recognize and help shoppers overcome purchase barriers. It should reflect a minimalist approach with message. A good rule to follow is five words or less. If you cannot stop them, you will never hold or close them. Know your key customers' equities and/or business priorities. Lay it all out in the brief. Brilliant briefs lead to brilliant creative.

Packaging

The package is both one of the most important in-store marketing components for a brand and the only one over which the manufacturer has complete control. However, because you do not control the retail environment or your customer's choices on your communications executions, your *packaging* should effectively tell shoppers what the brand is, what it does, and why to buy it. You can use the criteria in Table 6-7 to determine in-store stopping, holding, and closing power for a package, as well as the effectiveness of its equity/message delivery:

Table 6-7   Evaluating Packaging

Packaging Criteria	Qualities
Stopping Power: Does the package stand out on the shelf and visually engage the shopper?	Intrusiveness
Holding Power: Is the shopper drawn to engage with the product? Is the message relevant?	Relevance
Closing Power: Is the package persuasive enough to induce purchase?	Persuasiveness
Equity Building/Reinforcement: Is the package consistent with brand image and personality? Are relevant PODs highlighted?	Credibility
Shopper Friendliness: Is the package easy to handle and remove from shelf/cart? Is messaging visible as shelved?	Shoppability

In-Store Vehicles

To make the right customer plan and investment choices, it is important to know what types of vehicles and in-store locations (hot spots) are most effective in reaching shoppers. These vary from retailer to retailer and from market to market, so there is no substitute for testing for your customer and market. Developing customized vehicles for your key customers helps get their buy-in and support, particularly if they feel they have a voice in their design. With retailers for whom totally custom vehicles do not return the ROI, the menu concept from account-specific marketing can be used to tailor generic *shopper-based* vehicles to the needs of different retailers and their shoppers. Giving each customer choices of in-store vehicles designed or tailored specifically for them is an effective way to leverage their stores and ensure initiative awareness and trial.

You want to remember a few in-store vehicle principles:

- The vehicle and its messaging should Stop/Hold/Close.
- Discontinuity drives awareness. Use vehicles that interrupt and break through the clutter.
- Visual design influences awareness. Colors and shapes are what a shopper sees first.
- Signage that is eye-level or below, is repeated, and is sizeable drives awareness.
- Messaging should be relevant to shopper target (needs/purchase barriers).

Campaigns

Campaigns consist of any activity or set of activities unique to your customer and you in which a common business opportunity, target group, and communication idea are developed to bring joint equities to life with the goal of increasing joint value. There are key actions you want to take to ensure that you design a "sustainable campaign." A campaign is a joint equity-building marketing program between you and your customer that is based on shopper insights and will be executed for two years minimum. There are three important principles to consider when designing/planning a customer-specific shopper marketing campaign:

- The campaign should build upon a relevant customer strategy/opportunity. Addressing a "top priority" customer opportunity results in top management alignment and, ultimately, excellence in execution because the customer has a vested interest in its success.
- The campaign should be designed with the shopper in mind. The campaign strategy should be built with and around the shopper. A good way to identify a joint business opportunity is to explore areas where shoppers' needs are not being met or purchase barriers are negatively impacting sales. Often, exploring sales data is the starting point for this. When one sees sales declines or category sales that are less than would be expected relative to the retailer's market share, it is an indication that something is wrong in the eyes of the shopper.
- The campaign should be ownable for you. Campaigns that become key drivers of customers' business have the risk of being taken over by them. Hence the challenge is to keep the campaign ownable for your brands. There are ways manufacturers do this. They
    - Make their brands an integral and indispensable part of the campaign.

- Lead the efforts to renew the program; innovate to stay ahead of the pack, and continue to integrate new ideas into the program. This provides added value and retains the customer's interest in working with the brand.
- Integrate existing third-party alliances into the program. These assets are a unique advantage and cannot easily be duplicated.

Environmental Design

How shoppers think about, consider, and choose your brands can be influenced by the shopping environment. Shopper marketing has produced countless examples of chain drug and supermarket cosmetics departments ditching the steel gondolas and linoleum floors for an environment more like the cosmetics section of a high-end department store. In-store book departments now often have wooden shelving and easy chairs to give them a library feel. Produce departments—complete with misters and mood lighting— look like they are "ready for their close-up" in *Bon Appétit*. In these cases, the environment is revamped to make shoppers feel comfortable that they are in the best place to buy.

Environmental design is also used to help your shoppers find and buy your brands quickly and with greater ease. Understanding how your shopper views the category and dividing it into more manageable parts—clearly labeled—can be of enormous help for the shopper trying to navigate categories with large numbers of SKUs. Most manufacturers have developed a decision tree identifying how the category is shopped for use in their category management efforts. This can be used for clarifying assortment segments for the current category design. Conversely, category reinvention is an opportunity for you to direct new shopper behavior by highlighting a new category segment or a more efficient shelf layout. The purpose of environmental design is to identify and join shopper usage habits with your target shoppers' desired shopping experience.

One more plus for environmental design—it creates a strategic go-to-market partnership with your customers by focusing on category or departmental-level insights and solutions that stimulate increased traffic and closure. This leads to category/department growth and profitability for both you and your customer.

Developing the Plan

Before developing your plan, double-check your work to date to ensure that you have thoroughly excavated and isolated those points that will enable you to make a difference—for your firm, your brands, your key customers, and the mutual shopper. Be your own severest critic. Ask yourself the following, Have I...

- Developed an in-depth holistic picture of my current situation that serves as the business basis for the strategies and initiatives that I am proposing? Successfully mined the details and identified the proprietary research opportunities that will make us a preferred partner in the eyes of my key customers?
- Identified shopper-based issues and opportunities that *only* your brands can best address (that is, ensured "ownability"?—use IVA [initiative value assessment] to determine)?
- Formulated and prioritized strategies to address these opportunities in ways that provide balanced mutual benefits?
- Thought through the objectives and/or nature of the specific initiatives I have in mind to execute within the framework of these strategies?
- Costed-out the plan, estimated ROI, and established the measurement criteria relevant to all stakeholders?
- Ensured the plan aligns with the primary customer plan and is scheduled to link as closely as possible to trade spending initiatives?

At the conclusion of this step, what you have is an initial draft of your plan. The next step is to discuss it with your key customers before finalizing it to secure their input and ensure strategic alignment. The earlier you do this in this process, the more relevant your plan will be.

1. Start with a clear understanding of your customer's business strategy, competition, and shopper segments.
2. Understand your customer's category and department strategy relative to your brands and how your brands are performing in this customer relative to the competition and the market. Perform (or update) an in-store brand health assessment to identify specific issues.
3. Develop in-depth shopper understanding to identify strengths and opportunities for the category and department at the customer—prioritize unmet needs.
4. Perform an initiative value assessment to determine the extent to which your brands can help address the problem/capitalize on the opportunity.
5. Align with the customer on common business goals strategies and equities—collaborate to identify common issues and opportunities that your brands can effectively address.
6. Use shopper research to fill information gaps and develop relevant shopper insights and concepts to achieve aligned business goals.
7. Identify all vehicles through which to communicate the concept to target shoppers along the path to purchase. These could include in-store or other vehicles to reach target shoppers with your messages.

8. Synthesize and consolidate key findings/insights/agreements into the preliminary shopper marketing customer marketing plan. Reconvene with the customer to secure final agreement.

9. Secure input of the customer team. Integrate this with the primary customer business plan. Schedule to ensure coordination with trade events and finalize the plan.

10. Thoroughly communicate the shopper marketing plan to your shopper marketing agency and coordinate resources to execute with excellence.

11. Measure results—for the customer and for you. Use this for continuous improvement.

Remember, the quality and depth of support you receive will be directly proportional to the input your customer feels he has had into your plan *prior to* finalization!

The Shopper Marketing Customer Plan

You can build the shopper marketing customer plan by combining or summarizing information you have collected along the way in various worksheets as we demonstrate here. The steps in the process are:

- **Situation Assessment Key Findings**—Trends, brand, consumer, customer, shopper
- **Insights/opportunities**—Coming out of the situation assessment
- **Prioritizing opportunities**—Template for prioritizing based on your criteria
- **Strategy development**—How to capitalize on prioritized opportunities for mutual benefit
- **Plan**—Strategy, initiative, timing, metrics for success
- **Detail on initiatives**—Tactics, message, offer
- **Calendar**
- **Execute with excellence**

Situation Assessment—Key Findings

Summarize the key findings from your situation assessment in each area listed in Table 6-8 and use this for implications/insight development and establishing priorities.

Table 6-8   Assessment Summary Key Findings—Implications Summary

Socioeconomic Trends	Brand	Consumer	Customer	Shopper

Based on your key findings, draw implications that will help inform your plan. Use this for developing initiative strategies and prioritizing research needs (see Table 6-9).

Table 6-9   Implications Summary

Factors that influence current buying decisions	
Issues and opportunities I need to address	
Information gaps I need to fill	
Long- and short-term priorities	Short: Long:

Mutual Target Shopper Summary

Describe the mutual target shopper for each brand in your retailer. Use this for initiative development, messaging, and portfolio development (see Table 6-10).

Table 6-10   Mutual Target Shopper Summary

Brand	Mutual Target Shopper Summary/Retailer Segment

Identifying Equities

Identify the brand equities that are most relevant to your shopper in your retailer. Identify the retailer's equities that make your shopper choose this store. Use this for messaging and portfolio development (see Table 6-11).

Table 6-11 Equities Summary

Brand	Retailer
Examples:	Examples:
• Positioning	• Positioning—e.g., freshness, quality, value
• Taste	• Product assortment
• Performance	• Shopping experience
• Nutrition	• Shopper loyalty
• Preference	• Trust
• Convenience	• Community involvement
• Trust	• Platforms
• Longevity	
• Nostalgia	
• Positive associations	
• Endorsements	

Summarize Objectives

Enter brand objectives and retailer objectives from discussions with the retailer and/or your account team leader/key account managers. Enter shopper needs from your analysis of the mutual target shopper (see Table 6-12).

Table 6-12 Objectives Summary

Brand	Retailer	Shopper
Examples:	Examples:	Examples:
• Achieve 65% distribution of new product by X	Overall: • + Transaction size • Expand category penetration among HLS Category: • Improve promoted margins	• Overcome purchase barriers • Solutions for meal planning • Solutions for weight management • Solutions for family healh • Save me time • Save me money
• Drive 50% awareness of product improvement		
• Increase loyalty 5% among segment		
• Drive 10% trial among heavy competitive users		

Opportunity Evaluation Worksheet

Rank each opportunity on a scale of 5 (High) to 1(Low) based on your judgment of how well the opportunity meets the following criteria. So, for example, if the opportunity is ownable, score it as a "5" under "Is the opportunity ownable" (see Table 6-13). Then transfer scores to the Opportunity Ranking Worksheet (see Table 6-14).

Table 6-13   Opportunity Evaluation Worksheet Criteria

Is Opportunity Ownable?	Is Opportunity Sustainable?	Addresses Key Brand Objectives?	Addresses Key Customer Objectives?	Addresses Mutual Shopper Objectives?
Can we "own" this opportunity in this retailer?	Is this opportunity ongoing?	Financial objectives—volume and profit?	Financial objectives—volume and margin?	Saves time? Saves money?
Do we bring unique equities that other brands cannot replace (e.g., category leadership position, scale, contractual assets, etc.)?	Or can this opportunity be repeated over time, e.g., annual event? Can this opportunity be refreshed over time?	Awareness/trial? Loyalty? Specific target? Enhances relationship with CTC?	+ Transaction size? + Traffic? + Loyalty/frequency? Enhances relationship with HLS?	Solves a problem? Improves shopping experience?
Can the retailer hijack this opportunity and easily do it on its own?	Can this opportunity be expanded over time?		Provides source of differentiation?	
Can we bake-in elements that require our involvement for success?			Makes it easy to find and buy? Leverages retailer equities?	
Ex: 2 Points	2 Points	4 Points	3 Points	4 Points

Use this ranking to determine the priorities for your initiatives. Focus only on those that will deliver the most important balanced mutual benefits (see Table 6-14).

Table 6-14 Opportunity Evaluation Worksheet Template

Opportunity	Ownable?	Sustainable?	Brand Win?	Retailer Win?	Shopper Win?	Score

Customer Shopper Marketing Plan

Drawing on all of the previous analyses and thinking, develop your strategies, initiatives, and timing for each opportunity (see Table 6-15).

Table 6-15 Customer Shopper Marketing Plan

Opportunities	Strategies	Key Initiatives/Tactics	Timing
Ex: Expand underdeveloped baking category.	• Leverage varying shopper needs by highlighting range of expertise in our products.	• Back lobby solution center—near dairy—milk tie-in	October - December
	• Overcome purchase hurdle location with display identifying everyday store location.	• November feature (suggested)	
	• Leverage "nostalgia" equities, Halloween, Christmas	• Combination of print and online with November incentives and December continuity, recipes	
		• Extended FSI coupon coverage	
Opportunity 2			
Opportunity 3			
Opportunity 4			

Enter initiative details in preparation for forecasting, costing, and ROI estimation in the worksheet in Table 6-16.

Table 6-16 Initiative Detail

Opportunity	Messaging	Tactics	Offer	Vehicles

Estimating Volume/Costs

Now you must cost things out. Enter your estimated incremental cases and case margin in dollars for each participating brand. Calculate incremental revenue, enter estimated costs of the initiative, and then calculate an ROI estimate (see Table 6-17).

Table 6-17 Financial Estimate

Opportunity	Incremental Cases	Case Margin $	Incremental $	Estimated Cost	ROI
Participating Brand			Incr Cases × Case Margin $		Incr $/Est Cost
Participating Brand					
Participating Brand					
Participating Brand					
TOTAL					

Annual Plan

The annual plan should then look something like Table 6-18.

Table 6-18 Annual Shopper Marketing Plan

Q1	Q2		Q3		Q4	
TIMING	Initiative timing/run dates		Initiative timing/run dates		Initiative timing/run dates	
TITLE	Initiative title		Initiative title		Initiative title	
STRATEGY	Strategy		Strategy		Strategy	
INITIATIVE DESCRIPTION	Description		Description		Description	
BRAND(S) INCLUDED	Brand(s) included		Brand(s) included		Brand(s) included	
MESSAGE/OFFER	Message/offer		Message/offer		Message/offer	
INCR VOLUME BY BRAND	Brand	Incr Volume	Brand	Incr Volume	Brand	Incr Volume
	Brand	Incr Volume	Brand	Incr Volume	Brand	Incr Volume
	Brand	Incr Volume	Brand	Incr Volume	Brand	Incr Volume
	Brand	Incr Volume	Brand	Incr Volume	Brand	Incr Volume
COSTS BY BRAND	Brand	Costs	Brand	Costs	Brand	Costs
	Brand	Costs	Brand	Costs	Brand	Costs
	Brand	Costs	Brand	Costs	Brand	Costs
	Brand	Costs	Brand	Costs	Brand	Costs
	Trade Promotion Support					
	Brand	Support	Brand	Support	Brand	Support
	Retailer Events					
	Super Bowl				Frozen Food Month	

Execution Thoughts

As your initiatives get implemented, ask yourself and your team the questions listed in Figure 6-7.

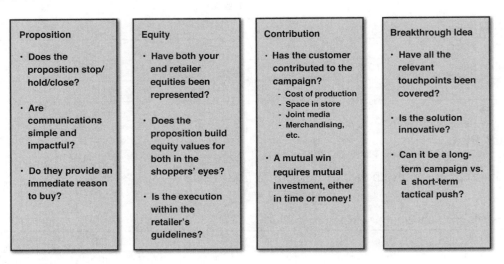

Proposition	Equity	Contribution	Breakthrough Idea

• Does the proposition stop/ hold/close?
 	
• Are communications simple and impactful?
 	
• Do they provide an immediate reason to buy?
	• Have both your and retailer equities been represented?
	
	• Does the proposition build equity values for both in the shoppers' eyes?
	
	• Is the execution within the retailer's guidelines?
		• Has the customer contributed to the campaign?
		  - Cost of production
		  - Space in store
		  - Joint media
		  - Merchandising, etc.
		
		• A mutual win requires mutual investment, either in time or money!
			• Have all the relevant touchpoints been covered?
			
			• Is the solution innovative?
			
			• Can it be a long-term campaign vs. a short-term tactical push?

Figure 6-7 *Plan check.*

Interesting Findings from Research

1. Brand is the only common element to the entire demand chain. Brand strategy management should be both a demand and supply chain priority in contrast to its general demand chain focus.[1]

2. Shoppers choosing from larger assortments often shift their choice from vice-type products (indulgences) to virtues and from hedonic to utilitarian options. These effects reverse, however, when situational factors provide accessible reasons to indulge, underscoring the role of justification.[2]

3. Failing to incorporate consumer search into an assortment planning process may cause a retailer to underestimate the substantial value a broad assortment has in preventing consumer search (going elsewhere to continue searching for a better product).[3]

4. A power aisle comprising a smaller number of stock keeping units (SKUs) and a correspondingly greater quantity of each item will convey a lower price image than will a power aisle comprising a greater number of SKUs and a correspondingly smaller quantity of each item.[4] (This article is a bit old but may still be true.)

Endnotes

1   Glaser, Stan (2008), "The Role of Branding in the Value Chain," *International Journal of Physical Distribution and Logistics Management*, 38 (9), 726-736.

2   Sela, Aner, Jonah Berger, and Wendy Liu (2008), "Variety, Vice, and Virtue: How Assortment Size Influences Option Choice," *Journal of Consumer Research*, 35, 941-951.

3   Cachon, Gerard P., Christian Terwiesch, and Yi Xu (2005),"Retail Assortment Planning in the Presence of Consumer Search," *Manufacturing & Service Operations Management*, 7(4), 330-346.

4   Smith, Peter and David J. Burns (1996), "Atmospherics and Retail Environments: The Case of the 'Power Aisle,'" *International Journal of Retail and Distribution Management*, 24 (1), 7-14.

7

Execution

The third stage in our four-stage shopper marketing process is execution. Executing shopper marketing plans involves four important concepts: collaboration with customers, empowering agencies, reporting results, and supply chain management as shown in Figure 7-1.

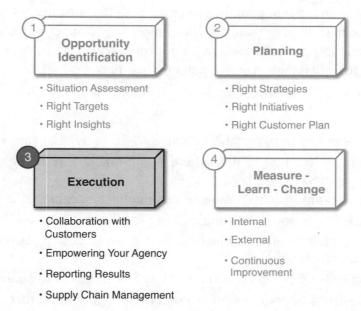

Figure 7-1 *Execution phase.*

Collaboration with customers means establishing a close and productive relationship with your key customer's marketing department and becoming a top-of-mind resource for all decisions affecting your brands and categories. The ultimate objective is to become a preferred partner. This is initially achieved by taking a nonparochial approach wherein the focus of introductory presentations is on helping your customers improve their business by better understanding their strengths and weaknesses from the shopper's point of view.

Empowering your agency means working with your shopper marketing agency as partners, communicating openly and effectively, and motivating them to go the extra mile on every initiative. It also means taking the time to write brilliant briefs so that there is no misunderstanding about what is required to achieve your objectives or on how your agency expects to be measured.

Reporting results means taking the time to detail and report the results of *every* shopper-based initiative and building an historical data base of these results. This is the key to being able to continuously improve over time.

Collaboration with Strategic Customers

Some CPG manufacturers have an inherent strategic advantage in that they are one of a handful[1] of suppliers that have products represented in almost every aisle. In the aggregate, this gives them significant potential leverage with key customers because they have the power and resources to help them address almost any shopper-based issue while simultaneously benefitting their brands in the process. This is, in fact, exactly what leading retailers look for when they evaluate potential partners.

Specifically, leading retailers ask about the following issues, which serve as selection criteria:

- Overall importance to the retailer's business? To individual categories?
- Capacity and willingness to invest human and financial resources in growth of retailer's business?
- Quality of relevant insights? Value-added intellectual capital?
- Understands issues and opportunities from retailer's standpoint?
- Has size and scale to afford to be objective about total store, departmental, and category recommendations?
- Strategic clarity, consistency, and flexibility? Willingness to adapt?
- Currently: Best shopper marketing programs—so important that it is now the door opener for many smaller companies that otherwise would not qualify.

What Retailers Want

No matter what the brand, category, problem, or opportunity, best practice companies find that most retailers want their shopper-based initiatives to achieve one of the following six objectives:

- Increase customer count (new customers).
- Increase trip frequencies (current customers).
- Increase transaction size (current customers).
- Increase productivity (human and financial).
- Reduce costs (costs of goods and operations).
- Differentiate on a nonprice basis (reinforce equity/increase loyalty/offer something unique in market).

Focus your initiative on the one objective agreed upon between you and your customer. This is what you will be measured on. Do not dilute the strength of the initiative in an attempt to address multiple issues simultaneously.

Figure 7-2 shows a general framework for collaboration. Your particular situation may require more meetings than this, but this gives you an idea of how it works.

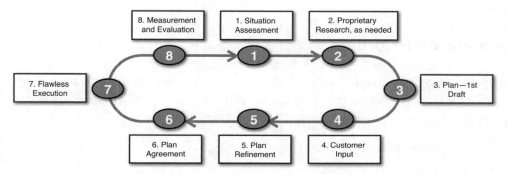

Figure 7-2 *Collaboration process.*

This process can be applied to collaborative product and package customization as well as promotional customization and aisle presentation work.

The Initial Meeting

The overarching objective of collaboration is to secure your key customer's input to and approval of your customer plan prior to finalization. Involving your customer in the early stages of the development of your plan and communicating frequently throughout the implementation of the plan obviously produces significantly better results for both parties. Specifically, use the strategies you developed as a result of the right strategies step as the starting point for initial discussions. Your objective is to secure your customer's input to these strategies and your rationale for having arrived at them. Be prepared to make adjustments based on this input and/or any new information your customer provides.

Depending on the customer, the department to see on shopper marketing subjects is likely to be your customer's marketing department, but this can differ among retailers. Regardless of with whom you are primarily working, the merchandising department's category managers need to be in the loop and give their approval for *any* initiative involving their specific category. A key part of effective collaboration is that no one is surprised.

Ensure that the subject matter is of sufficient scope and importance to your customer to justify his attention *relative to what you might surmise your competitors have been saying*. If necessary, do proprietary research to ensure that what you are discussing is "new news" and inherently relevant. And keep the conversation on a strategic level, staying on point. Some find it helpful to arrive with a list of questions about their own strategy choices to ensure this. This indicates a willingness to listen and a questioning frame of mind.

Agreement on Priorities

After you have reworked your strategies to incorporate your customer's input and insights, the next step is to mutually agree on priorities and performance measures. Your objectives at this point are to

- Review revised strategy choices.
- Agree on strategic priorities.
- Establish joint metrics for success.
- Manage expectations—do not overcommit.
- Determine role of each leverageable asset.
- Strive to integrate collective assets.
- Ensure fair investment on both sides.
- Commit to "test and learn" philosophy.
- Build respect and goodwill.

In prioritizing strategies, focus on those that deliver the most important mutual benefits, even leaning initially to those that benefit your customer more than your brands. Resist the temptation to execute more strategies than your resources can accommodate. It is better to do one right than two poorly.

There are some things to watch out for during this process. Securing mutual agreement on priorities and performance measures can sometimes be a sensitive discussion because of conflicting interests and objectives. For example, many discussions between manufacturers and retailers wind up trying to clarify whether objectives relate to

- Brand equity versus store equity
- Brand share versus category share
- Brand margin versus category margin
- Brand ROI versus category ROI
- Consumer versus shopper
- Manufacturer brands versus store brands

There are no "pat" answers to these issues (which may or may not come up), but many can be anticipated and addressed by conducting an Initiative Value Assessment (IVA) as a part of your overall preparation. This enables you to determine the value that your brands bring to your customer and agree on performance measures that you are reasonably sure you can achieve for both parties.

Final Approval

Once you have completed your customer plan and have determined the types of *initiatives* you have in mind to achieve your objectives, reconvene with your customer to get her final approval *before* proceeding to implement/commit funds.

Here, you want to review your entire plan so that your customer can develop a complete picture of the business reasons behind your recommendations. Clarify any points of difference or confusion. Highlight potential sensitive issues that you know may arise. You want to avoid unpleasant end game surprises.

Your objectives at this point also include securing your customer's input as to the *types* of initiatives you propose for executing the agreed-upon strategy, for example, how you plan to help achieve your customer's differentiation objectives, overcome specific purchase barriers or improve category "shoppability," and so on. This helps you secure preliminary approval and paves the way for the initiative when introduced.

Finally, agree on timing, roles, and responsibilities in implementation: who will do what, when, and where. Have this mapped out prior to the meeting. And agree on a schedule of regular formal review meetings.

Follow-up

After your customer has approved your plan, the number one priority is flawless implementation. You need to ensure that your shopper marketing agency thoroughly understands the agreed-upon strategic framework for initiative development and is apprised of the types of initiatives you have in mind to achieve these objectives. (The mechanism for this is the strategic brief—discussed in a moment.)

Conduct an initiative value assessment for every initiative that your agency proposes to ensure alignment with the plan's objectives and strategies and potential to deliver to your customer's expectations.

Ensure that Sales is continually in the loop. While they may have approved and/or integrated your plan into the basic customer plan at the beginning of the fiscal year, always double-check to remind them of the specific nature and timing of your initiatives.

Set up a system for measuring results based on the agreed-upon metrics. Track and measure every event and identify what worked versus what didn't and why. Communicate with your customer regularly throughout execution. This includes using the regularly scheduled review meetings to report results and analyze strengths and weakness on both sides. Use results to immediately improve the next initiative.

Common Subjects for Collaboration

Beyond the customer plan, Table 7-1 lists the most commonly discussed subjects between partners on shopper marketing. Note the nature and variety of subjects on which meaningful collaboration can take place.

Table 7-1 Common Topics of Discussion

Joint strategy development	• Problem/opportunity identification • New product launch planning • Top-to-top messaging/positioning • Functional involvement in strategy/planning • Co-marketing/equity alignment
In-store communication	• POP/media • Departmental/aisle/set design • Fixturing
Supply chain	• Module/shipper customization • Pallet configuration • RFID
Product customization	• Unique product formulation • Custom package design • Promotional package elements
Promotional tailoring	• Reinforce customer differentiation objectives—corporate/divisional/store • Retailer cause marketing • Cross-category/solution centers

Some topics are great collaboration door openers. Go in with an open, inquisitive, and problem-identifying/solving mindset. Be curious and not judgmental. Initially you are *not* trying to "sell." You are trying to *learn*. Try to learn

- Who their shoppers are—not just for your categories but in total
- How these differ from their competitors' shoppers
- How these shoppers behave in-store versus in-market/other channels (trip frequency/basket size/trip type)
- The primary shopper needs that their stores address—by segment
- Departmental/category barriers
- Shopper card analyses
- Insights on what shopper card analysis may not tell them
- What their shoppers—especially their HLSs—buy in *other* stores—and why
- What motivates their shoppers to buy—beyond price
- Success stories from noncompeting retailers on moving shoppers up the loyalty ladder
- Success stories from noncompeting retailers on expanding penetration within the store into more departments or categories
- Research on/knowledge of an important shopper segment
- Any proprietary research that results in actionable insights of mutual benefit

As part of this learning process, there are ten questions that manufacturers should ask retailers' marketing departments:

1. What do you want shoppers to think and feel about your stores?
2. Which of your equities do you think are most important to your shoppers or most unique to you?
3. What are your company's key objectives? What are your key objectives in your job?
4. What are your company's strategies for growth? From your point of view, how can manufacturers like us help you grow?
5. What marketing platforms or programs do you have that we should consider?
6. What in-store vehicles should I know are available? What are the marketing or merchandising "don'ts" I should know about?
7. Who is your most valuable shopper? Is your emphasis more on retention/expansion of your most loyal/highest spending shoppers or on building loyalty and spending among your shoppers that are not top tier?
8. Have you defined your shoppers into segments? If so, what are their demographics, psychographics, and behavioral characteristics? What key attributes differentiate the segments? How much of your volume does each segment represent? Which are you targeting to maintain? Which are you targeting to grow? Can you give me guidance on how our categories, products, and/or SKUs index by your segments so I can know better how we should align with you?

9. What metrics do you use to evaluate success—for yourselves, for your suppliers, and for products? Is there a scorecard?

10. How can we best work together?

Working Well with Agencies

Your shopper marketing agency can help you deliver better results at the point of sale through shopper understanding, strategic creative capability, and design of strong execution. You cannot do this without them! Your agency has experience in creating a compelling reason to buy to convert shoppers into buyers. The better ones today fully understand the path to purchase concept and seamlessly integrate out-of-store with in-store marketing communication, using multiple media and tying their work into other out-of-store agency brand building.

To create an agency relationship that produces outstanding results, we need to give the agency clear direction, yet not be so prescriptive that we quash the creativity and innovation that bring your initiatives to life. Here are ten tips for getting the best out of your agency:

1. Think of your agency as a strategic partner and an important creative asset, not just an executional entity. Take the time to provide your agency with an in-depth understanding of your firm/division, your intrinsic strengths/resources, and where you are and want to be with your customers and the shopper. This is often referred to as *on-boarding* and should be done any time a new agency is brought on board, when new people in the agency join the team, or when there have been significant changes within your company, its brands, and/or direction. Ensure the agency understands:

   - Customer history
   - Channel dynamics
   - Customer strategies, priorities, and merchandising protocols
   - Customer and shopper research
   - Brand equities/path-to-purchase objectives
   - Messaging principles

2. Be clear, complete, and specific in setting expectations, for example, how you will work together, the need for agency presence with customers, and so on. Give a focused definition of success. This may include sharing your target ROI, your target compliance, or some other result you are envisioning. Invite the agency to attend all shopper research presentations and ask them to actively participate in concept development.

3. Write the strategy brief yourself! Do not do this hastily or leave this to the last minute. *Never do this verbally*. Writing your own briefs is a disciplined way of forcing yourself to carefully think through what you want your initiative to accomplish.

4. Be prescriptive on essentials, for example, the initiative's objective, but allow the agency sufficient latitude to create a cohesive program that meets your objectives.

5. Make it meaty. Give the agency a rich picture of your target, driving insights, and what you want the target shopper to think, feel, and do.

6. Discuss the finished brief with your customer team to ensure that it is clear and captures the spirit of what you envision.

7. Be realistic on timing. Anticipate the length of time to get approvals both internally and with the customer or any partners. Make rush projects the rare exception.

8. Appoint one decision-maker for all creative submissions. After each submission, give the agency clear and actionable feedback. Make sure the agency fully understands your comments and reasons. Avoid situations where the agency is taking direction from more than one person. There may be a need for more reviewers than one (legal, brand marketing, in-store marketing and merchandising, and so on), but these should all channel their feedback to the one person designated as the primary agency contact point for creative submissions.

9. Show enthusiasm for risk-taking and bold experimentation. Encourage the agency to think outside the box!

10. Formally evaluate your agency once a year using a structured format. Be clear and constructive when sharing your evaluation and ask them to give you feedback. Ensure that you get your agency's view of what your organization could be doing better as well. Keep a professional arm's length from your agency representative. Meetings are not an occasion for socializing but for achieving objectives.

The Strategic Brief

As mentioned, the most critical communication between the manufacturer and the shopper marketing agency is the brief. It is also one of the most frequently avoided pieces of work—largely because it is time-consuming. A great brief needs to convey a lot of information—particularly in shopper marketing where you are often briefing on multiple constituencies. Brief formats are often devised between agency and brand to find the most workable format for both parties. As a result, some companies separate the strategic information for the brief—the target, overall brand and retailer objectives, and the like—

from the tactical information such as in-market dates, quantities needed, and budget for each particular initiative. The strategic brief can then be done once a year in great detail for the things that do not change and attached as reference to each creative brief that outlines the tactical details for specific initiatives.

Others cover the general information on brand, consumer, retailer, and shopper in onboarding materials and use a shopper marketing brief like the one shown in Figure 7-3 that is initiative-specific yet is still strategic in nature.

Category:
Brand:
Retail Environment:
Customer:
Date of Brief:
Final Art Delivery:

TYPE OF INITIATIVE:
☐ Brand Activation ☐ Multi-brand ☐ Multi-manufacturer ☐ Customer Initiative ☐ Retail Environment Innovation

PROGRAM OBJECTIVE: (What is the purpose of the program—e.g., volume, trial, loyalty, customer value, etc.—be specific and quantitative?)

REASON TO BELIEVE: (Benefit, Reason why, What value are you bringing?)

TARGET SHOPPER: (Demographics: Sex, Age, Education, Socioeconomic Level, Shopper segment, Ethnicity)

OUTCOME: (What is the desired shopper response in attitude and action?)

KEY BENEFIT		
SHOPPER	**CUSTOMER**	**EQUITY/BRAND**

SHOPPER INSIGHTS:
Attitudes: (Brand, Category, Retail Environment, Seasonal)
Behavior: (Shopping Intention/Trip Type, Who or where are they currently buying, Time at Shelf, Retail Touchpoints, Traffic Pattern)
Key Insight: (Unmet need, Opportunity, Brand, Shopper, Customer)
Retailer's Shopper Segment:
Barriers: (Shopper, Customer, Competition—what makes the SHOPPER deselect)

CONSIDERATIONS: (Mandatories, Formats, Government Regulations, Etc.)

DELIVERABLES: (Elements and timing, be specific on "by when")

BUDGET PARAMETERS: (Overall and creative)

CREATIVE PRINCIPLES:
Strategic (On Strategy, Equity Building)
Now (Simple, Fast)
Attention Grabbing (Disruptive)
Powerful (Relevant,. Engaging, Motivation)

Figure 7-3 *The strategic brief.*

Selecting Partners

Manufacturers are always trying to identify the best agencies for their shopper marketing-related partnerships. Likewise, these agencies, who until recently served a specialized niche in the marketing communications industry, are trying to identify the best manufacturers with whom to partner. One way both are getting a better idea of who the best partners are for doing shopper marketing is by participating in and reading the results of the annual *Hub Shopper Marketing Top 20* report.

The Hub Top 20 ranks the top 20 shopper marketing agencies as indicated by manufacturer representatives and the top 20 manufacturers as indicated by agencies. Each group evaluates members of the other group on 13 criteria.

Manufacturers rank agencies on the following criteria:

- Shopper marketing concept understanding
- Programming relevancy
- Key account knowledge
- Understanding shopper motivations
- Execution—on time and on budget
- Strategic planning
- Getting results
- Retailer relationships
- Programming innovation
- Growth culture
- Digital capabilities
- Global capabilities
- Research capabilities

Agencies rank manufacturers on these criteria:

- Uniformity of shopper marketing vision
- Integration and coordination among/between departments
- Understanding shopper motivations
- Clearest shopper strategy and objectives
- Best planning
- Best budgeting
- Retailer relationships
- Openness/willingness to share
- Accessibility to key decision-makers

- Digital capabilities
- Feedback and constructive criticism
- Best approvals process
- Global capabilities

This survey has been running annually since 2007. Table 7-2 lists the winners for 2013.

Table 7-2   The Hub Top 20 for 2013

Agencies	Brand Marketers
1. CatapultRPM	1. Procter & Gamble
2. Mars Advertising	2. Campbell's Soup
3. Acosta Mosaic Group	3. Kimberly-Clark
4. JWT/Ogilvy Action	4. Clorox
5. TracyLocke	5. Hillshire Brands
6. IN Marketing	6. Pfizer
7. Match Marketing Group	7. Nestlé
8. Arc Worldwide	8. Unilever
9. Saatchi & Saatchi X	9. ConAgra Foods
10. Draftfcb	10. The Coca-Cola Company
11. Mass Hispanic	11. M&M Mars
12. Blue Chip Marketing	12. SC Johnson
13. The Integer Group	13. Hershey's
14. Upshot	14. PepsiCo
15. TPN	15. Bacardi
16. Circle One	16. Barilla
17. G2	17. Hormel Foods
18. Collaborative Marketing Group	18. Kraft Foods
19. Alcone Marketing Group	19. Reckitt Benckiser
20. Leader Enterprises	20. Novartis

Evaluating Creative

As a shopper marketing professional, you should evaluate creative copy from your agencies on specific criteria. Some examples include evaluating it on

- **Strategy**—In line with marketing objectives, merchandising objectives, retailer objectives, and drives consumer pull.
- **Disruptiveness**—Breaks through the clutter, commands attention, and has stopping power.
- **Simplicity**—Easy to comprehend and doesn't require effort or thought by the shopper.
- **Engagement**—Connecting on a personal level: Surprising, entertaining, enjoyable, useful, intriguing—a reason to pay attention.
- **Relevance**—Addresses an occasion or solution. Shoppers tend to seek solutions by room, task, or occasion.
- **Speed**—A quick read with little interpretation, obvious value.
- **Motivating ability**—Breaks tie, compels purchase, creates an immediate desire to buy!
- **Equity building**—Drives longer term brand relationship. Is unique, ownable, and memorable.

Reporting Results

Detailed and accurate input on each initiative is key to improving the impact (ROI—return on investment and ROMO—return on marketing objectives) of future initiatives and greatly simplifying forecasting. Shopper marketing's role is to ensure that the data entered by the agency are accurate.

So what elements should be tracked and reported? At a minimum, you should capture the following information:

- Type(s) of initiative
- Objective of initiative
- Timing of initiative—start and end dates
- Brand(s) included
- Elements used
- Offer type(s)
- Value of offer(s)
- Retail compliance—that is, % of stores or % of retailer ACV (all commodity volume) where initiative was activated
- Costs
- Results

What Does Execution Success Look Like?

In terms of collaboration, you see strong relationships with all key members of your customer's marketing department or whoever handles shopper marketing at your retailer. You also see jointly developed customer plans and initiatives structured to deliver balanced mutual benefits.

In terms of agency empowerment, you should see executions that are on strategy, on target, on time, and on budget that delight, engage, and motivate the mutual shopper to purchase your brands.

In terms of reporting, you see a rich database of initiative results and underlying causal information that facilitates future planning and continuous improvement.

A Few Lessons on Messaging

We want to share with you a few case studies of shopper marketing messaging. The first is about integrating out-of-store advertising with in-store executions for the Land O'Lakes butter brand.

The brand developed an effective print advertising piece of a father, mother, and daughters enjoying the social experience of eating pancakes with butter with laughter and family togetherness. The ad used a sepia tone for nostalgia and highlighted the brand by placing the box of Land O'Lakes butter and a plate of pancakes with butter in the corner in four-color. There was story copy across the picture: "The lesson about sharing clearly pays off when it's pancakes with butter;" some ancillary copy nearby: "Pure natural Land O'Lakes butter makes the moment better;" and a tagline near the four-color call-out: "Where Simple Goodness Begins."

Two variations were developed for translating this ad to in-store—in this case as a shopping cart ad. The first variation was the picture of the family in the print ad with the four-color plate of pancakes and box of Land O'Lakes butter replaced by just the Land O'Lakes logo. The story copy remained, but the tagline was removed. The other variation eliminated the picture of the family and the story copy completely and instead used the four-color part from the original ad—the plate of pancakes and box of butter—and used the tagline: "Where Simple Goodness Begins" along the bottom with "Land O'Lakes Butter" and the logo in the left quadrant—all in larger type than had appeared in the print ad.

When viewed on a shopping cart, there was no question that the second variation was superior. Despite that we know women (the primary shopper for this product) relate well to the social situations, people, and family represented in the first variation, the message in that first variation simply got lost. It was too much for the busy shopper to process. The social situational print ad out-of-store worked well to build brand equity with a consumer having the time and attention to read it. But once in the store, messaging needs to *leverage* that equity, more than try to build it, and do it powerfully and quickly to close the deal now. It needs to quickly *remind* her of the print ad, but activate an immediate desire to purchase that brand while on this trip.

The lesson for in-store messaging: The simpler the better. The average US shopping trip lasts 20 minutes or less. Of that time, only 15% is actually spent on deciding which products to buy, the rest on navigating from aisle to aisle. The result is that 42% of supermarket shoppers have a decision time in front of the shelf of 5 seconds or less for buying individual products, 33% take 6 to 15 seconds, and only 25% take more than 15 seconds.[2] One needs to get to the point quickly.

Another case study focuses on the relevance of the messaging. In this case, the cough/cold section of a supercenter retailer was not performing up to expectations. A leading brand in that section teamed up with the retailer to gain some insight into why. What they learned was that even the store's loyal shoppers didn't want to face a big store or a big parking lot when they were sick; they wanted to get what they needed and get out quickly. How does one message when the shopper won't come to the store? In this case, they messaged for a time the shopper *was* in the store before they were sick. They developed a preparedness campaign to encourage shoppers to stock up for their inevitable cough/cold needs at the start of the cough/cold season. The message: By being prepared, there would be no emergency trips when they were feeling bad, and the shopper could take advantage of the store's lower prices. By changing the mutual target shopper's perspective and need state, the brand and retailer used messaging to make cough/cold shopping in that retailer relevant.

Next time you are in a store, take a look at the various messaging throughout the store. There will be plenty of it even in a "clean" store that does not allow manufacturer point of sale material. Try to identify who that target shopper is and whether the messaging is relevant for that target. Ask yourself whether the messaging is compelling or complex. If it is complex, would you interrupt your shopping trip to take the time to read it? If it is compelling, ask yourself why.

Compelling messaging captures the shopper's attention, draws the shopper in to learn more, and finally closes the deal. There are a number of different ways this hierarchy is described, perhaps the most common of which is *200-20-2*, referring to catching the shopper's attention at 200 feet—generally with something that breaks through the clutter; drawing the shopper in at 20 feet with a simple and strong message; and then getting into detail (as needed) at 2 feet when the shopper is right on your product or message. Those messages that grab your attention, call you to action immediately (that is, "try," "satisfy your craving," "indulge," "go on, have it"), and communicate powerfully and quickly with few words are most compelling.

Supply Chain Management

This book is not about supply chain management in retail. Many books cover that well. All we want to do here is highlight the implications shopper marketing has for supply chain management. Compliance, as it is referred to in industry, refers to the percentage of programs actually executed the way they were designed and contractually agreed to be executed. Compliance estimates on average range between a high of 50% to lows in the mid 20% range. There are many reasons for this such as store manager autonomy, complex and busy schedules at the store level, lack of understanding of the program's intent, and simply poor communication. To be fair, some brokers and agents claim to get compliance as high as 90% for their clients and do. But on average, this is an anomaly.

A key competency any firms engaged in shopper marketing absolutely must have is an expertise in supply chain management—the management of the flow of goods, information, and financial resources to ensure that the right products and displays are in the right place at the right time at the right prices. The following sections discuss some of the challenges shopper marketing can create.

Unique Demand

Shopper marketing programs often are specific to a brand-retailer partnership. When this is done, not only are the displays unique to a specific store, but sometimes the products themselves. This creates a distribution challenge when multiple stores in close proximity to each other require slightly unique products even though within their cases and containers they look similar. Keeping track of specific items destined for specific stores even though both seem to be Lay's brand potato chips of the same size adds a slightly higher tracking challenge to the system.

Coordination

Retailer-customized programs that are beyond simply restocking shelves require more detailed coordination among the brand and the retailer. Setting stores usually requires additional labor hours, and the parties responsible for this work must be negotiated. Displays need to be strong enough to not only hold the product but survive transportation to the stores. In addition, many programs involve multiple brands. Coordinating all of the vendor representatives to fulfill their part of the display can be an enormous challenge. The last thing you want as a shopper marketer is for your display to arrive and have it partially empty or filled with the wrong items.

Packaging

Packing often falls within the area of logistics or supply chain management as well as marketing. Sometimes packaging design changes are cosmetic for shopper marketing programs and do not affect transportation or display much. Other times changes do affect how products are packaged for transport and displayed, as in when products are bundled together.

Program Timing—Short Run Programs

Many shopper marketing programs are relatively short run initiatives. Yes, some do run continuously as when a section of the store is redesigned or a permanent display is created. But often they are designed around a calendar event. As such, supply chains need to be agile. Supply chain agility is a hot topic in research right now, and it focuses in part on how to structure and manage a distribution network that can adapt to changes and variance quickly and effectively. Realize that the more varied events you design for your individual strategic retail customers and the shorter their duration, the more stress you are placing on your supply chain's ability to respond effectively.

Forecasting

Shopper marketing programs add a great deal of variance to the demand side of the equation. This makes forecasting sales down at the stock keeping unit (SKU) level more difficult. Predicting the short- and long-term effects on sales of SKUs that are being modified slightly throughout the year and in different ways for different retailers without a clear understanding of what the expected effects are of all of the marketing media employed is challenging. Forecasting is about accuracy or minimizing error. Selling too much can be just as bad as not selling enough. Be sure to work carefully on helping planners forecast the effects of your programs. The last thing supply chain managers want is a surprising spike or dropoff in demand, with an emphasis on surprise.

Interesting Findings from Research

1. Manufacturers that establish successful order fulfillment service can affect retailer loyalty. Empirical evidence is provided on the relationships between relational order fulfillment service, operational order fulfillment service, satisfaction, affective commitment, purchase behavior, and loyalty. Such evidence not only focuses on the strategic importance of the operations management discipline in manufacturer-retailer relationships, but also extends previous operations management theory by taking a more complex view of the loyalty phenomenon.[3]

2. An empirical study is used to analyze the state of manufacturer-retailer relationships and the implications of these on efficient functioning of the grocery supply chain in Spain with efficient consumer response (ECR) as a backdrop. The study focuses on the order fulfillment or demand satisfaction logistics process and evaluates the willingness for collaboration among the enterprises using best practices and information and communication technologies (ICTs) associated with ECR.[4]

3. The "last mile" of the retail supply chain—that is, delivering products to the end-customer—highlights the need for recognizing product type differences in configuring order fulfillment processes in electronic business-to-customer (B2C) transactions. The results of the empirical analysis indicate that, on average, customers tend to have higher satisfaction levels with the order fulfillment process of convenience and shopping goods than with the order fulfillment process of specialty goods.[5]

4. The food value chain analysis (FVCA) methodology is introduced for improving consumer focus in the agri-food sector based on the lean paradigm, value stream mapping, and value chain analysis. This is a case study of a UK red meat supply chain explaining how the FVCA method enabled a team of researchers and practitioners to identify the misalignments of both product attributes and supply chain activities with the consumer needs. This paper explains how the FVCA methodology potentially realigned the processes along the supply chain with the true consumer requirements and why the supply chain effectiveness was improved; this follows with a description of the subsequent efficiency gains from application of the FVCA methodology. This paper further defines the demarcation between supply chain *effectiveness* and *efficiency*. This paper contributes to the debate on the importance of supply chain effectiveness by linking to consumer value at every stage of the supply chain.[6]

5. This study reports results from case studies of four Internet-ordering and home-delivery grocers and 2,440 of their customers. Each grocer follows a different operations strategy as determined by choice of where to fulfill customer orders (from existing stores or from a dedicated DC) and by choice of delivery method

(direct to the customer's home/office or indirect via customer pickup or third-party logistics provider). The survey data from customers are used to assess the degree of integration between marketing and operations and the relationship with customer behavioral intentions. The results indicate that eBusiness, product, and service quality all have a significant direct effect on customer behavioral intentions to purchase again. The relationships between the predictor variables and customer behavioral intentions differ across grocers. This supports the idea that grocers utilizing different operational strategies should focus attention on different facets of their business and provides insight as to where efforts should be directed.[7]

Endnotes

1 Nestlé, Kraft Foods, ConAgra Foods, Unilever, N.A., General Mills, Procter & Gamble Source: Cannondale Associates PoweRanking Survey, 2008.

2 Dickson, Peter R. and Alan G. Sawyer (1990), "The Price Knowledge and Search of Supermarket Shoppers," *Journal of Marketing*, 54, (3), 42-53.

3 Davis-Sramek, Beth, John T. Mentzer, and Theodore P. Stank (2008), "Creating Consumer Durable Retailer Customer Loyalty Through Order Fulfillment Service Operations," *Journal of Operations Management*, 26(6), 781-797.

4 Mejias-Sacaluga, Ana, and J. Carlos Prado-Prado (2002), "Integrated Logistics Management in the Grocery Supply Chain," *International Journal of Logistics Management*, 13 (2), 67-77.

5 Thirumalai, S. and K. K. Sinha (2005), "Customer Satisfaction with Order Fulfillment in Retail Supply Chains: Implications of Product Type in Electronic B2C Transactions," *Journal of Operations Management*, 23(3-4), 291-303.

6 Zokaei, A. Keivan and David W. Simons (2006), "Value Chain Analysis in Consumer Focus Improvement," *International Journal of Logistics Management*, 17 (2), 141-162.

7 Boyer, Kenneth K. and G. Thomas M. Hult (2005), "Extending the Supply Chain: Integrating Operations and Marketing in the Online Grocery Industry," *Journal of Operations Management*, 23(6), 642-661.

8

Measurement

Measurement in the world of shopper marketing has been a hot button issue full of debate and consternation for years. The basic problem is an age-old one that extends even further back than shopper marketing—how to measure the effectiveness of marketing expenditures.

Marketers always like to claim that their advertising expenditures, promotional campaigns, and investments in sales calls result in immediate or nearly immediate sales lift and contribute toward long-term brand equity building. In short, everyone wants a valid return on his investments.

The problem is that multiple variables get in the way. The first variable is time. The longer the time lag between exposure to some form of marketing communication and actual purchase behavior, the greater the chance of other variables affecting the behavior as well. Think of the last time you *planned* to buy a product but had to alter your plans. Things like available time at the moment, available funds, and a hundred situational factors might have gotten in your way. In fact, you might have intended to buy a specific brand—the brand was even written on your shopping list—and you failed to complete the mission.

Advertisers and marketers realize this and long ago backed off trying to draw causal paths between advertising expenditures and specific sales. They realize that a great deal of advertising affects attitudes, perceptions, feelings, and some level of predisposition to buy—intent. They know that what is highly correlated with our attitudes toward brands are the frequency with which we view an advertisement, our liking of the ad, and things like our judgment of how believable and relevant the ad claims are to our lives. In the aggregate, the more often people see a likeable and believable ad and the more people who see it, the higher the likelihood that positive attitudes will result and by extension increases in sales and brand equity. This reach and frequency goal has evolved to a rating system known as GRPs or gross rating points. Agencies for a long time would sell clients on their ability to reach a certain percentage of a target audience a specified number of times by selling them a GRP guarantee. GRPs wound up becoming one metric for making advertising buys.

But in the larger sense, all marketing managers are held accountable these days for the funds they spend to stimulate or manage demand. Measuring the impact of digital media has brought its own opportunities and challenges with click-through and other web analytics. But marketing effectiveness measurement has rarely been all that precise. Shopper marketing brings a positive and a negative angle to this issue simultaneously.

Metrics and Shopper Marketing

Shopper marketing brings into the equation all the marketing communication vehicles in the store. There are some positives to this. First, media exposure in the store is the closest you can get to actual purchase behavior. The time lag problem is reduced to as small as possible. The only place the lag might be shorter is in the online environment—sometimes. But the time between exposure to an end-cap display and product being placed in a shopping basket is nearly instantaneous.[1]

The problem lies in measurement of all the in-store media as distinctly different forms of exposure. A myriad of questions immediately come to mind:

- Do eyeballs on target, that is, viewing a sign, mean the same level of attention and information processing in the store environment as it does out of store? There are arguments both ways—more attention is paid to in-store signage and less attention.

- How many times does a shopper need to see a sign for it to be effective, and if the same out-of-store rules apply, for example, you need seven exposures, we're in trouble because shoppers do not walk by the same area seven times in a store!

- What media ought to be considered? Signs, coupon dispensers, demonstrations, packaging, digital displays, shelf talkers, floor stickers…?

- How do you "measure" an entire solution center, end-cap, or secondary placement display?

- How do we know if someone saw a vehicle? Heat maps, RFID sensors on carts or baskets, video-mining?

- How do we know if someone stood in front of our brand, that they were *looking at* our brand? And what information were they processing? Did they like it or hate it?

- What are the effects of changes in lighting, scents, colors, temperature, and all other atmospherics that impact all of a shopper's senses? How do these changes affect the effectiveness of other variables such as signage?

- Should we be measuring product placement as a variable and do so as precisely as placement down along an aisle as well as height—*relative to the optimal height for the target shopper*? The optimal height could easily be different for an elderly shopper than a teenage male.

There are so many questions about precise measurement when we talk about treating the store as a marketing environment. To calculate ROI, we need to also measure:

- The costs associated with creating/executing the initiative (including all supply chain costs, often overlooked!)
- The costs of measurement (also often overlooked)
- Compliance rate—not everything that is planned and designed actually gets executed at the store level. In many cases, compliance rates at from 45% to 85%. It doesn't make any sense to conclude that an initiative was ineffective by assuming it was executed in 100% of the stores.

Table 8-1 lists the basic vehicles that must be measured.

Table 8-1 Media Forms

Out of Store	In Store
• Print	• Interactive kiosks
• Television	• Video displays
• Radio	• Coupons
• Online	• Mobile
• Events	• Standard displays
• Mobile	• Sample/demonstrations
	• Signage on shelf
	• Speed to shelf (inventory flow)
	• Facings
	• Shelf position
	• Pricing

The problem was recognized a number of years ago. As a result, the PRISM (Pioneering Research for an In-Store Metric) project was born. The Nielsen Company, one of the world's largest consumer data collection companies, was heavily invested in this project, as was the In-store Marketing Institute, now known as the Path-to-Purchase Institute. If any company should know a lot about consumers and shopping, The Nielsen Company should (and does). Walmart was also heavily involved. Unfortunately, although early results were encouraging, the PRISM project was disbanded before development of a standardized process for measuring the effectiveness of shopper marketing with syndicated data.

This does not mean that we are at ground zero. Retailers learned over more than half a century what works, what doesn't, and why in stores. The measurement is not as precise as industry is asking for at this time, but we know a lot. Also, companies like The Nielsen Company and even smaller niche companies like dunnhumby, Foresight ROI, and Shopper Insights are constantly giving us insights to more efficient and effective measurement solutions. Just because we can measure something does not mean that we should. The payout may not be worth it. These companies and ones like them are helping the industry understand what is worth measuring and at what level of precision.

And one thing we do know: We're moving in the right direction. And we realize that it is not simply a spike in sales, that is, lift, that we are looking for. We are looking for long-term benefits as well when we talk about shopper marketing. We are trying to increase the brand equity of a specific retailer and so should see net effects over time from campaigns not simply spikes in sales due to events.

The purpose of all initiatives is to grow profitable volume. Short-term initiatives—for example, a two-week promotion—should show a short-term obvious spike in volume, frequently followed by a dip in volume as pantry-stock is filled. Key measurements for this are lift and ROI. But long-term initiatives—for example, fixturing that makes it easier for shoppers to find and buy your brand—are also expected to drive volume, reflected in a growth of base volume over time. Key measurements for the latter are brand preference and brand and category share gains (see Figure 8-1).

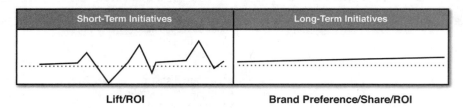

Figure 8-1   *Impact of short- and long-term initiatives.*

In addition to the short- and long-term impact on the brand, it is also important to measure the impact of your initiatives on the retailer. If you recall from our discussion of how retail works, there are three key levers to driving sales at retail: traffic, trips, and transaction size. If one can increase traffic to the store, more people are making purchases. This metric is also called *capture*. By increasing trips, one increases the *frequency* at which products are purchased. One might think an increase in trip frequency is a zero-sum proposition: that the shopper is merely allocating a fixed shopping budget across the period—for example, five trips @ $20/trip instead of four trips @ $25. Interestingly, that is rarely the case. The average basket size may be slightly lower, but shoppers frequently add items or buy an item they might have bought on a trip to another store, resulting in a net increase overall. As we look at transaction size or market basket value, there are three ways to drive sales with this lever: 1) increase the average number of items purchased per category—hence the growing prevalence of multiples, for example, 10 for $10; 2) increase the average value of the item purchased per category—in other words, trading the shopper up from a lower to higher priced item; and 3) increasing the number of categories purchased. One of the key growth strategies in many retailers is to increase the number of categories purchased. Converting a shopper who buys a category in another store to a loyal category shopper in your retailer is often the most productive lever long term. You are not asking the shopper to spend more but merely to shift where he buys that category, yet it adds the value of another category on a regular basis to the market basket. Retailer POS data, particularly if shopper level data is captured, is the source of these measures.

If we look at macro and micro means of measuring the impact of shopper marketing programs we can think in terms of the following:

Macro Measurement

- Share gain (here syndicated data are available)
- Extent of increased brand-retailer collaboration as a result of the program efforts
- Extent of strategic partnering improvement beyond category
- Impact on brand equity
- Impact on retailer category growth and profitability

Micro Measurement

- Percent of shoppers who see the program—adjusted for the expected compliance level!
  - Number of items printed/circulated
  - Number of shoppers who have an opportunity to see
- Extent shoppers engage a program
  - Visits to website (and a whole host of web analytics)
  - Tweets followed, forwarded
  - Dwell time at the display (but be careful, longer is not always better)
  - Percent who listen to, touch, smell, read, or pick up products or display media
- Percent who place items in the basket

To calculate ROI we must understand the "I" portion. What did the program cost? In this cost analysis shopper marketers examine the costs of the many media forms being used, costs of agency contracts, costs of displays, costs of display execution as in labor, and any incentives involved in the program. Some initiatives can be expensive. Take, for example, the initiative Tostitos ran leading up to the Super Bowl in the United States. Entrants were challenged to create their own Super Bowl commercial. The winning commercial aired during this National Football League final event, and the creator won 1 million dollars. This program also ran in several dozen other countries. The most powerful incentive in the United States to encourage participation was the possibility to have an ad aired. In other countries where the Super Bowl is not that significant, the prize money was the main incentive. However, this program, which involved complex social media as well as aspects all along the path to purchase to store shelves unique to each retail partner, exceeded 8 million dollars. This is clearly not the norm, but does highlight the importance of achieving a solid return on the investments you make. Cost areas often overlooked include supply chain management, packaging, and other labor.

It is in the context of ROI that marketing mix modeling (MMM) plays a powerful role. You can think in terms of regression formulas but a bit more complex. These models capture relevant media used in a program and estimate the impact on dependent variables like sales lift.

One of the leading companies working in this area is Foresight ROI. Foresight estimates that there is more than a half a billion dollar opportunity in shopper marketing if best practices are followed and that shopper marketing has greater reach than prime time television at one-fifth the cost. Shopper marketing events also seem to return better than trade events on average. That said, they need each other. Shopper marketing programs must integrate with trade programs. The advice Foresight would give includes funding high performance customers, differentiating by segment and even customer, collaborating and managing communications throughout the path to purchase—all the kinds of things we have been discussing in this book.

Concerning the path to purchase, programs that involve the entire path are far more profitable than at-home only or in-store only programs. It also seems that brands with strong equity perform better in shopper marketing programs than others.

Predictive modeling can be used to remove the guesswork from programs. These tools can be used to know what you can expect from each media form and the interaction among numerous combinations of media.

Expected Impact

What can be expected from diligent efforts at shopper marketing? In short, to move from an unacceptable .85:1 ratio to a 5:1 ratio, which far exceeds the 2.5:1 target marketing managers seek for traditional advertising (see Figure 8-2).

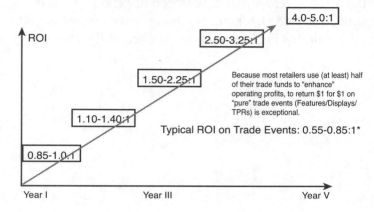

**Average Best Practice ROIs on combined
Trade/Shopper Initiatives over Time**

4.0-5.0:1

2.50-3.25:1

1.50-2.25:1

ROI

Because most retailers use (at least) half
of their trade funds to "enhance"
operating profits, to return $1 for $1 on
"pure" trade events (Features/Displays/
TPRs) is exceptional.

1.10-1.40:1

Typical ROI on Trade Events: 0.55-0.85:1*

0.85-1.0:1

Year I   Year III   Year V

Figure 8-2   *Expected impact over time.*

The final measurement thought we leave you with is the idea of continuous improvement. The idea is to measure and then adapt and learn from what worked and what did not. Incorporate the learning into your insights and your planning process for the following year. Do more of what worked. Adapt or stop doing those things that did not. Figure 8-3 depicts this thought process.

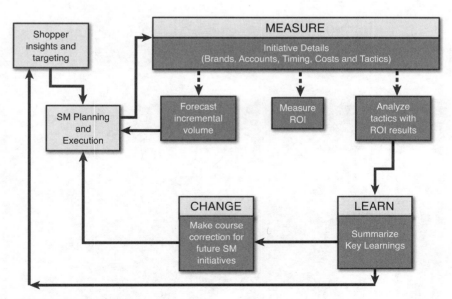

Figure 8-3   *Measure-learn-change process.*

Endnote

1   We know that only a very small percentage of products placed in shopping baskets get removed before checkout. So being in the basket is quite close to actual purchase, although this is also being researched still today.

Part II
The Scholar's View

Part II of the book is devoted to exploring a little bit deeper the scholastic research that supports some of the thinking and guidelines offered in Part I. There are only a few chapters, but they are quite different from the chapters in Part I. Here we help you understand both the way academics, also referred to within the profession as *scholars*, think and findings from academic research in areas relevant to shopper marketing. It is not our intention to showcase all the research that might be relevant; that would be impossible. Instead, our intent is to share the kinds of research being done so that you can seek out contemporary work that might help you with your specific challenge at hand. This work is being done constantly on campuses and within academic-business partnerships around the globe. Much of the best work winds up in academic journals, which serve as the sources of what we present here.

Chapter 9, "What Do Academics Actually Do and How Do They Think?" addresses philosophy of science, in other words the various ways scholars think, that is, their perspectives, world views. This is important because those perspectives are linked to the type of research questions they ask and the methods they rely on to answer those questions. That chapter can be exciting when you begin to recognize that all of our research is influenced by the way we look at the world. If you are a researcher, you may not even realize that you have a world view.

The remaining three chapters provide findings from research in the following areas:

- Chapter 10, "Exemplars of Shopper Marketing Relevant Academic Research"
  - Market opportunity identification
  - Core topics:
    - Strategic brand management
    - Retailing
    - Consumer behavior

- More specific topics:
    - Shopper behavior and store environment
    - Private brands and brand equity
    - Product assortment and shelf management
    - Online and multichannel shopping
    - Segmentation
    - Reference price and promotion
    - Shopper paths
    - In-store advertising
    - Mobile marketing
    - Shopper satisfaction and loyalty
- Chapter 11, "Connecting Supply Chain Management to Shopper Marketing"
- Chapter 12, "Conclusion"

You should have a more rigorous understanding of how academics think, what they do, and the kind of findings they generate by reading Part II. This should help you understand a bit more how we sometimes know why certain strategies work and why others do not. You will also hopefully develop a deeper appreciation for the work that academics provide to support business and society. The first section hits on this very point—what do academics actually do anyway?

9

What Do Academics Actually Do and How Do They Think?

Academics, or scholars, conduct research that primarily either builds or tests theoretical models. They have the potential to make significant contributions to your thinking and practice. But to use them and their knowledge most effectively, you should know a little bit about what they are incentivized to do and how they think. This chapter is about that. Most academics are interested in generalizable knowledge, meaning that models or frameworks can apply to various situations and contexts, and ideally models that remain stable over a period of time. So, for example, although they may not be interested in a specific marketing fad, they may very well be interested in how fads in general emerge and fade away. Or they may not be as interested in how a particular package affected a specific market segment's purchase behavior during a specific campaign as they are in how humans react to and what they feel about specific colors, shapes, and so forth that drive other behaviors, that is, knowledge that could apply to many packaging decisions over decades.

Academics are also interested in being thorough, digging deeply, and being precise. This means anomalies and interesting, unique aspects of what they study are also of interest, but often because theory would not normally predict the anomaly and thus it becomes interesting. The topics of study are often referred to generally as *phenomena*. So academics spend a great deal of time studying important and interesting phenomena to understand and in some cases predict how things work. The more knowledge about a particular phenomenon we develop, the better advice we can give to people living in or managing that particular phenomenon. In the field of marketing, many phenomena have been explored for nearly a hundred years and more emerge each year because the field is dynamic.

How is this knowledge generated? Business generally and marketing in particular is an applied discipline. This means marketing draws on theories, knowledge, and methods from more basic fields such as psychology, social psychology, sociology, anthropology, economics, ecology, behavioral economics, and neurology, as well as methods from statistics, calculus, hard sciences for experimental design, and so forth. Usually academics have areas of interest on which they focus and a set of research method tools they prefer to use. This helps them become experts in particular areas that may seem narrow but are usually quite deep. Where the MBA degree creates a solid manager across all aspects of business, a PhD in business drives an academic to become an expert in a particular aspect of her field. Ideally, the methods chosen to study a phenomenon are driven by the research questions the researcher is asking about that phenomenon. Some methods are better at building theory, while others are better at testing theory. Usually qualitative methods are best for building theory while testing theory draws on quantitative methods. The scientific method needs both and many ways of collecting and analyzing data.

Results from these research studies are usually published in scholastic journals after passing through a rigorous double blind review process. This means after research projects are completed, a manuscript describing the project and findings is sent to a journal whose mission and readership align with the project for review. The manuscript is sent to several academic reviewers who do not know the manuscript's authors. After a month or more, authors receive the reviews with the reviewers' identities hidden. If the manuscript is salvageable, meaning it has potential and merit, the authors are allowed to revise it and return it for a second round of reviews. This process may take three or four rounds for many journals and for the top rated journals, only 8% to 10% of the work submitted ends up in print and sometimes takes one to four years to get into print! This is precisely why phenomena must not be fads and must be relatively stable and long-term. Only academics and scholars in industry read these scholastic journals regularly. They are a means of documenting a conversation among scientists. This also ensures that what gets published is of the highest quality in terms of theoretical usage, development, and testing. It ought to be relevant to business somewhere—in theory.

Although this book is not designed to make you an academic, you ought to know with whom you are working when working with academics. You need to know what to expect and what not to expect. Many academics enjoy working with business professionals to help them solve their business problems by studying what works and why as well as offering improvement suggestions. Many if not most have business experience of their own and know what business managers are facing. The knowledge academics have at their disposal may or may not help a manager's particular organization directly and immediately because that manager's problem is context specific. So the advice may need some adaptation, which some academics are proficient at handling while others are not. Due to the way academics identify phenomena and research questions to pursue they sometimes can be drawn away from immediate, contemporary business issues, problems, and phenomena. In some areas, academics might be ahead of business in their thinking by recognizing patterns or how things are working before practitioners do. This is because academics are incentivized to slow down and study in detail what a business manager might simply not have the time to study. At other times, due to the pace at which business moves, academics can be left a bit behind the business world. In the field of shopper marketing there exists this kind of gap, that is, academics have been a bit behind. That said, a significant body of research does apply to bits and pieces of what is now being pulled together under the shopper marketing concept.

The term *shopper marketing* first appeared in traditional, rigorous scholastic journals around 2011 while it was accelerating since 2004 in practice. Some in academia might argue that seven years is not much of a gap in the scientific world, but in business terms that's eons. That said, a great deal of the research available currently can apply to this shopper marketing world, and Part II of this book helps shed some light on the kinds of research that is out there. Before we get to the actual findings, you ought to be aware of another important issue when it comes to academics. Within the academic world itself there are different, and some might say divisive views on both what to study and how to study it. Academics tend to adopt one of many philosophical perspectives or world-views that affects all of their decisions. Our view here is that an eclectic view to knowledge generation is needed.

The next section describes the most prevalent philosophical views that exist about knowledge generation and what they contribute. As a practitioner drawing on and paying for research projects, you ought to be as eclectic as possible, drawing on numerous, sometimes conflicting, perspectives and methods. Only in this way will you discover that piece of knowledge none of your competitors have taken the time to find or had the capabilities to find. This will give you an edge, and having an edge is worth everything in business. This next section gets a bit heavy in terms of scientific philosophy. Despite how important we feel it is to your understanding of what kind of knowledge is available to you, feel free to come back to this section later and jump right to the actual examples of shopper marketing relevant academic knowledge.

Philosophical Views and Eclectic Marketing Inquiry

A philosophical perspective is sometimes referred to as a paradigm or world view[1] and means a specific ontological (nature of truth) and epistemological (nature of our ability to find truth) orientation.[2] It also includes the choices one makes in conducting inquiry, similar to "scientific style."[3] Most marketing scholars are well aware of the philosophy of science debates that have invigorated many disciplines. The experienced marketing scholar, many new scholars, and most marketing practitioners often do not find much value or interest in these debates, and as such, fail to see (or remember) the interconnections between perspectives and the methods chosen to study particular marketing phenomena. One cannot reach the full potential of a mixed method approach to the study of marketing phenomena without a solid understanding of the linkages between those methods and the ways they can be employed under the guidance of a variety of philosophical perspectives. Our aim is not to revisit various philosophy of science debates, but rather to highlight nine perspectives, comment on their ontological and epistemological positioning, and present the traditional methods (and their variants) most often adopted by each. We hope to refresh marketing scholars' memories and inform practitioners of these important linkages.

Eclectic Marketing Theory and Practice

Eclectic marketing theory and practice (EMTP) is the integration of multiple perspectives and methods for the study of marketing phenomena of interest. Eclectic theory and practice is "not a demand for integration of theories or resolution of disagreements… rather it is an attempt to account for many representations related to an area of study."[4] In this sense, the goal is for comprehensive understanding of marketing.

The Dilemma

Research and practice can occur within one philosophical perspective. However, some of the more insightful research findings and practical innovations come from EMTP. The vast majority of marketing research and practice occurs in the cell described as single method and single perspective, that is, Quadrant 1, in Figure 9-1. When marketing research teams want to venture off into the other three cells, they confront a dilemma—reconciling researchers' different opinions on the appropriate method and perspective to study the focal phenomenon. Reconciling and combining methods (that is, Quadrant 2) is not so difficult if adopted in a way consistent with one perspective. Reconciling and combing multiple perspectives (that is, Quadrants 3 and 4) on the other hand is another matter entirely. Some marketing scholars argue that certain perspectives are incommensurable and that attempts to account for conflicting perspectives amounts to some form of relativism. However, many marketing scholars have concluded that thorough investigation of incommensurability in philosophy of science debates has found no justifiable evidence of this problem. As a result, multiple perspectives from multiple disciplines are sometimes encouraged and have become increasingly accepted in marketing.

Even if marketing scholars and practitioners accept multiple philosophical perspectives, few incorporate scholars holding different perspectives from their own within specific research projects, with the opportunity cost of limiting the possible theoretical and practical insights from those projects.

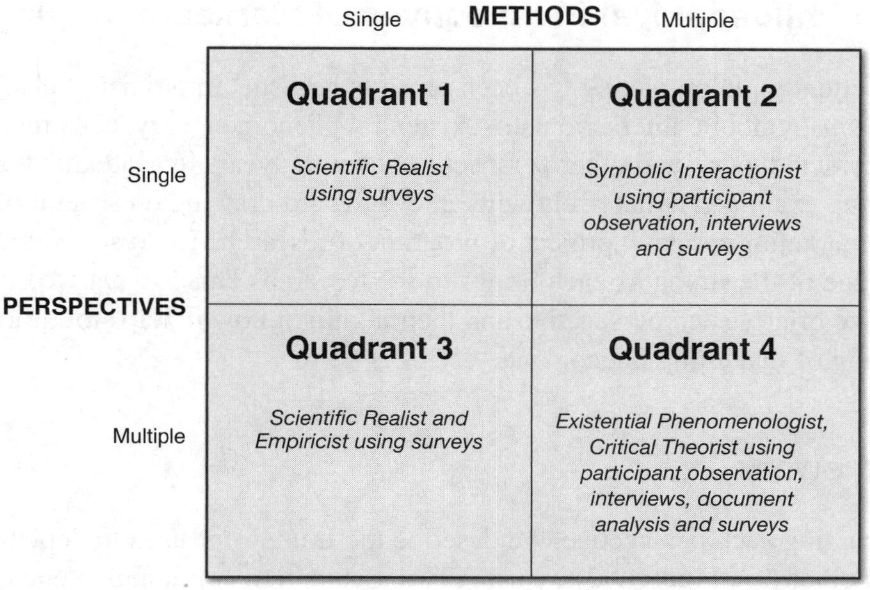

METHODS

Single   **METHODS**   Multiple

	Single	Multiple
Single	**Quadrant 1** *Scientific Realist using surveys*	**Quadrant 2** *Symbolic Interactionist using participant observation, interviews and surveys*
Multiple	**Quadrant 3** *Scientific Realist and Empiricist using surveys*	**Quadrant 4** *Existential Phenomenologist, Critical Theorist using participant observation, interviews, document analysis and surveys*

PERSPECTIVES (vertical axis)

Figure 9-1 *Perspective Method matrix.*

A philosophical perspective involves a researcher's assumptions about the nature of reality and ways of knowing. The marketing debate through the last four decades, like similar debates in other disciplines, has raised the awareness of issues related to diverse philosophical perspectives and had the effect of motivating marketing scholars to be more eclectic in their views. Specifically, over the years many marketing scholars have expanded their horizons and adopted or incorporated philosophical perspectives and methods traditionally used elsewhere (for example, sociology, cultural anthropology, literary criticism, history). In fact, business disciplines as a whole have become more tolerant of and actually are increasing their assimilation of a wide array of philosophical and methodological orientations in large part due to the concerted efforts of scholars trying to understand and accept diverse research perspectives. The underlying assumption here is that marketing phenomena are multifaceted and understanding the whole requires understanding the multiple facets. To do this, diverse marketing researchers, both in academia and practice *must* come together and leverage their expertise to address marketing phenomena of interest. There are fine examples of this within marketing,[5] management,[6] supply chain management,[7] and even accounting.[8] These and similar studies, although providing evidence that EMTP is possible, demonstrate that a working level understanding and leverage of diverse philosophical perspectives is required. The next section offers this working level knowledge.

The Nine Philosophical Perspectives of Marketing Inquiry

Significant attention in marketing has been given to realism, empiricism, falsification-ism, relativism, symbolic interactionism, existential phenomenology, constructivism, semiotics, critical theory, and other perspectives over the years in academic texts.[9] Yet, rarely are they examined collectively with an eye toward drawing on several of them within one marketing research project or program of research. To do so requires a working knowledge of the strengths each brings to the research. This is what we do here, that is, summarize briefly each perspective and then highlight how it helps to inform our understanding of marketing phenomena.

The Framework

Before discussing each perspective, we describe the framework used to depict them relative to each other (see Figure 9-2) by using two assumption continuums: one concerning the relationship between reality and the mind and the other concerning the role researchers believe their own values should play while examining phenomena of interest. The first dimension concerns *ontology*, the nature of the world itself, and is a common dimension used to depict philosophical perspectives.[10] The second dimension concerns *epistemology*, the researcher's mental position while investigating that world. This discussion differs from many multiperspective discussions in that it addresses each perspective uniquely and independently, highlighting the fact that although in many ways the perspectives overlap and the boundaries blur, there are subtle and important differences among them that enable each to provide a unique contribution to marketing inquiry.

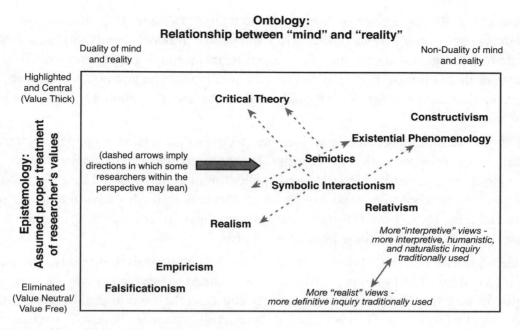

Ontology:
Relationship between "mind" and "reality"

Duality of mind and reality

Non-Duality of mind and reality

Highlighted and Central (Value Thick)

Epistemology: Assumed proper treatment of researcher's values

Critical Theory

Constructivism

Existential Phenomenology

(dashed arrows imply directions in which some researchers within the perspective may lean)

Semiotics

Symbolic Interactionism

Relativism

More "interpretive" views - more interpretive, humanistic, and naturalistic inquiry traditionally used

Realism

Empiricism

Eliminated (Value Neutral/ Value Free)

Falsificationism

More "realist" views - more definitive inquiry traditionally used

Figure 9-2 *Relative positions of nine perspectives.*

Dimension One: Reality/Mind Relationship

Debate over the relationship between reality and the mind is a common demarcation. Various perspectives have been described as residing on a continuum anchored by two polar extremes. On one extreme, reality exists in the objective world external to and separate from the individual's mind (that is, perception of it), and that reality is consistent across situation and time. On the other extreme, all reality exists only *within* the individual's mind as she constructs it, and it is time and context bound; she may construct it differently at different times and in different contexts. The continuum reflects the basic difference between the duality assumption of mind and reality as separate versus the nonduality assumption of the human mind as the architect of reality.

Not many researchers reside at either end of the continuum. Typically, the more realist views, those of contemporary social science, fall toward the left of the continuum in Figure 9-2, where most of the phenomena explored are assumed to be fairly consistent across time and context and of an objective nature (for example, separate from those who perceive it). Even latent constructs are assumed to exist. The problem lies in attempts to measure them. Therefore, observable items are identified and measured that are thought to be indicators of unobservable variables.[11] The term *realist* more aptly depicts a host of perspectives such as scientific realists, fallibilists, falsificationists, empiricists, and combinations of these. It assumes that although reality changes, aspects of it do not change so quickly that they cannot be measured. Furthermore, realism recognizes that although there may in fact be a reality that one attempts to measure, researchers' understandings of it probably will not be able to completely and accurately depict it.

Toward the middle ground lie various perspectives that acknowledge people actively construct their own perceptions of realities, but those realities might have a structure or pattern to them that can be identified and applied to multiple people. These philosophical views seek to understand how people construct meaning through social interaction and documentation. These perspectives include critical theorists, relativists, symbolic interactionists, semioticians, and some phenomenologists.

The right end of the continuum reflects individual construction of reality, that is, nonduality of mind and reality. Individuals are assumed to behave the way they do because of how they individually and actively construct their world as they live it. It does not matter if a "true" reality exists since people act on what they believe is truth, and that belief is time and context bound. The focus is on how different realities emerge for individuals. Perspectives include more subjective views such as existential phenomenology and constructivism.

Dimension Two: Treatment of Researcher's Values

Related to the reality/mind relationship dimension is the continuum of the assumed role a researcher's values should play in the research process, depicted on the vertical dimension of Figure 9-2. This dimension concerns epistemology—ways of knowing. At one end, the researcher assumes his own values and biases get in the way of good research, depicting the more realist oriented views. At the other extreme, researchers' values should be highlighted and are central to the research. Closer to this end are critical theorists who might attempt to find the humanly constructed structure of society that oppresses one group of people. Their goal might be to find and highlight that oppression to the oppressed, thus instigating change within that culture or group. In the middle lie the views that researchers cannot remove their own values from research, and in fact, should take advantage of them as a means of interpreting a phenomenon or text. According to these views, researchers must get "close" to the participants of a study in their worlds to comprehend those worlds.

An Overview of the Nine Perspectives

Extensive methodological details are beyond the scope of this book. However, researchers' perspectives lead them to rely on the methods that best address the unique kinds of questions each perspective generates. Therefore, the kinds of methods often relied on by followers of each perspective are provided in Table 9-1. A researcher's philosophical perspective drives the generation of certain kinds of research questions. It is in attempts to answer these research questions that researchers should then turn to the most appropriate methods, both quantitative and qualitative. Many of the nine perspectives discussed here rely on both qualitative and quantitative methods. The *application* of these methods is what often differs among the perspectives.

Realism

Realism is described first because it represents a perspective held by a large portion of current marketing scholars. It emerged primarily from logical empiricism and includes multiple divisions (for example, classical realism, scientific realism, fallibilistic/critical realism, instrumentalism). Realism attempts to describe reality as it "really" exists. A true reality is assumed to exist, and it often differs from individuals' perceptions and interpretations of it. The aim is to align understanding of the world with how it really behaves. Progress and improvement are assumed to be necessary in science, and progress is seen as the continuous construction of a staircase toward the truth. Thus, conditions that lead a researcher to turn to this perspective are theory construction, theory testing (verification), development of models representing an objective reality, and theory modification.

The aim of scientific realism is to develop lawlike generalizations about phenomena that can be verified through empirical testing. From a social science perspective, it assumes that many phenomena are relatively stable across time and context, and theories are comprised of both observable and unobservable variables (latent variables). It is stochastic when dealing with social phenomena, due to the inherent complexity of social issues. The scientific method is the primary protocol relied on for conducting research, where all attempts are made to remove researcher bias and value involvement, fully recognizing that this objectivity is merely a goal.

The probabilistic quantitative approaches are where scientific realists excel. A great deal of work in marketing has improved the development of how concepts are measured and addressed the issues of reliability and validity. Realists force marketing scholars and practitioners to think about what is controllable and observable, and help them operationalize ideas and theories. The use of the scientific method is intended to yield intersubjectively verifiable results, thus giving researchers and practitioners greater faith that something like the supported hypotheses might really exist. Scientific realism contends "the job of science is to use its method to improve our perceptual (measurement) processes, separate illusion from reality, and thereby generate the most accurate possible description and understanding of the world."[12] The primary intent is to build and validate theory.

Table 9-1   What the Nine Perspectives Bring to the Table

Perspective	Comments on Perspective	Research Question Examples (Some Shopper, Some Business Focused)	This Perspective Forces Us to Think About...	Methods Often Used
Realism	Attempts to predict, focuses on causality, scientific method central to process.	What causes retail customers to be satisfied with brand manufacturers? How can marketing managers influence the shopping experience?	Constructs, relationships among them, theoretical explanations	Exploratory interviews, structured interviews, unobtrusive observation, surveys, case studies, experiments, quantitative content analysis
Empiricism	Relies on empirical evidence of theory's ability to depict reality.	What are the direct effects of specific in-stock levels on shopper loyalty?	Measurement of what we can observe, control, manipulate	Laboratory experimentation, simulation, surveys, modeling
Falsificationism	Develop crucial experiments to falsify grand theories.	Under what conditions can one customer be found that was not satisfied with a specific marketing campaign that should have been according to theory?	The limitations of our theories	Observation, crucial experiments
Relativism	Attempts to place all research in perspective. Many variations. Some question the ability of theory to represent reality. Others question findings themselves.	How did past researchers' culture and perspectives influence their interpretation of market research findings and thus their recommendations?	The paradigms under which we design, we design, conduct, and interpret the findings of research	Historical analysis, ethnography, interviews, content analysis
Symbolic Interactionism	Aim is to understand the meanings that emerge through interaction, which includes the researcher's interaction with the text.	How do shoppers construct meaning within their interactions with other shoppers and store personnel?	How people develop and attach meanings to things, people, themselves, and behaviors through interactions	**Iowa School:** Semantic differential scales, **Chicago School:** field studies, depth interviews, ethnography, ethnomethodology, grounded theory

Perspective	Comments on Perspective	Research Question Examples (Some Shopper, Some Business Focused)	This Perspective Forces Us to Think About...	Methods Often Used
Existential Phenomenology	Aim is to understand the essence of an experience by bracketing out unrelated issues and getting to core meanings. Seeks idiosyncratic knowledge first.	What does it mean for shoppers to experience incredibly (dis)satisfying retail environments?	The experiences of individuals, the central core of an experience, idiosyncratic knowledge	Videotapes, journals, in context depth interviews, hermeneutic interpretation, ethnography, participant observation, experience oneself
Constructivism	Aim is to understand how individuals actively construct their own realities.	How do the past experiences and life-worlds of key retail customer decision-makers reveal themselves in their views of shopper marketing initiatives?	How humans are unique in their ability to actively construct and reflect on their own worlds that constitute their reality	Depth interviews, participant observation, experience oneself
Semiotics	Aim is to understand the meaning of the symbols a group of people use.	What symbols connote high or low brand quality to shoppers and how do shoppers use them to construct meaning and communicate with others?	The symbols that permeate cultures and organizations	Interviews, text-based content analysis, hermeneutics, quantitative content analysis, ethnography
Critical Theory	Aim is to identify the location of a presumed social structure that might be oppressing some people and benefiting others to instigate change in the system.	How are social and environmental structures impacting shoppers' evaluations of retailers?	The hidden structures within society that limit people's options, restrict people from considering and creating a "better" society	Theory-driven interpretive essays, structured interviews, observation

Empiricism

Empiricists assume that the foundation of all knowledge is experience, where science starts with observation and inductively proceeds in a gradual process toward general principles.[13] It emerged as Bacon, Locke, Hume, and Mill brought the true inductive-deductive procedures of Aristotle back into use as classical empiricism (logical empiricism is associated with Hemple, Nagel, and Braithwaite). Empiricism relies on assumptions of an objective reality that can only be known through the senses. These senses are in response to attributes inherent in objects. There is a structure of relationships in the real world, which can be determined. Additionally, behavior can be predicted and conditioned to respond to events or stimuli in the environment. Thus, empiricists are more deterministic as compared to the stochastic realist perspective. Empiricists tend to focus predominantly on observable variables within a theory and strive for complete objectivity.

The primary distinction between empiricists and realists is in the rigidity with which empiricists hold to objective, rational inquiry and attempt to develop true explanatory and predictive knowledge of an external reality. Theory must reference empirical evidence. Thus, conditions that lead a researcher to turn to this perspective are theory testing (verification), maximum control for and manipulation of observable variables, and theory modification.

Empiricists teach marketing scholars the rigor necessary for the design and conduct of experiments, and practitioners the criteria to evaluate the applicability of such experiments. They teach the importance of measurement and detailed description. Empiricism forces the marketing scholar to think about what can be controlled, and the impact those variables have on observable, measurable outcomes. Empiricists teach that it is sometimes best to know a lot about a piece of a phenomenon than to know a little about the entire phenomenon.

Falsificationism

Falsificationism is more of an extreme philosophy toward theory testing. The realist view that knowledge is built one step at a time is seen as relatively slow, and possibly misleading, progress. Realists are seen as constantly sidetracked on fruitless studies. Instead, the falsificationist's aim is to develop precise and grand theories that are extremely falsifiable yet resist falsification.[14] The more precise and potentially more falsifiable the theory, the better. Findings that fail to reject such a theory (that is, support it) are the strongest evidence for it. Platt[15] indicated that efficient and rapid progress in science is attained through the use of logic trees where crucial experiments are designed that enable rapid elimination of entire streams of research that would eventually prove fruitless. Through the conduct of these crucial experiments, rival hypotheses can be tested, enabling exclusion of those that fail.

Falsificationists assume there is an external reality, and the researcher's values should be kept out of any inquiry into it. In addition, true breakthroughs in knowledge only occur when a grand theory no longer holds up to empirical testing. The scientific aim is to take these theories and rigorously attempt to find situations where they do not work. Falsificationists attack the problem from a completely different angle than theory verificationists where knowledge is gained through constant and gradual relaxation of restrictive assumptions to increase theory generalizability. Falsification is intended to be rapid, destructive, and enlightening. Thus, conditions that lead a researcher to this perspective are theory testing (falsification versus verification) and seeking the boundaries of a theory's application.

Falsificationist thinking helps the marketing scholar explore ways to disprove theories rather than find support for them. It drives researchers to seek efficiency in science by stepping back and thinking about the many rival, yet plausible explanations for a phenomenon and only pursuing the ones that make the most sense.

Relativism

Relativism has many dimensions (for example, historical, rationality, reality, cognitive value, critical epistemic, aletheic, subjective, objective, and conceptual relativism).[16] The "naïve" relativist, depicting an extreme, would state that all reality is relative to the individual perceiving it. When a perceiver leaves the room, the room may cease to exist. In practice, the view is usually less extreme. According to historical relativism, research findings and methods must be assessed within the historical perspective of the researchers who conducted the work. Relativists, and particularly critical relativists, assume that knowledge production is impacted by the broader culture in which it is embedded. There may be an external reality, but science cannot find it, especially through the scientific method. Relativism emphasizes description rather than prediction.

Relativism recognizes that a group of researchers develop an understanding of phenomena relative to the time, setting, and values in which they exist. Thus, conditions that lead a researcher to turn to this perspective are the examination of conditions (for example, historical, cultural, personal) that influence particular research studies or define the limitations of the study.

Additionally, relativists believe that it is impossible to remove one's values in research. They do not propose the use of them to one's advantage in the conduct of research as do some perspectives (for example, symbolic interactionists, constructivists), or encourage the use of them to judge and critique as in still other perspectives (for example, critical theorists). Yet they do place great emphasis on the view that these values always influence any research study. As such, all research must be viewed in recognition of the values that influenced it.

Relativists inspire marketing scholars to reflect on the perspectives under which they are currently operating. Researchers begin to examine the conditions under which they are designing, conducting, and interpreting the results of their studies. Researchers think of the assumptions they bring as well as the limitations. By thinking in terms of a relativist, marketing researchers are driven to question the way they think about all of their work, and practitioners are driven to think about their application of that work.

Symbolic Interactionism

The three premises presented by Blumer,[17] one of the fathers of qualitative symbolic interactionism, are 1) people act toward things based on the meanings the things have for them, 2) objects' meanings emerge from interaction with other people, and 3) the meanings are altered by the person's continuous interpretation of them as the person encounters the objects. It is the interaction of people with each other, as well as objects in various situations, that enable people to form meanings of the world—which, in turn, drives behavior. Symbolic interactionists assume that people construct their reality through continuous interaction and as a result things have specific social meanings. Groups of people may develop similar meanings, however, and these meanings can remain fairly consistent across time but are probably uniquely attached to certain situations. Symbolic interactionism sees meaning creation as an evolutionary process where mutual understandings are arrived at through interaction and the use of symbols (for example, voice and gestures) and where fitting of interpretations results in coordinated action.

To understand behaviors, the researcher must understand the meanings and interpretations formed by the individuals researched. This necessitates recognition of one's own values and realizing their role in the interpretation process. The researcher is interacting with the subjects being studied in some cases, thus forming meanings about the meanings the subject holds. It is impossible, and undesirable, to remove one's own values from this perspective. Thus, conditions that lead a researcher to turn to this perspective are seeking to understand socially constructed meanings as formed through interaction, theory development, exploratory and discovery research, and depth of understanding.

There are also variations, or slants, one might take as a symbolic interactionist, often referred to as the Iowa School and the Chicago School.[18] The Iowa School (reflected by the arrow in Figure 9-2 pointing toward realism) adopts a realist perspective in its approach to symbolic interactionism, thus leading to the use of more quantitative methods. These researchers see meaning as fairly stable and attempt to classify people who form similar meanings through similar types of interactions. The Chicago School (reflected by the arrow pointing toward existential phenomenology) adopts a more phenomenological approach to symbolic interactionism, thus using more interpretive methods. These researchers see meaning as created and described by individuals through their interactions with self and others. Symbolic interactionism can also take on a structural slant (represented by the third arrow pointing toward critical theory), focused on the meanings of groups who interact within and across socioeconomic layers.

Thinking like a symbolic interactionist forces marketing researchers and practitioners to focus on the meanings of things and how people engaged in social behavior construct those meanings—to see the logic behind why certain groups of people interpret objects and behavior differently. Researchers and practitioners begin to look at the process of meaning construction versus the static state of current meaning.

Existential Phenomenology

Existential phenomenology is a combination of Kierkegaard's[19] 1838 existentialism and Husserl's[20] phenomenology, each of which falls under the broader heading of subjectivism. There are details that distinguish existentialism from phenomenology, the former rejecting phenomenological essences to focus on the gestalt of being alive, the latter focusing on how the individual interacts with external objects to develop individual meanings of the world.

The existential phenomenological view[21] is on the individual and the individual's construction of reality. It is the study of the individual's "life world" and daily existence. It assumes people act based on how they interpret their world and give meaning to it. Phenomenology generally seeks to uncover the essence of things (including experiences) as seen from a psychological point of view. To focus on a thing's "essence" is to reveal the central core of an experience, such that without that core, the experience would cease to be what it is. Anything that presents itself to a person's consciousness, be it an object, person, or experience (real or imagined), is of interest to phenomenology.[22] Reality for people emerges through their experiences.

The existential phenomenological problem in studying people's experiences is that researchers know too much (or think they do) when they begin to investigate a phenomenon. The aim is to bracket out what the researcher knows, or at least recognize its influence on one's interpretation, and attempt to discover the phenomenon from a fresh and new perspective—that is, from the perspective of the person who actually experienced it. It is assumed that we can only know what we experience by attending to the perceptions and meanings that awaken us.[23] It may even mean a mandate to experience the phenomenon, which is an existential view. It may mean merely focusing on the people themselves and how they experience a phenomenon. The researcher is often an active participant in the process of representing multiple realities. Meaning emerges through interaction of the researcher's and the participant's views. A key is to focus on the details of the participant's experience and feelings and not encourage the participant to rationalize *why* he felt the way he did.

Existential phenomenology seeks contextually based, holistic understandings of human beings in nondualistic terms. Marketing researchers following this perspective seek to understand the essence of people's life worlds, to understand what it is like to experience something from the experiencer's point of view (for example, shopping, consuming, managing), to reveal idiosyncratic knowledge, holistic perspectives, uniqueness, and diversity among individuals (for example, consumers, buyers, marketers).

Thinking like an existential phenomenologist helps marketing scholars and practitioners focus on the experiences of individuals. It drives researchers and practitioners to stop thinking in terms of entire segments of static variables and start thinking about the experiences people have and how those experiences unfold and define people's worlds. Specifically, it forces attention on those experiences that heighten people's awareness of themselves as living, human beings. It raises one's own assumptions and understandings to the conscious level. It means that, first and foremost, researchers and practitioners must understand how each unique individual constructs her world in her mind.

Constructivism

Constructivism holds that positivist views are flawed. *Reality* is something that exists only in the context of a mental construct.[24] Constructivists feel that the only way to deal with human behavior and minds is subjectively. They rely on hermeneutics and dialectics. The first addresses the individual's construction of reality. The second then compares and contrasts this interpretation with other constructs belonging to the same or other individuals. The aim is to form a single framework that recognizes the existence of multiple realities. There is a strong assumption of subjectivity and active, individual constructions of reality. There is also a strong assumption that researchers must use their own constructs to compare to the participant's constructs. Thus, conditions that lead a researcher to turn to this perspective are seeking holistic, idiosyncratic perspectives, discovery research, and seeking to understand diversity and uniqueness among consumers.

Constructivist thinking forces marketing researchers and practitioners to reflect on each individual's construction of reality and possibly how those reality constructions differ for one individual across contexts and time. It helps the marketing scholar and practitioner realize that life and the experiences that comprise it are constantly changing. Each of us is always actively constructing the worlds in which we live and behave accordingly. The more researchers understand the uniqueness in each construction of reality, the more they appreciate the richness and complexity of life. It forces a focus on the dynamic individual in contrast to the static group. It seeks to understand, not predict.

Semiotics

Semiotics focuses on the meanings and symbols people use to communicate with each other and themselves.[25] It assumes that social interaction and meaning are constructed through symbols and signs. Signs can be words, pictures, objects, or products.[26]

Semiotics can have a realist, structural, or phenomenological slant (reflected by the arrows in Figure 9-2). For example, from a realist slant, semioticians empirically explore the relationships among signs and symbols and other constructs that might be behavioral or psychological. From the structural slant, semioticians explore the consumption and meaning of products while remaining aware of the structural underpinnings and agendas that underlie them. It continually tests preconceptions brought into the research. From a phenomenological slant, semiotics explores the emergence of the meanings of symbols as formed through actual experiences.

Semiotics "explores how reality, words, gestures, myths, products/services, and theories acquire meaning."[27] Meaning becomes the central focus in human behavior. Thus, conditions that lead a researcher to turn to this perspective are seeking to interpret the signs, symbols, and language related to a phenomenon.

Thinking as a semiotician helps marketing scholars and practitioners see the symbols within cultures and how perceptions of them influence behavior. Researchers and practitioners begin to see the meanings of corporations, logos, images, job titles, brand names, and product types. If one thinks in terms of symbols and their meanings in various societies, entirely new dimensions emerge and with them research questions and practical innovations.

Critical Theory

Although several perspectives can be critical in nature and take a critical view of the text being explored, *critical theory*[28] aims to transform reality by raising people's awareness of the structures in which they exist. There is an external reality, as well as a conflicting subjective perception, that reflects the human construction of the world.

In socioeconomic constructionism, the words people use to describe the world in which they live reflect the point in history and position in the structure that drove them. Hermeneutic methods are used to uncover misunderstandings and miscommunications. It is critical and skeptical of social institutions.[29] From this perspective, the researcher highlights and makes central his own values and uses that perspective to uncover oppressed groups of people. Basic forms might focus on social class (as in Marxism), racial groups, gender (as in feminism), or combinations of these ideologies. At a basic level, the focus is on ideological power and hegemonic functions.

Modern Marxism encompasses far more than Marx's classical social class distinctions between working and ruling classes but still assumes that a social structure underlies other issues, and it is this structure that is the most important aspect of society to understand. The ruling parties in society, those with power, emphasize racial and gender issues, either intentionally or unintentionally, to mask the true structural demarcation, which is primarily economic. This economic demarcation must be revealed and brought to the attention of those people who are disadvantaged. Feminism is another complex form of critical theory that focuses on the gender and race issues of structural control. It too has many viewpoints, such as liberal feminism, women's voice/experience feminism, and poststructuralist feminism.[30] In both Marxism and feminism, reality is dialectic in nature and changes as the structure of societies change. In fact, by the extreme perspectives, it is incumbent upon the researcher to identify the way in which the structure is operating and then *motivate* the oppressed or repressed group to discard the structure. It is critical in that not all forms of knowledge and ways of knowing are equal. The aim is to identify ways in which to improve human existence.

In literary criticism, critique is aimed at literary works as text. The literary texts in which scholars would be interested include publications of scholarly research and theory, as well as more applied texts, such as advertisements. Literary criticism can examine text in at least three modes: psychobiographical, editorial, and structural. According to Stern,[31] literary criticism is "the overall term for studies concerned with defining, classifying, analyzing, interpreting and evaluating works of literature."

Critical theory falls in the middle range concerning the mind and reality, recognizing that both objective and subjective realities exist. However, this perspective lies at the far end of the researcher values continuum, giving these values a central role. In effect, critical theory encourages reflection and contemplation about the past, present, and future of society. "Through the process of critique and dialogue, the critical researcher tries to help people imagine alternative social organizations that facilitate the development of human potential free from constraints."[32] It is a critique of society that encourages consumers to visualize a better world and consume in a way to enact that world. Critical theory helps marketing researchers begin to see hidden structures in society, and forces the marketing scholar and practitioner see more ethical and moral issues.

Revisiting the Four Quadrant Matrix

With this summary of nine perspectives, we can now revisit the four quadrant matrix in a little more detail. Quadrant 1 in Figure 9-1 represents research projects built upon a single perspective and using a single method—for example, when a scientific realist uses surveys, or a semiotician uses quantitative content analysis. A major strength of this kind of project is that it is efficient. When researchers hold the same perspectives and agree on the use of one research methodology, usually because the researchers are experts in that methodology and that methodology seems to be the most appropriate to answer the research questions, attention is focused on the research issue. Although all thorough research can be time consuming, project design and implementation is straightforward relative to projects in the other three quadrants. A major weakness is that these projects provide narrow views of the phenomenon of interest. This is not necessarily bad, especially if the research question is narrow. They also tend to build on research results emerging from projects conducted by researchers holding similar perspectives and using similar methods as the current project, and as such, risk ignoring (either by design or unintentionally) research conducted under different, especially conflicting, perspectives. Finally, these projects are the most susceptible to method bias concerns because they do not triangulate multiple methodologies.

Quadrant 2 represents a project built upon one perspective, but utilizing multiple methods. This is traditional triangulation research. An example would be a symbolic interactionist relying on ethnography and using participant observation, interviews, and surveys to address an issue. Another example would be an empiricist conducting multiple studies via laboratory experiments, natural experiments, and surveys. A third example would be a scientific realist using exploratory interviews to build theory, followed by several surveys and experiments to validate the theory. A major strength of these projects is that they reduce method bias. When conducted by more traditional positivistic researchers, or "contemporary social scientists," these projects assume a central reality upon which various methods triangulate. When conducted by interpretivist researchers, these projects assume multiple social realities, which multiple methods help elucidate. Although not as efficient as Quadrant 1 projects, Quadrant 2 projects provide more effective method triangulation but are not distracted by philosophical debates. The major weakness of these projects is that, like Quadrant 1, they are narrow in their depiction of phenomena because they take place within a single perspective.

Most disciplines employ scholars engaged in projects that tend to fall into Quadrants 1 and 2. It is difficult to ascertain merely from the journals to which quadrant a project belongs because (1) researchers often do not articulate their perspectives and (2) it is often difficult to determine whether a published article is a standalone study or one in a series of studies within a larger program of research. However, Quadrant 1 and 2 projects are logical choices due to their efficiency, due in large part to their philosophical consistency.

Quadrant 3 represents a project relying on multiple perspectives, yet one method. An example might be an empiricist and a scientific realist conducting an experiment together. Here different, but usually complementary perspectives (for example, multiple positivist, interpretive, or humanist perspectives) combine their backgrounds and assumptions to design a project relying on a single method. Another example might be a scientific realist and a structuralist conducting a theory building study using in-depth interviews. This kind of project is most likely to take place when researchers who hold different but similar philosophical perspectives have used, or at least accept the viability of, a variety of similar methods, allowing them to choose one for the project in question. A strength of these projects is their incorporation of multiple perspectives of the environment. Quadrant 3 projects begin to step back and question the assumptions behind the research and the way one views a particular phenomenon. Their strength is in considering multiple views about a phenomenon and possibly multiple realities. A weakness of Quadrant 3 projects is that they fail to take full advantage of differing assumptions because they rely on a single methodology, which only reveals a narrow interpretation of the phenomenon of interest.

Finally, Quadrant 4 represents projects that leverage multiple perspectives and multiple methods (that is, EMTP research). An example would be an existential phenomenologist, critical theorist, and symbolic interactionist using observation, interviews, and surveys in a multistaged research project. An actual example is a multiyear project in which the authors are currently involved. The initial study was a grounded theory study exploring the nature and processes of changes in customers' desired value (for example, new supplier requirements) from the perspectives of buyers and buying influencers within automobile manufacturers. The perspectives of realist, empiricist, structuralist, and symbolic interactionist are all represented on the EMTP team of six scholars. Data in the initial study were comprised of primarily audiotaped depth interviews, supported by observations and company documents. Interpretation of the data was accomplished from a number of perspectives. Ongoing studies within this project involve additional naturalistic inquiry as well as validation studies of appropriate pieces of the emergent theory.

The strength of Quadrant 4 projects is that they take advantage of differing perspectives to generate a variety of questions about a particular phenomenon because each researcher views the social world from a different orientation. Like Quadrant 3 projects, the distinctly different questions generated from different perspectives lead to thinking about a phenomenon from many angles. Unlike Quadrant 3 projects, however, Quadrant 4 projects recognize that these questions demand mixed methods. Thus, Quadrant 4 projects offer the potential for maximum triangulation (that is, effectiveness). They are efficient in that studies stemming from conflicting perspectives can be conducted simultaneously with a mutually agreed upon goal of combining the results as multiple views of the central phenomenon, not conflicting views on a single truth. Coordinated, simultaneous studies are more time efficient than sequential studies that respond to previous studies. A weakness of Quadrant 4 projects is that the researchers must take time to understand the multiple perspectives with their underlying assumptions. Quadrant 4 projects demand that open minds accept alternative perspectives as offering unique insights to a particular phenomenon. Even if results of multiple studies within a project are directly contradictory, researchers must be willing to explore the differences as possible multiple interpretations of the phenomenon. Beyond demanding greater time and energy for understanding co-researchers' perspectives, Quadrant 4 studies possess the greatest risk for conflict. The risk of conflict is highest when the most diverse perspectives are juxtaposed. However, the process of working through conflicting perspectives often leads to the greatest insights.

The EMTP Process

Merely recognizing and appreciating the unique contributions of nine philosophical perspectives and the methods on which they rely does not constitute EMTP. EMTP takes place when scholars invite diverse perspectives to join a research team. EMTP calls for active, personal engagement where ideas are aired and debated, and research is designed and implemented while jointly and cooperatively trying to understand phenomena holistically. There are numerous texts offering guidelines for designing and conducting many forms of both qualitative and quantitative studies. Unlike these texts, the EMTP guidelines presented here are not focused on methodology, but rather focus primarily on mental orientation. They are offered to assist scholars to embrace divergent viewpoints and in "maintaining flexible, inquisitive, resilient minds...[that] acknowledge the mutual coexistence of potentially contradictory research paradigms."[33] This section describes EMTP as a multiphase process that can guide marketing researchers in systematically viewing phenomena from various perspectives, designing and conducting studies that together offer holistic insights to those phenomena, which can subsequently benefit practitioners (see Figure 9-3).

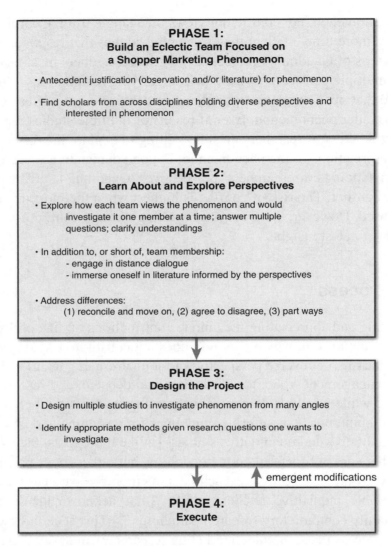

Figure 9-3 *Building an eclectic research team (the EMTP process).*

Phase 1: Build an Eclectic Team

Within a research program, there are many phenomena to potentially explore. Contemplation of these phenomena generates specific research questions. The selection of phenomena to explore typically comes from observation and/or the literature. However, as our discussion thus far has emphasized, each researcher is likely to see only a narrow aspect of the potential research because each researcher is limited by her philosophical perspective. Researchers within other disciplines and holding differing perspectives are likely to view the same research differently. Armed with a realization that one's view from the beginning is limited by one's perspective, the eclectic scholar is driven to seek out diverse views on the phenomenon of interest. Scholars come across diverse views in their literature searches concerning specific issues. The eclectic researcher ensures that literature across disciplines and perspectives is amply represented. Phase 1 of EMTP calls for more than merely an eclectic approach to literature reviews, however. EMTP calls for active dialogue from the start among interdisciplinary researchers on the phenomenon of interest. Thus, in Phase 1 the principal researcher must assemble a potential team of interdisciplinary scholars willing to embark on a journey of inquiry focused on a key phenomenon. It is likely that intense debate will emerge among this budding team concerning exactly what the phenomenon of inquiry is, how it will be defined, and possibly whether it is even a relevant issue. This is exactly what the eclectic researcher hopes will happen. The initial debate will solidify in everyone's mind exactly *what* needs to be researched.

Assembling a diverse team for EMTP demands that one reach out to those with different perspectives in different disciplines. One must look beyond colleagues conducting similar work in a similar manner, beyond colleagues with whom one sees eye to eye, and beyond colleagues who attend one's presentations at conferences. The primary objectives are to find scholars who (1) are likely to see the phenomenon in which one is interested differently and (2) are likely to be interested in researching the phenomenon in which one is interested. The team must be comprised of passionate, open-minded scholars because working with a team of scholars who see the world differently for the higher cause of holistically studying an important issue demands such passion and open-mindedness. Scholars who refuse to acknowledge the complementary contributions of diverse perspectives will not last long on an EMTP team. One finds these diverse, passionate, open-minded scholars by examining the journals of other disciplines and visiting other departments. One motivates potential team members by selling them on one's idea of eclectically studying a particular issue. Team members do not personally adopt a single perspective or merge perspectives into some hybrid perspective. They merely acknowledge the value of other team members' perspectives to the inquiry process.

During Phase 1, team members begin to get to know one another as they clarify the phenomenon of interest. The principal researcher's initial hunch that team members view the phenomenon differently is confirmed as researchers steeped in their traditions begin to speak. It is during these early stages of the research project that team members become fully aware that everyone does not view the world in the same manner and that EMTP demands extensive time focused on exploring perspective differences before designing any individual studies.

Phase 2: Learn and Explore

Phase 2 is where researchers take time to send the phenomenon of interest to the background and raise the perspectives through which team members view the phenomenon to the foreground. In Phase 2, the idea is to understand more deeply the ontological and epistemological orientations of team members—the more diverse the better. It is in this phase that the risk of team dissolution is highest. Researchers may feel as if their assumptions and orientations are being called into question or fail to see the value certain members bring to the table and, as such, may depart the project. The principal researcher must facilitate open dialogue among team members and guard against dissolution. The challenge is to encourage diverse perspectives yet also keep engagement. As part of the dialogue, each team member clearly articulates his perspective and what that perspective brings to understanding the phenomenon of interest. Team members should strive to understand perspectives different from their own. Even the most eclectic researchers may only be aware of some perspectives. Active dialogue breathes life into these perspectives and their similarities and differences.

A backup to actual team membership may be dialogue with relevant researchers via telephone or email. Another avenue is to immerse oneself in literature informed by the relevant perspective. However, active membership provides far more value than secondary interpretation. Enthusiastic and competent scholars bring a wealth of knowledge not only about their perspectives, but about what others in their discipline are doing and changes that have occurred since studies have been published. The results of a combined intellect of active, engaged scholars far surpass what can be accomplished merely through secondary analysis of the work of those same scholars.

Whether in active dialogue with team members or trying to understand perspectives through a secondary route, there are questions one is trying to answer: (1) How would a researcher following this perspective think about this phenomenon? (2) What questions might she ask and how would those questions be phrased? (3) What information would be gained if answers were sought to these questions? (4) What methodologies would be appropriate for answering these questions? Answers to these questions help the team members mentally manipulate the phenomenon and explore how a particular perspective might guide inquiry. The procedure here is to "turn the microphone" over to each team member. That individual then addresses each of these questions. Other team members attempt to see the phenomenon through the speaker's lenses. After each team member has had her initial say, open dialogue about what was said emerges. A continuous process of clarification and questioning solidifies the multitude of angles that can and should be taken in the investigation of the phenomenon of interest. A few follow-up questions might include (1) Which of these research questions, if answered, would make a significant contribution to marketing research, practice, or pedagogy? (2) Which of these research questions has not been addressed before? (3) Which of these research questions excites us the most? (4) Which of these research questions is/are feasible for us to pursue now? Researchers essentially have three options when differences inevitably emerge: (1) reconcile differences and jointly investigate the phenomenon, (2) agree to disagree, remain a research team, and conduct multiple, simultaneous or sequential studies, or (3) part ways and investigate the phenomenon independently.

Phase 3: Design Studies

In this phase, the team designs multiple studies incorporating multiple methods such that the phenomenon is investigated from as many perspectives as possible. The point is to identify points of disagreement and choose a route to take. Some researchers may defer to others on a given point. For example, a structuralist may want to investigate how a social structure relates to a consumption phenomenon, and an existential phenomenologist may prefer to investigate personal experiences of consumption. In this case, one may defer to the other for the given study. Both researchers may jointly conduct one study, agreeing to conduct a follow-on study within the larger project from the other perspective. The research team may also decide to allow the studies to emerge as the project proceeds, deciding on the appropriate methods for each study based on the results of the previous one.

By virtue of bringing together a team of EMTP researchers, one is likely to discover a diverse set of methodological preferences, as well as diverse expertise in using them. An EMTP team will hold diverse perspectives but will also be comprised of experts across a wide variety of methodologies. This expertise enables the phenomenon of interest to be explored from many angles. The aim is to plan for systematic leveraging of the expertise.

The overall goal of Phase 3 is to develop a plan for the project. Teams in this phase attempt to cover all possible angles that ought to be explored concerning the phenomenon of interest. They design multiple studies, prioritize them, and divide into subteams where possible to simultaneously carry them out. Realistically, some studies may be modified, some added, and some deleted as new data emerge throughout the project (that is, the emergent modifications arrow in Figure 9-3). The plan is dynamic, but, the key is to have a plan.

Phase 4: Execute Studies

In this phase, researchers carry out the studies designed in Phase 3, and practitioners put the findings to use. Each method chosen is followed according to its guiding tenets, whether qualitative or quantitative. When deviations are desired, the team discusses the desired adjustments. As results become available, they are discussed with the team and placed within the larger context of the overall plan developed in Phase 3.

One important task of multiple study research is integrating the results. It may be useful to designate one or more researchers as findings integrators. These researchers analyze results across studies, comparing and contrasting the implications. In some instances, results may support other results. In other instances, results may complement each other, adding new dimensions to the team's understanding. In a third instance, findings may be conflicting, leading to dialogue and additional studies to reconcile the conflicts.

Another important task of research is auditing both the process and findings of studies. Team members are designated as auditors of other team members' processes and findings while they simultaneously conduct their own research. There are numerous guidelines for conducting such audits. It is sometimes difficult in heavily interpretive work for an outside auditor to "see" what the interpreters see, but the auditors should be able to see how interpretations were made and data were collected.

The primary goal of Phase 4 is to leverage the expertise and size of the team. An interdisciplinary team brings together scholars with diverse perspectives, methodological expertise, and writing skills. The team should coordinate its activities and focus individuals' attention in ways that leverage this diversity and tap their interests. Otherwise, the team is nothing more than a larger group of researchers who may actually slow down the research process or slip back into executing a series of narrowly focused studies.

Summary Comments on Eclectic Inquiry

This chapter emphasizes the need for EMTP research to develop holistic understandings of marketing phenomena. EMTP was defined as research involving teams of researchers holding diverse ontological and epistemological perspectives relying on diverse methods to investigate central phenomena. EMTP is not desired merely for the sake of variety. Eclecticism is only valuable in that it helps researchers move beyond their traditional boundaries and explore research questions in innovative ways, resulting in more holistic, comprehensive understanding of important phenomena. The act of forcing oneself to think about a phenomenon in completely different ways ought to generate profoundly different hypotheses, results, and implementations. Leveraging diverse, potentially conflicting views and expertise from multiple disciplines is a key to insightful research. Diverse perspectives must be actively sought, assembled, and managed as a unified team if true EMTP research is to take place. Without full recognition and management of the differences and complementary nature of multiple perspectives, EMTP will stall before it gains momentum. As a result, research will be incomplete and disjointed.

Endnotes

1   Gioia, D. A. and Pitre, E. (1990), "Multiparadigm Perspectives on Theory Building," *Academy of Management Review,* 15 (4), 584-602; Guba, E. G. (1990), *The Paradigm Dialogue,* Newbury Park, CA: Sage; Hunt, Shelby D. (1990), "Truth in Marketing Theory and Research," *Journal of Marketing,* 54 (July), 1-15; Hunt, Shelby D. (1991), *Modern Marketing Theory,* Cincinnati, OH: South-Western Publishing Co.; Kuhn, Thomas S. (1970), *The Structure of Scientific Revolutions*, 2nd ed. Chicago: University of Chicago Press.

2   Spiggle, S. (1994), "Analysis and Interpretation of Qualitative Data in Consumer Research," *Journal of Consumer Research*, 21 (December), 491-503.

3   Hirshman, Elizabeth C. (1985), "Scientific Style and the Conduct of Consumer Research," *Journal of Consumer Research*, 12 (September), 225-239.

4   Gioia, D. A. and Pitre, E. (1990), "Multiparadigm Perspectives on Theory Building," *Academy of Management Review*, 15 (4), 584-602.

5   See for example: Arnould, E. J. and Price, L. L. (1993), "River Magic: Extraordinary Experience and the Extended Service Encounter," *Journal of Consumer Research,* 20 (June), 24-45; Celsi, R. L., Rose, R. L. and Leigh, T. W. (1993), "An Exploration of High Risk Leisure Consumption through Skydiving," *Journal of Consumer Research,* 20 (June), 1-23; Mentzer, John T. and David W. Schumann (2006), "The Theoretical and Practical Implications of Marketing Scholarship," *Journal of Marketing Theory and Practice*, 14 (No. 3), 179-190; Sirci, A. K., Ward, J. C. and Reingen, P. H. (1996), "Microcultural Analysis of Variation in Sharing of Causal Reasoning about Behavior," *Journal of Consumer Research*, 22 (March), 345-72.

6   Gioia, D. A. and Pitre, E. (1990), "Multiparadigm Perspectives on Theory Building," *Academy of Management Review,* 15 (4), 584-602; Morgan, G. and Smircich, L. (1980), "The Case for Qualitative Research," *Academy of Management Review*, 5 (4), 494-500; Tsoukas, Haridimos (1994), "What Is Management? An Outline of A Metatheory," *British Journal of Management*, 5, 289-301.

7   Flint, Daniel J., Everth Larsson, Britta Gammelgaard, and John T. Mentzer (2005), "Logistics Innovation: A Customer Value-Oriented Social Process," *Journal of Business Logistics*, 26 (No. 1), 113-147; Golicic, Susan L. and John T. Mentzer (2005), "The Drivers of Interorganizational Relationship Magnitude," *Journal of Business Logistics*, 26 (No. 2), 47-71.

8   Searcy, DeWayne L. and John T. Mentzer (2003), "A Framework for Conducting and Evaluating Research," *Journal of Accounting Literature*, 22, 130-167.

9   Alspector-Kelly, Marc (2001), "Should the Empiricist Be a Constructive Empiricist?" *Philosophy of Science,* 68 (4), 413-431; Calder, Bobby J. and Tybout, Alice M. (1987), "What Consumer Research Is…," *Journal of Consumer Research,* 14 (June), 136-40; Denzin, N. K. (2001), "The Seventh Moment: Qualitative Inquiry and the Practices of a More Radical Consumer Research," *Journal of Consumer Research*, 28 (September), 324-30; Easton, G. (2002), "Marketing: A Critical Realist Approach," *Journal of Business Research*, 55, 103-9; Marsden, D. (2001), "Rethinking Marketing and Natural Science," in *Rethinking European Marketing*, Thirteenth EMAC Proceedings, ed. Einar Breivik, Andreas Falkenberg, and Kjeil Gronhaug, Bergen, Norway, 75; Niiniluoto, I. (1999), *Critical Scientific Realism,* Oxford: Oxford University Press; Thompson, C. J., Locander, W. B. and Pollio, H. R. (1989), "Putting Consumer Experience Back into Consumer Research: The Philosophy and Method of Existential-Phenomenology," *Journal of Consumer Research*, 16 (September), 133-146.

10 Hirshman, E. C. and Holbrook, M. B. (1992), *Postmodern Consumer Research,* Newbury Park, CA: Sage.

11 Bagozzi, R. P. (1984), "A Prospectus for Theory Construction in Marketing," *Journal of Marketing,* 48 (Winter), 11-29.

12 Hunt, S. D. (1990), "Truth in Marketing Theory and Research," *Journal of Marketing,* 54 (July), 1-15.

13 Alspector-Kelly, M. (2001), "Should the Empiricist Be a Constructive Empiricist?" *Philosophy of Science,* 68 (4), 413-431.

14 Bechtel, W. (1988), *Philosophy of Mind: An Overview for Cognitive Science,* Hillsdale, NJ: Lawrence Erlbaum Associates; Chalmers, A. F. (1982), *What Is This Thing Called Science?* St. Lucia, Qld: University of Queensland Press; Popper, K. R. (1962), *Conjectures and Refutations*, New York: Harper. Popper, K. R. (1972), *Objective Knowledge.* Oxford, UK: Clarendon.

15 Platt, J. R. (1964), "Strong Inference," *Science,* 146 (October), 347-53.

16 Muncy, J. A. and Fisk, Raymond P. (1987), "Cognitive Relativism and the Practice of Marketing Science," *Journal of Marketing*, 47 (Fall), 20-33.

17 Blumer, H. (1969), *Symbolic Interactionism: Perspective and Method,* Berkeley, CA: University of California Press.

18 Stryker, S. (1990), "Symbolic Interactionism: Theories and Variations," in *Social Psychology: Sociological Perspectives*. Eds. Morris Rosenberg and Ralph Turner. New Brunswick: Transaction Publishers, 1-29.

19 Kierkegaard, Soren A. (1838), *From the Papers of One Still Living,* Copenhagen: Gad.

20 Husserl, E. (1960), *Cartesian Meditations: An Introduction to Phenomenology,* Atlantic Highlands, NJ: Humanities Press.

21 Heidegger, M. (1927/1962), *Being and Time,* New York: Harper & Row.

22 Van Maanen, M. (1990), *Researching Lived Experience: Human Science for an Action Sensitive Pedagogy*. New York: State University of New York Press.

23 Patton, M. Q. (1990), *Qualitative Evaluation and Research Methods*, 2nd. ed. Newbury Park, CA: Sage.

24 Guba, E. G. (1990), *The Paradigm Dialogue,* Newbury Park, CA: Sage; Guba, E. G. and Lincoln, Y. (1989), *Fourth Generation Evaluation*, Newbury Park, CA: Sage.

25 Blumer, H. (1969), *Symbolic Interactionism: Perspective and Method,* Berkeley, CA: University of California Press; Floch, Jean-Marie (1988), "The Contribution of Structural Semiotics to the Design of a Hypermarket," *International Journal of Research in Marketing,* 4 (1988), 233-252.

26 Mick, D. G. (1986), "Consumer Research and Semiotics: Exploring the Morphology of Signs, Symbols and Significance," *Journal of Consumer Research,* 13 (September), 196-223.

27 Haley, J. E. (1992), *Aids Communication in a Rural Community: An American Cultural Studies Perspective*, Dissertation. University of Georgia.

28 Guba, E. G. (1990), *The Paradigm Dialogue,* Newbury Park, CA: Sage; Niiniluoto, Ilkka (1999), *Critical Scientific Realism,* Oxford: Oxford University Press.

29 Greene, J. C. (1990), "Knowledge Accumulation: Three Views on the Nature and Role of Knowledge in Social Science," in *The Perspective Dialogue*, E. G. Guba, ed., Newbury Park, CA: Sage.

30 Bristor, J. M. and Fischer, E. (1993), "Feminist Thought: Implications for Consumer Research," *Journal of Consumer Research,* 19 (March), 518-36.

31 Stern, B. B. (1990), "Literary Criticism and the History of Marketing Thought: A New Perspective on 'Reading' Marketing Theory," *Journal of the Academy of Marketing Science*, 18 (Fall), 329-36.

32 Murray, Jeffrey B. and Ozanne, Julie L. (1991), "The Critical Imagination: Emancipatory Interests in Consumer Research," *Journal of Consumer Research,* 18 (September), 129-144.

33 Hirshman, E. C. and Holbrook, M. B. (1992), *Postmodern Consumer Research,* Newbury Park, CA: Sage.

10

Exemplars of Shopper Marketing Relevant Academic Research[1]

In addition to the gaps between academic researchers themselves, the more critical gap lies between academics and practitioners. Part II of this book is designed to help close that gap. Shopper marketing research specifically is currently underrepresented in the marketing literature[2] and the supply chain management literature. This means that few scholars are directly contributing to the resolution of the many shopper marketing challenges. That said, many areas within the academic marketing and supply chain management research landscapes can and do apply to shopper marketing. The next two chapters offer some examples of where that is the case.

Market Opportunity Analysis

Companies that are market oriented, meaning that they have a culture and set of capabilities that place emphasis on collecting customer and competitor intelligence, sharing that knowledge throughout the organization, and then acting on it are the kinds of organizations scanning their market environments for opportunities.[3] Research since 1990 on market orientation has borne out that these firms usually enjoy superior financial and market performance.

These firms are likely to follow any of a number of strategic models, such as the competitive strategy frameworks offered by Michael Porter (at Harvard) or George Day (at Wharton) over the years, or customer value strategies long proposed by Bob Woodruff and his colleagues (University of Tennessee).[4] Most of these frameworks at a general level suggest that managers:

- Study the macro environment such as the economic condition, social/cultural data, regulatory data/changes, and geographic/environmental opportunities and limitations
- Study supplier-related capabilities, opportunities, and threats

- Study immediate customer strategies, capabilities, and opportunities such as those of a retail customer to a brand manufacturer
- Study end-users for what they value, behaviors, attitudes, and so forth, which in this context would mean shoppers
- Study competitors' strategies and capabilities

Only by examining opportunities in light of this information can an estimate of the attractiveness of various opportunities or a demand forecast be made. There are numerous outstanding textbook sources for strategic planning,[5] strategic brand management,[6] consumer behavior,[7] and retailing[8] that may be helpful to you. Within strategic marketing texts you find topics such as strategy formulation; market opportunity analysis; understanding markets, competitors, and customers; tactical considerations; quality management; supply chain execution; and financial reporting. Within strategic brand management texts you find frameworks for establishing brand identities and positions, brand architecture, designing programs, measuring and interpreting brand performance, and growing, expanding, and even eliminating brands in sustainable ways. Within a standard consumer behavior text you learn about psychology such as motivation, ability, attention, knowledge, attitudes, and memory. You are exposed to consumer's decision-making processes, culture, individual and social influences, symbolic consumer behavior, adoption of innovations, and even public policy as it relates to consumer welfare. Finally, retailing texts cover retail marketing strategy, store location, financial strategy, customer relationship management, merchandising, category management, human resources, and store management. Much of this information across all of these topics can be used to help managers identify market opportunities. This book does not attempt to replicate the standard information provided in those sources, even though those texts do incorporate findings from some of the latest relevant academic research findings at the time. What we do here is identify some important core concepts as well as categories of research within marketing relevant to shopper marketing offering some interesting research findings within each to help you think through your particular shopper marketing management challenges.

Core Concepts

The core concepts section here merely presents some commonly known aspects of marketing relevant to shopper marketing. They are the kinds of concepts that would appear in almost any textbook on the topic.

Strategic Brand Management

Brand management is well understood in the academic field of marketing and in practice. A brand, consisting of a name, term, symbol, design, or combination of those that tend to be associated formally with a particular product or service offered by an organization, can and is managed by teams who try to create, enhance, refine, and maintain a specific image in the marketplace. A *brand* differs from a *product*. Products can be any physical good, service, retailer, person, place, and so on. Products provide core benefits from their core attributes and can be augmented by additional attributes. Brands on the other hand go further. They create perceptions of and feelings toward specific products in the marketplace. A brand image helps shoppers, consumers, and business customers have confidence in what they get, which reduces decision risk. If we know one thing about the mind from psychology and neurology it's that the human mind prefers to be efficient; it would prefer to not work too hard if given a choice unless that "work" involves enjoyment in activities like puzzle solving or story completion. When brands are managed well, they accumulate brand equity, which means because customers (shoppers, consumers, or business customers depending on the context) place value on them, the brand has monetary value to its owner. For example, some of the most valuable brands include Apple ($98 billion), Google ($93 billion), Coca-Cola ($79 billion), IBM ($78 billion), Microsoft ($59 billion), and McDonald's ($41 billion).[9] Other top 100 brands known to be included by brand managers in shopper marketing programs include Samsung, Disney, Gillette, H&M, Pepsi, Pampers, Kellogg, Budweiser, Nescafe, L'Oreal, Sony, Danone, Colgate, Nestlé, Johnson and Johnson, Kleenex, and Starbucks.

Brand equity is built by creating perceived differences that result in different outcomes for one brand above and beyond others. This is achieved by identifying and creating brand positioning, understanding brand values, planning and implementing brand marketing programs, measuring and interpreting the brand's performance, and managing activities that help to sustain and grow the brand.[10] This process involves creating a brand architecture that enables a brand to "occupy" a unique position in customers' minds that is worth paying for time and time again. As we discussed earlier in this book, brands are built on the concepts of need satisfaction, performance characteristics, imagery, judgments, and feelings that eventually culminate in overall connections with oneself or one's organization. In contemporary marketing and brand management thinking, brand equity is not built solely by nor controlled entirely by a brand's owner; it is built through communities of customers engaging each other and the brand.

Shopper marketing has extended a brand manager's strategic role into the retail environment. It has also extended a retailer manager's role into not only managing its own retail banner brand equity and private label equity but also playing a role in the broader market environment. It is not as much that brand management has changed entirely as it is the key decision-makers involved have changed. This means that academics researching brand management processes should now be discussing extended brand management teams and process that reflect the following kinds of changes:

- Alignment of brand positioning with retailer positioning *before campaigns are run*
- Brand positioning in consideration of shopping mindsets and behaviors
- Brand communication within the store
- Brand communication taking into consideration other brands within specific stores, both potential complementary brands and competing brands, both inside and outside of category
- Inclusion of different kinds of consumer research to include shopper research
- Coordination and strategic collaboration with additional and new types of agencies, that is, shopper marketing agencies
- Inclusion of broker agencies and supply chain management in plans for execution assurance
- Alternative measures of brand health derived from retail-level data

Which brings us to the next core concept, retailing management.

Retailing Management

There are many outstanding retailing centers on university campuses around the country at places like Kellogg School of Management at Northwestern, Texas A&M University, Kelley School of Business at Indiana University, The University of Arkansas, Wharton and Western Michigan University, to name only a few. There are numerous textbooks on all aspects of retailing and numerous retailing departments. As with strategic brand management, we merely point out here some commonly known core concepts.

First of all, retailers provide time and place utility. This means they offer brands shoppers need and want in a useful or even pleasant way in a location that is relatively convenient at times when they are desired. Despite the explosion of online retailing, many shoppers enjoy physical locations as well. Although we have previously described retailers as primarily financial institutions, recognize that the competition for shoppers' time and loyalty is fierce in virtually every retail channel and vertical, that is, grocery, mass merchant, apparel, and so on. Retailers are competing by managing as best they can:

- Their store brand image
- The service levels through processes and personnel

- Merchandise assortment (including private label if appropriate)
- Store environments (including displays, layout, and all sensory stimuli)
- Store location
- Pricing
- Customer communications

Retailers learn what they ought to do with each of these through their own research on shoppers and competitors. Historically, retailers have relied heavily on brands for some of this research, but more and more, larger retailers are conducting or contracting for their own research. This becomes more important the more a retailer's merchandise assortment includes private label brands. Retailers segment their shoppers like brand manufacturers segment their consumers, and no retailing textbook would be complete without a discussion of segmentation and targeting. But retailer research can be extensive these days, well beyond customer segmentation. Retailing is where the rubber meets the road. To be both effective and efficient in closing the deal for brands, transactions through which the retailer makes its money, retailers must manage numerous costs. An important one is labor.

Store personnel must not only be functionally able to manage a store's operations, but also be able to interact with shoppers in ways that enhance shoppers' experiences with the retailer. This affects hiring, training, and management processes. Retailer floor employees are crucial to a retailer's success. One area being researched by academics as well as practitioners is the role of technology in this environment. How can technology enhance customer service? At what points and in what ways should technology replace store personnel, and when and where should it augment or provide additional tools for store personnel? These questions have not been fully answered in the literature or in practice.

Retailers are also highly concerned with the supply chain, which includes purchasing decisions, delivery parameters, and inventory management. All of this requires careful integration of supply and demand management. Shopper marketing programs need to be integrated with numerous retailer strategies and initiatives, and timing is crucial. The challenges shopper marketing places on retail supply chain execution have not been addressed fully yet either in the academic literature.

Consumer Behavior

The last core concept we introduce here relevant to shopper marketing is consumer behavior. Like the strategic brand management and retailing, consumer behavior has a rich history in the academic world and as such is supported by hundreds of books and articles used in the education of budding marketers. At one point, marketing research grew out of economics where a market was literally a place where goods and services could be exchanged. The study of marketing focused on economic aspects of providing time and place utility. However, it quickly became apparent that in competitive markets, exchanging goods and services required persuasion, and this required an understanding of people, that is, how they make decisions, their attitudes, their emotions, their perceptions, and their behaviors. Thus, psychology, social psychology, sociology, anthropology, and ecology to name a few became important to marketers. These disciplines gave birth to the field known as consumer behavior. Consumer behavior courses have become the virtual core of a marketing degree on university campuses.

Any consumer behavior textbook covers many of the following kinds of topics:[11]

- Consumer culture and macro topics
  - Societal structures
  - Social norms and influencers
  - Diversity
  - Social class
  - Households
  - Values and lifestyles
  - Psychographic profiles
  - Cohorts and social groups
- Psychology at a more micro level
  - Motivation
  - Attention, interest, and desire
  - Perception
  - Knowledge and learning
  - Attitude formation and change
  - Memory
  - Sensory stimulation
  - Personality
  - Emotions and mood
  - Self-identity
- Consumption and shopping decision-making processes
  - Problem recognition
  - Information search
  - Judgments and evaluations
  - Variety and novelty seeking

- Security and risk management
- Post-decision processes
- Outcomes of purchase decisions
  - Adaptation
  - Cognitive dissonance (buyer's remorse, post-purchase tension)
  - Satisfaction
  - Diffusion of innovations
  - Symbolic behaviors

This is not an exhaustive list either. Within this, almost all marketing students recall frameworks such as Maslow's Hierarchy of Needs (physiological, safety, social, egoistic, and self-actualization) or values and lifestyles segments (survivors, believers, strivers, makers, thinkers, achievers, experiencers, and innovators). There are many more, and frankly some are overused. Academic literature has a wealth of knowledge in all these areas. Similarly, state of the art research methods for studying consumers and shoppers emerges from this area. One of the best academic associations focused on consumer behavior is Advances in Consumer Research. This association publishes the *Journal of Consumer Research*, the premier journal publishing academic concepts and research findings in consumer behavior. They also hold numerous conferences. An area within this field that shopper marketing professionals ought to stay abreast of is known as *consumer cultural theory* or CCT. Numerous cross-disciplinary conferences and articles within CCT have shopper marketing relevance.

The consumer behavior research relevant to shopper marketing has begun to highlight shopping behavior, attitudes, perceptions, decision-making processes, segmentation, motivations, and social behaviors *within* the consumer field. So according to marketing scholars, shopper behavior research (to include cognitions, emotions, and so on in addition to behavior) lies within the consumer behavior field. Contrastingly, in practice, it is critical to distinguish *between* consumption behavior and shopping behavior. This is largely due to marketing's, and in particular brand management's, history of focusing communications heavily on use of products and services rather than shopping for them.

So, given that our intent is solely to remind you of some core concepts about which you can find research results and practical guidance, we next share with you some exemplars of this kind of research. The following section shares specific research results from individual studies published in academic journals. Usually an idea must be supported numerous times before it is worthy of being published in a textbook. But by then, everyone knows it. By staying abreast of individual research projects, you might be able to obtain a knowledge-edge over your competitors.

Specific Examples Beyond the Core

Scholars and shopper marketing professionals are working together,[12] but more scholarly research is needed to address shopper insights, marketing planning, execution, and measurement. A fair amount of research is available on shopper behavior,[13] retail strategies,[14] and innovation in a shopper marketing context.[15] Looking more broadly, and as suggested in our discussion of the core concepts, much of the work in retailing, merchandising, brand management, cross-functional and interorganizational coordination, and supply chain management *could* apply if framed within the context of shopper marketing.

The next sections provide some examples of research findings, some of which were introduced in Part I of this book, that fit into the categories of

- Shopper behavior and the in-store environment
- Private brands and brand equity
- Product assortment and management
- Online and multichannel shopping
- Segmentation
- Reference price and promotion
- Shopper paths
- In-store advertising
- Mobile marketing
- Satisfaction and loyalty

The information provided here comes from manuscripts published in some of the top journals in marketing as well as other context-specific and relevant journals. These sources include but are not limited to

- *Journal of Marketing*
- *Journal of Marketing Research*
- *Journal of Consumer Research*
- *Marketing Science*
- *Journal of Retailing*
- *Journal of Consumer Psychology*
- *Journal of Marketing Management*
- *Advances in Consumer Research*
- *Journal of Advertising Research*
- *Journal of Business Research*
- *Service Industries Journal*

- *Brand Management*
- *International Journal of Research in Marketing*

If you are so inclined, feel free to access these journals and ones like them through your nearby university and in many cases via the Internet for abstracts at least.

Shopper Behavior and the In-Store Environment

In-store shopping behavior may be motivated by mood,[16] the joy of a bargain,[17] the pleasure of the in-store experience,[18] or impulse.[19] An initial purchase can provide a psychological impulse for shopping momentum that prompts purchases of unrelated items.[20] Impulse shopping, the sudden and powerful urge to buy immediately, has gained a lot of attention in practice as well. Some drivers of impulse buying seem to be promotions, momentum, the presence of others, and power distance beliefs of the shopper.[21] Practitioners have even begun to draw on neurology and behavioral economics to build on these scholastic bases.

Music, lighting, and the overall excitement projected in a store impact the amount of time shoppers spend in a store, as well as their emotional connection to a store.[22] Shoppers also take cues from a store's social environment, the overall ambiance of the store,[23] and from the moods and credibility of retailer salespeople.[24] Positive social conditions and ambiences have a tendency to reduce price sensitivity and increase pleasure of the shopping experiences. By understanding in-store environmental factors and cues that affect shopper spending, both retailers and manufacturers can develop more effective programs.

One study found that consumers have a unique way of anchoring their estimates of how much product they have in inventory in their homes.[25] They tend to anchor their estimates based on an average and not actual amount of product remaining in their cupboards. This study found that consumers tend to overestimate low levels and underestimate high levels. It is these estimates that seem to drive purchase behavior not actual inventory levels. So what might this mean? It means that tracking actual inventory levels of consumers to determine points at which they may turn into shoppers for products would not be accurate. It is the perception that matters. This kind of finding is consistent with what we know about human psychology concerning shortcuts we use as opposed to actual calculations. Anything we can do to make that task of thinking faster and easier, we will devise for ourselves. So using average estimates is not necessarily surprising, but it is contrary to popular beliefs about how consumers create their shopping lists and shop.

In addition to inventory levels at one's home, there is an effect of inventory levels on the shelf on shopping behavior as well. We know that sold-out products or out of stocks have various effects. One example of this kind of research found that the presence of information about sold-out products can prompt shoppers to make a purchase of an alternative product.[26] In other words, instead of deferring until later, they purchase now, but a different brand. Researchers hypothesize that this may be because the sold-out product creates a sense of urgency (an immediacy effect) or enhances the perceived attractiveness of similar products (informational cascades effect). This notion of scarcity to create a sense of urgency has been explored through a number of studies. The challenge for brands and retailers is in determining how to communicate that scarcity and stimulate shopper urgency.

Also product awareness related, how and when shoppers are exposed to various brands affects their choices.[27] Specifically, when shoppers have higher levels of incidental exposure to consumers with specific brands they are more positively inclined to choose those brands. However, more exposure is not always better. The relationship curve is an inverted U shape, with choice declining as exposure frequency increases beyond a certain level. Also, if the consumers a shopper was exposed to were "out-group" members, so not considered to be like them or part of their cohort, the effect was constant. Whereas "in-group" members enhance the exposure effects. These results justify efforts by marketers to increase exposure of their brands in social settings that have tight cohorts.

This area of exposure to certain kinds of environmental stimuli is a common playground for consumer behaviorists. It has been found that similar to social priming, brands can act as primers, meaning that brand exposure can elicit automatic responses in consumers and shoppers.[28] This is where we find that people primed with Apple logos behave more creatively than those primed with the IBM logo. It has also been found that whether the brand is goal-relevant influences various effects of the priming. Building on similar research, brand manufacturers and retailers are spending time exploring what to prime for shoppers and how to do so.

Also related to shopper decision making, some contemporary research explores the role of ethics or social responsibility. For example, a study conducted in the UK to identify the range of issues shoppers consider in this area found that these issues are indeed important and that they vary by shopping occasion.[29] Specifically, although important, some shoppers will back off their desires if the product imperative is high, and typical motivators such as product quality, customer service, and promotions are still critical. This means that retailer merchandising decisions and even branding decisions must always take into account these conventional characteristics when placing emphasis on ethical and social responsibility initiatives.

Researchers study context as well as issues (for example, social responsibility). For example, how shoppers behave in rural communities as compared to urban ones may be important for retailers moving from one to the other or merely entering a rural community. One study found that rural shoppers are more satisfied and loyal to retailers who feel like a part of the local community in large part because shoppers in small communities are often related by bloodline, extended family, or other community tie.[30] So initiatives that support the local community such as athletic team sponsorships might be more effective with shoppers in these communities than special promotions or radical merchandising.

These same authors also found that initial purchases shoppers make create momentum that affects subsequent purchases within a retail environment. This work seems to support a theory of implementation and deliberation mindsets. So once shoppers begin to shop, this helps them implement subsequent shopping. That said, this flow can be interrupted. So the challenge might be to estimate the kind of momentum shoppers are likely to have as they enter particular stores and begin to shop and either enhance it if one's product fits within that flow or interrupt and divert it if not.

Another important shopping context involves shopping with others versus alone. Some evidence suggests that shopping with peers increases the urge to purchase while the presence of family members decreases it.[31] If impulsiveness is socially acceptable within the group, shoppers are more likely to do so. Family members may engender feelings of responsibility and affect shopping behavior. This also depends, however, on the cohesiveness of the group and how susceptible the shopper is to social influence and desires to comply with social norms. Retailers may be able to influence how shoppers shop, but even if they cannot, this kind of research might explain differences in shopping behavior they experience with their shoppers.

If we move from context aspects of shopping behavior, we find researchers exploring psychological states specifically. For example, consumers' moods and emotions have long been rich areas of research for consumer behaviorists. Along these lines, we know that happy shoppers spend more money and tell more people about their positive experiences. Building on this foundation, research has investigated shoppers' mood regulation, specifically different kinds of shoppers and how well they tap into their own moods.[32] Some actively tap into positive memories to repair negative moods. In this sense, retailers can prime positive past experiences. Retailers who desire to create hedonic and experiential environments and experiences are advised to invite exploration through interesting layouts and products and abstract symbolism. Whereas a utilitarian value focus would emphasize more direct and concrete layouts and communication. This research also found that people who pay attention to their moods are more likely to desire and pursue hedonic shopping, whereas utilitarian shopping is likely to be pursued by those who do not monitor their moods or are not intimately familiar with their moods.

And not all research investigates how shoppers actually shop. Some explores how shoppers can disrupt shopping environments. For example, some research has found that psychological traits like obstructionism may impede shoppers from behaving in accordance with societal norms and as such be disruptive and dysfunctional in the retail environment. This work also finds though that customer care and the retail environment can significantly reduce dysfunctional behavior.

This area of shopper behavior and the in-store environment is easily the richest and most extensive area within which retail-focused marketing academics conduct their research. The phenomena and research questions seem endless. So attempting to capture all the latest research here is impossible. We offer some findings here to orient your thinking to the kinds of work being done daily across the country and globe at academic institutions. You can access this research in a variety of ways such as direct interaction with faculty, access to university databases, or access through search engines such as Google Scholar. However, "free" access through the Internet may require you to purchase copies of written articles or subscribe to the journal association. You can also obtain research summaries from organizations like the Marketing Science Institute in Boston. The point is the information is there if you have the desire to hunt it down. It doesn't usually find you until an author like Malcom Gladwell summarizes it in a popular press book—or we do here.

Before we move on to private label brands and brand equity as well as other topics, let's take a look at a few other shopper behavior studies. Let's talk about vice! Some researchers have been spending time exploring how shoppers shop for what they call "virtue" and "vice" products. As you can imagine, virtue products are the ones the shopper feels she *ought* to buy; they are utilitarian, necessary in some way. Vice products on the other hand are self-satisfying products, hedonic, to please oneself. One looked into self-control to show that shoppers voluntarily ration their purchase quantities of products likely to be consumed on impulse. Specifically, vice-seeking shoppers do not respond to price reduction promotions by increasing purchases like virtue-seeking shoppers do.[33] The idea of playing games with oneself to overcome self-perceived weaknesses is a common area of exploration in psychology and as a result consumer behaviorists.

Much of the work on shopping behavior related to shopper marketing has to do with the store environment obviously. Along those lines, researchers investigate why shoppers have favorite retail stores, their motivations, loyalty, and behavioral patterns all as they relate to service quality. One study supported empirically that retailers who stage experiences are the most successful.[34] This study also was able to classify shopper motivations as experiential stimulation, bargain hunting, image maintenance, and pampering, findings consistent with what brand manufacturers and market research organizations have found.

Regarding environmental factors, research explores the effects of in-store lighting, with one study finding two decades ago that although brighter lighting influenced shoppers to examine and handle more merchandise, sales were not affected.[35] In fact, quite a bit of the in-store environment research was at its peak in the mid 1990s. One study looking into many elements of the environment showed that ambient and social elements provide cues that shoppers use for quality inferences and that the environment, service quality, and merchandise quality lead shoppers to develop their store images.[36] There is so much research in the retail environmental influence area hitting on the effects of music, merchandising, lighting, texture, space, crowds, service quality, product assortment, layout, and so forth that summaries of this research have emerged over time.[37] So maybe the research summary articles are a good place to begin in areas that have received a lot of attention. Let's turn our attention to a few other topics.

Private Brands and Brand Equity

The growth of private label brands, beginning with grocery channels, has captured the attention of academic researchers. And this is not only a US phenomenon; it has exploded in places as different as Thailand as well. However, they had a disjointed start evidently in eastern countries. One study found that compared to US shoppers, Thai shoppers enjoy shopping more, are less time pressured, shop with others more, and seem to use price more as an indicator of brand quality and that these factors have an effect on brand images.[38] This kind of work stimulates questions about other culturally based shopper segments and their attitudes or behaviors regarding brand types.

Another project found private label brand promotions and national brand promotions attract shoppers with distinctly different psychological profiles, implying that in some cases, these brand types are not competing for the same shoppers.[39] However, two of the most important sources of variation in private label brand share across markets, retailers, and categories are intercategory differences and perceptions of risk associated with the purchase.[40] The lower the perceived risk of making a mistake, the more private label purchase increases.

Brand equity has been measured or assessed for quite some time now. Brand equity can reflect a financial value of a brand to its manufacturer based on its value to customers. It can appear as part of goodwill in financial statements or be evaluated by an outside organization such as Interbrand, which offers rankings and evaluations of the most valuable and respected brands. Brand managers want to know how valuable their brands are above and beyond a functionally equivalent and competing product/brand. Some academic researchers address this issue as well. The revenue premium a national brand obtains compared to competing private label brands can be calculated in a straightforward and objective manner according to some researchers relying mostly on publically available data.[41] Another study in this area used store level data to make brand equity estimates and specifically a random coefficients logit demand model to track estimates over time.[42] By also tracking new product innovations, advertising, and sales promotions, they found that the estimates are effective at capturing the high equity of strongly positioned brands and brands that command price premiums in niche markets. Related to brand equity itself, some research explores how brands and categories compare in terms of the extent to which retailer spending is passed through to consumers as opposed to applied to promotion and other costs. One study found that brands with higher market shares and brands that contribute more to retailer profits in the category receive higher pass-through.[43] Some researchers explore brand equity directly from consumers' perceptions. For example, the importance of brands to consumers' decision making within categories, that is, brand relevance in category (BRIC), was conceptually developed and tested in a sample of nearly 6,000 consumers in 20 product categories across 5 countries.[44]

Finally, research on the long-term effects of marketing strategies and marketing mix variables on brand sales reveals several interesting pieces of information.[45] Specifically, the long-term effects of discounting are one-third the magnitude of the short-term effects; other aspects of the marketing mix have reversed effects; all aspects of the marketing mix such as advertising, price, promotion, product, and place have positive short-term effects on sales, mostly distribution and product line length; base sales are positively affected by advertising but negatively by discounting over the long term; and the average 90% decay of the mix effect on base sales is about six weeks. Although a brand manager wanting to replicate these specific processes should review the original work cited here or their authors, the point is that academics do develop processes and measures for assessing brand equity in a variety of ways.

Product Assortment

Large product assortments may benefit shoppers by providing choices, but they also challenge shoppers to use extensive cognitive processes in making their purchase decisions.[46] These "costs" imposed on shoppers can diminish a category's attractiveness. That said, under high-risk conditions, larger assortments tend to be favored. These effects also seem to be moderated by a shopper's desire for stimulation.

When comparing two approaches to shelf management within a store, specifically customizing shelf sets based on store-specific movement patterns and product reorganization to facilitate cross-category merchandising or ease of shopping, the sales gains for the latter exceed those of the former.[47] So twenty years ago we had some indicator that what we now refer to as solution centers within the shopper marketing context are a good idea.

One study on category management processes discovered that it does not seem to find the optimal solution to management of the category and provides less variety and higher prices than optimal.[48] That said, the authors recommend that category management be used and evaluated based on basket profits from point-of-sale data as opposed to the typical accounting profit method.

Online and Multichannel Shopping

Shoppers' mental orientations such as shopping enjoyment, brand consciousness, price consciousness, shopping confidence, convenience/time consciousness, in-home shopping tendency, and brand loyalty, seem to be related to the searches for information when shopping online.[49] Specifically, when shopping for apparel items online, the orientation of college shoppers, an exploding demographic for online shopping, shoppers with different orientations shop differently. Additionally, women tend to shop more hedonically and be more brand savvy than men in this study. Both of these findings support what industry suggests regarding the importance of identifying shoppers' mental orientations, modes, and needs states as well as noting the effects of gender.

Research conducted in the Netherlands reported that online buying was affected by sociodemographics and spatial characteristics of people, their Internet experiences, and their attitudes toward in-store shopping.[50] This study compared Dutch shoppers with US shoppers, delved into the Dutch shoppers, and suggested that online shopping is not necessarily a substitution for in-store shopping but one of complementarity. Consistent with this finding of past Internet experiences affecting online buying, a different study found that satisfaction with previous purchases, website security and privacy policies, and service quality were determinates of trust in a website.[51] This study also compared four different profiles of online shoppers and the effects of various website attributes on their behaviors and attitudes.

Numerous studies compare references for shopping online versus in-store and the drivers of those differences. For example, for some shoppers, the service quality of salespeople at a store does not affect their preference for shopping there versus online.[52] When comparing 128 different aspects of the shopping experience for both physical and virtual stores, including the role technology plays in shopper satisfaction, a study found that shoppers were generally satisfied with the level of convenience, quality, selection, and value provided by retailers but were less satisfied with levels of service provided, availability of product information, and the speed of the shopping process.[53] This study reported that technology can be used to enhance the shopping experience, but it must be tailored to shopper segments and product categories. Research on the relationship between online and in-store shopping finds that searching online increases the frequency of shopping trips, which then positively influences buying online.[54] Additionally, time pressure has an effect on online buying, and online searching has a negative effect on in-store shopping duration. Finally as an example, we also know a little bit about the relationship between compulsive shopping and how online compares to in-store preferences. Compulsive shoppers tend to prefer to shop online in some cases.[55] Numerous studies compare online with in-store shopping, but we also have research on multimedia, multi-channel channel shopping and are finding various shopper segments based on preferences for different media and shopping channels. That said, one study in the grocery context in Germany found that most shoppers prefer one channel type within a buying process depending on their shopping motives and situation.[56]

Segmentation

Customer segmentation has to be one of the longest running areas for research within the marketing discipline. Not one marketing text fails to address the key concepts of segmentation and positioning within segments. As we move into the field of shopper marketing, segmentation focuses more on need states, motives, and use occasions as segment descriptors. But sometimes the traditional approaches still reveal interesting and useful findings. For example, a study conducted in Scotland revealed that rural and urban shopper segments have different demographic composition, which tends to affect their shopping attitudes and behaviors.[57] Rural shoppers tend to place more emphasis on quietness, scenery, sense of community, privacy, and a slower pace. They tend to dislike higher prices, lack of choice, poor leisure facilities, and decentralization. Urban shoppers place higher emphasis on social activities and dislike traffic, pollution, and noise levels. It could be argued that rural shoppers dislike these as well, and as such, live in rural areas. The message here is that some research suggests that retailers should adapt their shopping environments uniquely to rural environments and urban ones.

Not a great deal of segmentation work within academia currently addresses shopping segmentation as compared to consumer segmentation; however, some consumer segmentation is still relevant. For instance, situational segmentation such as the multiproduct snack segments of solitary snacking, socializing ensemble, high gravity socialization, and morning home snack may have high correlations with specific shopping behaviors and as such be useful in designing shopper marketing programs.[58] They certainly tell us something about preferred product types and categories.

One study that directly focused on shopper segmentation revealed six different grocery shopping segments connected to functional, experiential, and social motivators.[59] Shopping motivations in this study seem consistent with motivations identified more than a dozen years earlier. It appears that motivations for shopping at a high level may be relatively stable while demand within them keeps rising. The eleven motivators identified in this study included six functional (convenience, product and personnel quality, price, reliability, assortment, and promotions), three experiential (discovering new products, store atmosphere, demonstrations, animations, and tasting experiences), and two social (meeting people, social interaction with store personnel). The shopper segments explored were convenience shoppers, low-price shoppers, social shoppers, intense social shoppers, experiential shoppers, and recreational shoppers. Again, these are consistent with segments industry practitioners use.

Costs—Reference Price, Search Costs, and Promotion

Reference price and promotion research focuses largely on the impact of mental budgets, price sensitivity, and promotions on in-store purchase decisions. Much of the shopper marketing literature addresses in-store promotions that impact shoppers' mental budgets, concluding that shoppers have flexibility to make spontaneous decisions in response to in-store marketing campaigns.[60] Research suggests that consumers come to a store armed with reference prices from advertisements, mobile devices, or Internet sites,[61] and that price sensitivity is heightened in-store more so than online. Thus, organizations have the opportunity to create in-store promotions tied to price and specific events.[62]

Households of shoppers who shop on both online and in-store environments for the same product categories seem to be less price sensitive in the online environment than they are in the store. This is true across 12 vastly different product categories, be they large or small, sensory or utilitarian, packaged or nonpackaged goods.

Back when EDLP (Every Day Low Pricing) was the rage in the mid 1990s, research found that a 10% EDLP category price decrease led to a 3% volume increase, while a 10% Hi-Lo price increase led to a 3% sales decrease.[63] An EDLP policy reduced profits by 18% while a Hi-Lo policy increased profits by 15%. And every price reduction of 10% requires a sales increase of 39% to maintain existing profit levels. Findings like these are critical to retailers' pricing strategies. It is customary for researchers to not only report results but also provide any appropriate normative advice (recommendations) while remaining within the limitations of the research study. For example, a different study around the same time as the EDLP one showed that imprecisely worded discounts in brand promotions offered in the form of a low-probability lottery can lead to higher purchase intentions and profits than equally costly conventional promotions offering precise discounts on an entire stock.[64]

Research has shown that when shoppers spend money on searching for the right products, reductions in those search costs have a significant effect on search decisions while when consumers spend time (as opposed to money) on search, a decrease in time does not have an effect on search decisions.[65] This implies that when we think about shopping behavior both the monetary and time costs shoppers invest while searching for information and products must be considered, but the effects will differ.

It has been found that the long-term retailer pass-through of promotions is 65% and that large categories yield strong retailer response, while tight categories yield strong competitor responses to pass-through promotions.[66] Smaller brands face disadvantages in the form of obtaining lower retailer pass-through, lower retailer support, and lower benefits from competitors' brand promotions, while their promotions generate higher benefits to competitors. This form of research helps brands of various power levels (for example, market share) determine the kinds of price promotions they should employ. Building on the length of the effect of promotions theme, a study of more than 100 brands across seven categories for seven years demonstrates that some promotions can have a long-term effect, especially for small brands. Brands with higher equity and more product introductions seem to gain the most in terms of permanent and cumulative sales improvement from marketing promotions.[67] Similarly, retailers can improve their pricing decisions by understanding the effects of demand conditions and past pricing on current pricing decisions.[68]

Shopper Paths

Shopper marketing research would not be shopper research if someone did not explore shopping paths. Most marketers are well aware of Paco Underhill's[69] work on shopping and shopping environments or the work by Herb Sorensen.[70] But individual studies continue to be executed in this well-discussed research area. Store environments can create unique shopper experiences and as such help retailers differentiate from the competition.[71] Regarding shopping paths, for example, research finds major differences in shopping traffic patterns within a store depending on the time of the day[72] and that shoppers rarely follow any "up and down the aisle" patterns.[73] The perimeter seems to be the anchor area or "home base" with brief excursions being made into aisles as needed. And now some of this shopping path research is being applied to virtual stores as well.[74]

In-Store Advertising

Shopper marketing views the store as full of media and a place where in-store advertising could take place. Researchers asked whether in-store marketing works, and found that the number of facings has a consistent and positive effect on shoppers' attention levels and evaluation of brands, which influences choice.[75] This effect is strongest for regular users of a brand, low market share brands, and for young and highly educated shoppers who value both brands and low price. That said, shelf position effects were mixed in this study. Oddly, positioning brands on the top shelf and near the center of the shelf seemed to improve both attention and evaluation of the brand, but positioning them in the middle shelves helps attention but not evaluation. This seems contrary to common notions of shelf positioning, which often state that middle or slightly lower than eye-level is an optimal location. We point this out because not all research arrives at the same conclusions or supports the same recommendations. Marketers must combine results from multiple studies to develop their own conclusions and interpretations.

In the shopper marketing context, package design can act as a form of advertising. Specifically, package design can evoke brand values that in turn affect purchase intentions, but the effects are impacted by culture.[76]

However, the messaging objectives, content, and delivery ought to be different from out-of-store advertising. Academic research is exploring in-store advertising as well. And this advertising is not limited to displays or devices within merchandising the retailer constructs; it can be location-driven content that appears on shoppers' mobile devices. This form of mobile marketing is referred to as micromobility marketing and seems to be effective when interesting and relevant information is provided whether it is pull or push driven.[77]

As one final comment on in-store advertising, consider this. There are an estimated one quadrillion (a 1 with 15 zeros) media exposures annually in stores around the world.[78] Herb Sorensen is considered one of the leading experts in understanding the store environment. He explained that in a typical 20 minute shopping trip, a shopper reads only 8% to 10% of the messaging. Communication with those products purchased is about color, shape, and iconic images. Adding to this, impulse shopping accounts for 40% of all money spent, 80% of visual impressions are packaging related, and most exposures do not lead to sales.

Mobile Marketing

Mobile marketing research focuses on the benefits of marketing through mobile Internet devices within the store environment.[79] Hosbond and Skov[80] found that mobile Internet devices used in-store can provide relevant and interesting content to shoppers, thus enhancing the success of marketing campaigns.

Shopper marketing in this decade clearly involves mobile Internet devices such as smartphones with every marketer trying to figure out effective ways to include them in their campaigns. Early research in this area identified numerous motivators for even relying on mobile devices as a shopping vehicle and specifically to make purchases through a mobile device. One study in Taiwan, for example, identified 24 factors that motivate shoppers to shop online using a mobile device with the top five being to avoid traffic and parking problems, avoid self-shipping hassles, time convenience, privacy, and disturbance freedom.[81] This research stream looked into mobile coupons,[82] mobile marketing campaigns,[83] location-based advertising on mobile devices,[84] and the usage of comparison sites on mobile devices.[85] Mobile devices are extensions of shoppers and extend shoppers' worlds wherever they are. The paradigm has changed from one of consumers entering a retailer's environment to one of the retailer entering the consumer's.[86]

Satisfaction and Loyalty

We end this section with a discussion of satisfaction and loyalty research.[87] Customer satisfaction research began in the mid-1960s. But more recently, research relevant to shopper marketing focused specifically on shopper satisfaction with retailers and its drivers. And some interesting findings are emerging despite the general topic being well explored. For example, when shoppers are asked to state their expectations prior to shopping, they tend to focus on the negative aspects of the shopping experience and perceive the experience more negatively than when they are not asked about their expectations beforehand and are simply asked to rate the experience afterwards.[88] This is interesting, but what drives retailer satisfaction and does it relate to store loyalty? It turns out that, as one might expect, shoppers who have positive experiences with and perceptions of personal interactions, the value of merchandise, the store environment, merchandise variety, and complaint handling are more satisfied, and this contributes to both attitudinal and behavioral (actual sales) loyalty.[89] This finding is consistent with other research, which finds that shopping enjoyment (measured with numerous items) has a positive effect on retailer repatronage.[90] Research like this, which tries to tease out drivers of retailer and shopping experience satisfaction, continues. There are studies on the impact of congruency between retailer image and self-image,[91] gender and age cohort such as Gen Y.[92] In some cases it may be efficiency, in others economic value, while others hedonic pleasure. Within this literature are a growing number of studies on the design and impact of retailer loyalty programs.[93]

Endnotes

1 Special acknowledgment is offered for content in this section of the book to Drs. Hannah Stolze (Florida State University) and Dianne Mollenkopf (University of Tennessee).

2 Shankar, V., Inman, J. J., Mantrala, M., Kelley, E., and Rizley, R. (2011), "Innovations in Shopper Marketing: Current Insights and Future Research Issues," *Journal of Retailing*, 87S, S29-S42.

3 Narver, J. C. and Slater, S. F. (1990), "The Effect of a Market Orientation on Business Profitability," *The Journal of Marketing*, 54, 20-35; Jaworski, B. and Kohli, A. (1993), "Market Orientation: Antecedents and Consequences," *Journal of Marketing*, 52, 53-70.

4 Woodruff, R. and S. Gardial (1996), *Know Your Customer: New Approaches to Understanding Customer Value and Satisfaction*, Cambridge, MA: Blackwell Business.

5 Cadotte, E. R. and H. J. Bruce (2003), *The Management of Strategy in the Marketplace*, Mason, OH: Thomson/South-Western.

6 Keller, K. L. (2008), *Strategic Brand Management*, 3rd ed., Upper Saddle River, NJ: Pearson/Prentice-Hall.

7 Hoyer, W. D. and D. J. MacInnis (2007), *Consumer Behavior*, 4th ed., Boston, MA: Houghton Mifflin Co.

8 Levy, M. L. and B. A. Weitz (2012), *Retailing Management*, New York, NY: McGraw-Hill/Irwin.

9 Interbrands website: http://www.interbrand.com/en/best-global-brands/2013/Best-Global-Brands-2013-Brand-View.aspx; January 20, 2014.

10 Keller, K. L. (2008), *Strategic Brand Management*, 3rd ed., Upper Saddle River, NJ: Pearson/Prentice-Hall.

11 Hoyer, W. D. and D. J. MacInnis (2007), *Consumer Behavior*, 4th ed., Boston, MA: Houghton Mifflin Co.

12 Chandon, P. J., Hutchinson, W., Bradlow, E. T., and Young, S. H. (2009), "Does In-Store Marketing Work? Effects of the Number and Position of Shelf Facings on Brand Attention and Evaluation at the Point of Purchase," *Journal of Marketing*, 73, 1-17; Flint, D. J. (2012), "Shopper Marketing's True Potential," In M. Stahlberg & V. Maila (Eds). *Shopper Marketing: How to Increase Purchase Decisions at the Point of Sale*, 2nd edition, London: Kogan Page, 175-180; Flint, D. J., Lusch, R., and Vargo, S. (2013), "The Supply Chain Management of Shopper Marketing as Viewed Through a Service Ecosystem Lens," *International Journal of Physical Distribution and Logistics Management*, online, print forthcoming; Inman, J. J., Winer, R. S., and Ferraro, R. (2009), "The Interplay Among

Category Characteristics, Customer Characteristics, and Customer Activities on In-Store Decision Making," *Journal of Marketing*, 73, 19-29; Underhill, Paco (2000), *Why We Buy: The Science of Shopping*. New York: Simon & Schuster.

13 Dhar, R., Huber, J., and Khan, U. (2007), "The Shopping Momentum Effect," *Journal of Marketing Research*, XLIV, 370-378; Inman, J. J., Winer, R. S., and Ferraro, R. (2009), "The Interplay Among Category Characteristics, Customer Characteristics, and Customer Activities on In-Store Decision Making," *Journal of Marketing*, 73, 19-29; Underhill, Paco (2000), *Why We Buy: The Science of Shopping*. New York: Simon & Schuster.

14 Jerath, K. and Zhang, Z. J. (2010), "Store within a Store," *Journal of Marketing Research*, XLVII, 748-763; Shankar, V. and Bolton, R. N. (2004), "An Empirical Analysis of Determinants of Retailer Pricing Strategy," *Marketing Science*, 23, 28-49.

15 Shankar, V., Inman, J. J., Mantrala, M., Kelley, E., and Rizley, R. (2011), "Innovations in Shopper Marketing: Current Insights and Future Research Issues," *Journal of Retailing*, 87S, S29-S42.

16 Reynolds, K. L. and Harris, L. C. (2009), "Dysfunctional Customer Behavior Severity: An Empirical Examination," *Journal of Retailing*, 85, 321-335; Swinyard, W. R. (2003), "The Effects of Salesperson Mood, Shopper Behavior, and Store Type on Consumer Services," *Journal of Retailing and Consumer Services*, 10, 323-333.

17 Arnold, M. J. and Reynolds, K. E. (2009), "Affect and Retail Shopping Behavior," *Journal of Retailing*, 85, 308-320.

18 Cox, A. D., Cox, D., and Anderson, R. D. (2005), "Reassessing the Pleasures of Store Shopping," *Journal of Business Research*, 58, 250-259; Jin, B. and Kim, J. (2003), "A Typology of Korean Discount Shoppers: Shopping Motives, Store Attributes, and Outcomes," *International Journal of Service Industry Management*, 14, 396-419.

19 Beatty, S. E. and Ferrell, E. M. (1998), "Impulse Buying: Modeling Its Precursors," *Journal of Retailing*, 74, 169-191; Jones, M. A., Reynolds, K. E., Weun, S., and Beatty, S. E. (2003), "The Product-Specific Nature of Impulse Buying Tendency," *Journal of Business Research*, 56, 505-511.

20 Miller, N. J., Kean, R. C., and Littrell, M. A. (1999), "Exploring Consumer and Retailer Exchange in Rural Communities: Part II," *Family and Consumer Sciences Research Journal*, 28, 99-121.

21 Luo, X. (2005), "How Does Shopping with Others Influence Impulsive Purchasing?" *Journal of Consumer Psychology*, 15, 288-294; Stilley, K. M., J. J. Inman, and K. L. Wakefield (2010a), "Spending on the Fly: Mental Budgets, Promotions, and Spending Behavior," *Journal of Marketing*, 74 (3), 34-47;

Stilley, K. M., Inman, J. J., and Wakefield, K. L. (2010b), "Planning to Make Unplanned Purchases? The Role of In-Store Slack in Budget Deviation," *Journal of Consumer Research*, 37, 264-278; Zhang, Y., Winterich, K. P., and Mittal, V. (2010), "Power Distance Belief and Impulsive Buying," *Journal of Marketing Research*, 47, 945-954.

22 Areni, C. S. and Kim, D. (1994), "The Influence of In-Store Lighting on Consumers' Examination of Merchandise in a Wine Store," *International Journal of Research in Marketing*, 11, 117-125; Katcheva, V. D. and Weitz, B. A. (2006), "When Should a Retailer Create an Exciting Store Environment?" *Journal of Marketing*, 42, 253-263; Yalch, R. F. and Spangenberg, R. C. (2000), "The Effects of Music in a Retail Setting on Real and Perceived Shopping Times," *Journal of Business Research*, 49, 139-147.

23 Baker, J., Grewal, D., and Parasuraman, A. (1994), "The Influence of Store Environment on Quality Inferences and Store Image," *Journal of Academy of Marketing Science*, 22, 328-339; Baker, J., Grewal, D., and Levy, M. (1992), "An Experimental Approach to Making Retail Store Environmental Decisions," *Journal of Retailing*, 68, 445-445; Baker, J., Parasuraman, A., Grewal, D., and Voss, G. B. (2002), "The Influence of Multiple Store Environment Cues on Perceived Merchandise Value and Patronage Intentions," *The Journal of Marketing*, 66, 120-141; Grewal, D., Baker, J., Levy, M., and Voss, G. B. (2003), "The Effects of Wait Expectations and Store Atmosphere Evaluations on Patronage Intentions in Service-Intensive Retail Stores," *Journal of Retailing*, 79, 259-268.

24 Swinyard, W. R. (2003), "The Effects of Salesperson Mood, Shopper Behavior, and Store Type on Consumer Services," *Journal of Retailing and Consumer Services*, 10, 323-333; Swinyard, W. R. (1993), "The Effects of Mood, Involvement, and Quality of Store Experience on Shopping Intentions," *Journal of Consumer Research*, 20, 271-280; Swinyard, W. R. (1995), "Impact of Shopper Mood and Retail Salesperson Credibility on Shopper Attitudes and Behavior," *International Review of Retail Distribution and Consumer Research*, 5, 488-503.

25 Chandon, P. J., Hutchinson, W., Bradlow, E. T., and Young, S. H. (2009), "Does In-Store Marketing Work? Effects of the Number and Position of Shelf Facings on Brand Attention and Evaluation at the Point of Purchase," *Journal of Marketing,* 73, 1-17.

26 Xin, Ge, Messinger Paul R., and Jin Li (2009), "Influence of Soldout Products on Consumer Choice," *Journal of Retailing*, 85 (3), 274-287.

27 Ferraro, Rosellina, Bettman James R., and Tanya L. Chartrand (2009), "The Power of Stranger: The Effect of Incidental Consumer Brand Encounters on Brand Choice," *Journal of Consumer Research*, 35 (Feb), 729-741.

28 Fitzsimons, Grainne M., Tanya L. Chartrand, and Gavan J. Fitzsimons (2008), "Automatic Effects of Brand Exposure on Motivated Behavior: How Apple Makes you 'Think Different,'" *Journal of Consumer Research*, 35 (June), 21-35.

29 Megicks, Phil, Juliet Memery, and Jasmine Williams (2008), "Influences on Ethical and Socially Responsible Shopping: Evidence from the UK Grocery Sector," *Journal of Marketing Management*, 24 (5/6), 637-659.

30 Miller, Nancy J., Rita C. Kean, and Mary A. Littrell (1999), "Exploring Consumer and Retailer Exchange in Rural Communities: Part 1," *Family and Consumer Sciences Research Journal*, 28 (1), 71-98.

31 Luo, Xueming (2005), "How Does Shopping with Others Influence Impulsive Purchasing?" *Journal of Consumer Psychology*, 15 (4), 288-294.

32 Arnold, M. J. and Reynolds, K. E. (2009), "Affect and Retail Shopping Behavior," *Journal of Retailing*, 85, 308-320.

33 Wertenbroch, Klaus (1998), "Consumption Self-Control by Rationing Purchase Quantities of Virtue and Vice," *Marketing Science,* 17 (4), 317-337.

34 McCabe, Deborah Brown, Mark S. Rosenbaum, and Jennifer Yurchisin (2007), "Perceived Service Quality and Shopping Motivations: A Dynamic Relationship," *Services Marketing Quarterly*, 29 (1), 1-21.

35 Areni, Charles S. and David Kim (1994), "The Influence of In-Store Lighting on Consumers' Examination of Merchandise in a Wine Store," *International Journal of Research in Marketing*, 11 (2), 117-125.

36 Baker, Julie, Dhruv Grewal, and A. Parasuraman (1994), "The Influence of Store Environment on Quality Inferences and Store Image," *Journal of the Academy of Marketing Science*, 22 (4), 328-339.

37 Lam, Shun Yin (2001), "The Effects of Store Environment on Shopping Behaviors: A Critical Review," *Advances in Consumer Research*, Association for Consumer Research, Valdosta, GA, 28 (1), 190-197.

38 Shannon, Randall and Rujirutana Mandhachitara (2005), "Private-Label Grocery Shopping Attitudes and Behaviour: A Cross-Cultural Study," *Brand Management*, 12 (6) 461-474.

39 Ailawadi, Kusum L., Scott A. Neslin, and Karen Gedenk (2001), "Pursuing the Value-Conscious Consumer: Store Brands Versus National Brand Promotions," *Journal of Marketing*, 65 (January), 71-89.

40 Batra Rajeev and Indrajit Sinha (2000), "Consumer-Level Factors Moderating the success of Private Label Brands," *Journal of Retailing*, 76 (2), 175-191.

41 Ailawadi, Kusum L., Donald R. Lehmann, and Scott A. Neslin (2003), "Revenue Premium as an Outcome Measure of Brand Equity," *Journal of Marketing*, 67, 1-17.

42 Sriram, S., Subramanian Balachander, and Manohar U. Kalwani (2007), "Monitoring the Dynamics of Brand Equity Using Store-Level Data," *Journal of Marketing*, 71, 61-78.

43 Besanko, David, Jean-Pierre Dube, and Sachin Gupta (2005), "Own-Brand and Cross-Brand Retail Pass-Through," *Marketing Science*, 24 (1), 123-137.

44 Fischer, Marc, Franziska Volckner, and Henrik Sattler (2010), "How Important Are Brands? A Cross-Category, Cross-Country Study," *Journal of Marketing Research*, 47 (5), 823-839.

45 Ataman, M. Berk, Harald J. Van Heerde, and Carl F. Mela (2010), "The Long-Term Effect of Marketing Strategy on Brand Sales," *Journal of Marketing Research*, 47 (5), 866-882.

46 Boyd, Eric D. and Kenneth D. Bahn (2009), "When Do Large Product Assortments Benefit Consumers? An Information-Processing Perspective," *Journal of Retailing*, 85 (3), 288-297.

47 Dreze, Xavier, Stephen J. Hoch, and Mary E. Purk (1994), *Shelf Management and Space Elasticity* (graduate school thesis), The University of Chicago, Chicago, IL.

48 Cachon, Gérard P. and Kök, A. Gürhan, (2007), "Category Management and Coordination in Retail Assortment Planning in the Presence of Basket Shopping Consumers," *Management Science*, (Jun) Vol. 53 (6).

49 Seock, Yoo-Kyoung, and Bailey, Lauren R., (2008), "The Influence of College Students' Shopping Orientations and Gender Differences on Online Information Searches and Purchase Behaviors," *International Journal of Consumer Studies*, Vol. 32.

50 Farag, Sendy, and Krizek, Kevin J. (2006), "E-Shopping and Its Relationship with In-Store Shopping: Empirical Evidence from the Netherlands and the USA," *Transport Reviews*, Vol. 26 (1).

51 Martin, Sonia San and Carment Camarero (2008), "Consumer Trust to a Web Site: Moderating Effect of Attitudes toward Online Shopping," *Cyber Psychology & Behavior*, 11 (5), 549 – 554.

52 Sharma, Arun and R. Krishnan (2002), "Clicks Only, Clicks and Bricks, and Bricks Only: Are Retail Salespeople an Important Factor in Choice?" *Journal of Marketing Management*, 18 (3/4), 317-336.

53 Burke, Raymond R. (2002), "Technology and the Customer Interface: What Consumers Want in the Physical and Virtual Store," *Journal of the Academy of Marketing Science*, 30 (4), 411-432.

54 Farag, Sendy, and Krizek, Kevin J. (2006), "E-Shopping and Its Relationship with In-Store Shopping: Empirical Evidence from the Netherlands and the USA," *Transport Reviews*, Vol. 26 (1).

55 Kukar-Kinney, Monika, Nancy M. Ridgway, and Kent B. Monroe (2009), "The Relationship Between Consumers' Tendencies to Buy Compulsively and Their Motivation to Shop and Buy on the Internet," *Journal of Retailing*, 85 (3), 298-307.

56 Schröder, Hendrik and Silvia Zaharia (2008), "Linking Multi-Channel Customer Behavior with Shopping Motives: An Empirical Investigation of a German Retailer," *Journal of Retailing and Consumer Services*, 15 (6), 452-468.

57 McEachern, Morven G. and Gary Warnaby (2005), "Food Shopping Behaviour in Scotland: The Influence of Relative Rurality," *International Journal of Consumer Studies*, 30 (2), 189-201.

58 Gehrt, Kenneth C. and Soyeon Shim (2003), "Situational Segmentation in the International Marketplace: The Japanese Snack Market," *International Marketing Review*, 20 (2), 180-194.

59 Geuens, Maggie, Malaika Brengman, and Rosette S'Jegers (2001), "An Exploratory Study of Grocery Shopping Motivations," in *European Advances in Consumer Research*, Vol. 5, Andrea Groeppel-Klien and Frank-Rudolf Esch (Eds.), Provo, UT: Association for Consumer Research, 135-140.

60 Stilley, K. M., J. J. Inman, and K. L. Wakefield (2010), "Spending on the Fly: Mental Budgets, Promotions, and Spending Behavior," *Journal of Marketing*, 74 (3), 34-47; Stilley, K. M., J. J. Inman, and K. L. Wakefield, (2010), "Planning to Make Unplanned Purchases? The Role of In-Store Slack in Budget Deviation," *Journal of Consumer Research*, 37, 264-278; Tang, C. S., S. D. Bell, and T. Ho, T. (2001), "Store Choice and Shopping Behavior: How Price Format Works," *California Management Review*, 43, 56-74.

61 Broeckelmann, P. and Groeppel-Klein, A. (2008), "Usage of Mobile Price Comparison Sites at the Point of Sales and Its Influence on Consumers' Shopping Behavior," *The Internationl Review of Retail Distribution and Consumer Research*, 18, 149-166.

62 Chu, Junhong, Pradeep Chintagunta, and Javier Cebollada (2008), "A Comparison of Within-Household Price Sensitivity Across Online and Offline Channels," *Marketing Science*, 27 (2), 283-299.

63 Hoch, Stephen J., Xavier Dreze, and Mary E. Purk (1994), "EDLP, Hi-Lo, and Margin Arithmetic," *Journal of Marketing*, 58 (4), 16-28.

64 Dhar, Sanjey K., Claudia Gonzalez-Vallejo, and Dilip Soman (1995), "Brand Promotions as Lottery," *Marketing Letters*, 6 (3), 221-233.

65 Monga, Ashwani and Ritesh Saini (2009), "Currency of Search: How Spending Time on Search Is Not the Same as Spending Money," *Journal of Retailing*, 85 (3), 245-257.

66 Pauwels, Koen (2007), "How Retailer and Competitor Decisions Drive the Long-Term Effectiveness of Manufacturer Promotions for Fast Moving Consumer Goods," *Journal of Retailing*, 83 (3), 297-308.

67 Slotegraaf, Rebecca J., and Koen Pauwels (2008), "The Impact of Brand Equity and Innovation on the Long-Term Effectiveness of Promotions," *Journal of Marketing Research*, 45, 293-306.

68 Srinivasan, Shuba, Koen Pauwels, and Vincent Nijs (2008), "Demand-Based Pricing Versus Past-Price Dependence: A Cost-Benefit Analysis," *Journal of Marketing*, 72, 15-27.

69 Underhill, Paco (2000), *Why We Buy: The Science of Shopping*. New York: Simon & Schuster.

70 Sorensen, H. (2009), *Inside the Mind of the Shopper: The Science of Retailing*, Upper Saddle River, NJ: Wharton School Publishing.

71 Lucas, J. (2012), "Shopper Marketing, the Discipline, the Approach" in M. Stahlberg and V. Maila, (Eds.), *Shopper Marketing: How to Increase Purchase Decisions at the Point of Sale*, London: Kogan Page, 13-26.

72 Skogster, Patrik, Uotila Varpu, and Lauri Ojala (2007), "From Mornings to Evenings: Is There Variation in Shopping Behavior Between Different Hours of the Day?" *International Journal of Consumer Studies,* 32, 65-74.

73 Larson, Jeffrey S., Eric T. Bradlow, and Peter S. Fader (2005), "An Exploratory Look at Supermarket Shopping Paths," *International Journal of Research in Marketing*, 22, 395-414.

74 Vrechopoulos, Adam P., Robert M. O'Keefe, Georgios I. Doukidis, and George J. Siomkos (2004), "Virtual Store Layout: An Experimental Comparison in the Context of Grocery Retail," *Journal of Retailing*, 80 (1), 13-22.

75 Chandon, Pierre, J. Wesley Hutchinson, Eric T. Bradlow, and Scott H. Young (2009), "Does In-Store Marketing Work? Effects of the Number and Position of Shelf Facings on Brand Attention and Evaluation at the Point of Purchase," *Journal of Marketing*, 73 (November), 1-17.

76 Limon, Yonca, Lynn R. Kahle, and Ulrich R. Orth (2009), "Package Design as a Communications Vehicle in Cross-Cultural Values Shopping," *Journal of International Marketing*, 17 (1), 30-57.

77 Hosbond, Jens H. and Mikael B. Skov (2007),"Micro Mobility Marketing: Two Cases on Location-Based Supermarket Shopping Trolleys," *Journal of Targeting, Measurement & Analysis for Marketing*, 16(1), 68-77.

78 Sorensen, H. (2008), "Long Tail Media in the Store," *Journal of Advertising Research*, 48 (3), 329-338.

79 Broeckelmann, Philipp and Andrea Groeppel-Klein (2008), "Usage of Mobile Price Comparison Sites at the Point of Sale and Its Influence on Consumers' Shopping Behaviour," *International Review of Retail, Distribution and Consumer Research*, 18 (2), 149-166.

80 Hosbond, J. H. and Skov, M. B. (2007), "Micro Mobility marketing: Two Cases on Location-Based Supermarket Shopping Trolleys," *Journal of Targeting Measurement and Analysis for Marketing*, 16, 68-77.

81 Jih, Wen-Jang Kenny and Suzanne D. Su-Fang Lee (2003-04), "An Exploratory Analysis of Relationships Between Cellular Phone Users' Shopping Motivators and Lifestyle Indicators," *Journal of Computer Information Systems*, 44 (2), 65-72.

82 Gray, Steven (2009), "The Formative Years: The Mobile Couponing Craze Takes Shape," *International Journal of Mobile Marketing*, 4 (1), 12-14.

83 Leppäniemi, Matti and Heikki Karjaluoto (2008), "Mobile Marketing: From Marketing Strategy to Mobile Marketing Campaign Implementation," *International Journal of Mobile Marketing*, 3 (1), 50-61.

84 Banerjee, Syagnik and Ruby Roy Dholakia (2008), "Mobile Advertising: Does Location-Based Advertising Work?" *International Journal of Mobile Marketing*, 3 (2), 68-74.

85 Broeckelmann, Philipp and Andrea Groeppel-Klein (2008), "Usage of Mobile Price Comparison Sites at the Point of Sale and Its Influence on Consumers' Shopping Behaviour," *International Review of Retail, Distribution and Consumer Research,* 18 (2), 149-166.

86 Shankar, Venkatesh, Alladi Venkatesh, Charles Hofacker, and Prasad Naik (2010), "Mobile Marketing in the Retailing Environment: Current Insights and Future Research Avenues," *Journal of Interactive Marketing*, 24 (2), 111-120.

87 See Noble, S. M., Griffith, D., and Tandoh, M. (2006), "Drivers of Local Merchant Loyalty: Understanding the Influence of Gender and Shopping Motives," *Journal of Retailing*, 82, 177-188; Tandoh, M., Griffith, D. A., and Noble, S. M. (2009), "When Do Relationships Pay Off for Small Retailers? Exploring Targets and Contexts to Understand the Value of Relationship Marketing," *Journal of Retailing*, 85, 493-501.

88 Ofir, Chezy and Itamar Simonson (2007), "The Effect of Stating Expectations on Customer Satisfaction and Shopping Experience," *Journal of Marketing Research*, 44 (1), 164-174.

89 Terblanche, N. S. and C. Boshoff (2006), "The Relationship between a Satisfactory In-Store Shopping Experience and Retailer Loyalty," *South African Journal of Business Management*, 37 (2), 33-43.

90 Hart, Cathy, Farrell, Andrew M., Stachow, Grazyna, Reed Garry, and John W. Cadogan (2007), "Enjoyment of the Shopping Experience: Impact on Customers' Repatronage Intentions and Gender Influence," *The Service Industries Journal*, 27 (5), 583-604.

91 He, Hongwei and Avinandan Mjkherjee (2007), "I Am, Ergo I Shop: Does Store Image Congruity Explain Shopping Behaviour of Chinese Consumers?" *Journal of Marketing Management*, 23 (5-6), 443-460.

92 Sullivan P. and J. Heitmeyer (2008), "Looking at Gen Y Shopping Preferences and Intentions: Exploring the Role of Experience and Apparel Involvement," *International Journal of Consumer Studies,* 32, 285-295.

93 Demoulin, Nathalie T. M. and Pietro Zidda (2009), "Drivers of Customers' Adoption and Adoption Timing of a New Loyalty Card in the Grocery Retail Market," *Journal of Retailing*, 85 (3), 391-405; Kwon, Wi-Suk and Sharron J. Lennon (2009), "What Induces Online Loyalty? Online Versus Offline Brand Images," *Journal of Business Research*, 62 (5), 557-564.

11

Connecting Supply Chain Management to Shopper Marketing[1]

This chapter is about execution of shopper marketing initiatives, an area in need of research support. We merely highlight some critical areas of interest from the literature. While capturing shoppers' attention and influencing their purchase decisions are important objectives of shopper marketing efforts, in-store marketing strategies are often not fully diffused (passed on) to frontline employees and, therefore, are not executed in the store well, if at all.[2]

Current research in supply chain management that might be relevant to shopper marketing complements that of marketing relevant literature but focuses more on operational issues such as inventory management, forecasting, stock keeping unit rationalization, and relationships between retailers and manufacturers. Packaging, often seen in terms of marketing for communication reasons, is also studied extensively by supply chain management and logistics scholars. Additionally, topics of shelf position and aisle location discussed earlier are researched by operations management scholars.

Shopper marketing tactics such as product customization by manufacturers for specific partner retailers have the potential to completely disrupt a supply chain.[3] The goal of a retail channel is to provide the optimal quantity and assortment of goods and services needed to increase shoppers' satisfaction.[4] Retail channel research sometimes comes from the operations perspective, which explores the optimal product assortments and the forecasting of future inventory needs and product demand.

Retailers frequently attempt to attract shoppers by offering large product assortments.[5] However, the paradox of choice means that assortments can overtax shoppers and can result in suboptimized solutions. Product assortment decisions relate to category management, but as we stated, research suggests that category management does not provide an optimal solution for product mix. Basket assortment reflects the mix of products a shopper buys within one trip. Research into basket assortment takes many forms, can often involve experimental work,[6] and can help marketing professionals include the best products in shopper marketing programs as well as estimate the impact of such programs on product categories.

Retail Forecasting

Leading retailers pay extra attention to their supply chains to reduce stockouts, find more efficient ways of moving goods from manufacturers to customers, and improve the shopping experience, in part through superior forecasting.[7] Collaborative planning and forecasting between retailer and manufacturer are key ways these companies excel and have become a common focus for retailing research over the last ten years.[8] But shopper marketing often focuses on shorter-term and retailer-customized programs, increasing the forecasting challenge. Research in this area examines multiple forecasting methods. For example, stochastic demand methods enhance retailers' profit maximization, while collaborative judgmental forecasting by retailers and manufacturers leads to less error and more consistency over time.[9] In turn, manufacturers must collaborate more closely with retail customers to gain access to information needed to more effectively and efficiently serve retailers and to assist in forecasting the effects of shopper marketing programs.[10]

Retail Channel Execution

Shopper marketing takes place in the retail channel, not simply within stores, and is dependent on the relationships between retailers and manufacturers, intermediaries, ad agencies, and wholesalers. This research involves topics like coordination and collaboration, interorganizational relationships, and supply chain agility. Additionally, transportation and specifically network design, ideal modes of transportation, routing and scheduling, complexities of urban logistics, and so on are also key components of supply chain management research relevant to shopper marketing challenges.

Related to execution is the role of the manufacturer's sales team. The manner in which account management with retailers is conducted is changing rapidly as a result of shopper marketing.[11] The funds that account management teams have to allocate to their specific customers (for example, trade funds) are being reallocated away from price-based promotions and short-term tactical displays to more strategic initiatives. Thus, relationships move to more strategic levels and involve multiple categories and functions within the retailer. Shopper marketing efforts also force account managers to coordinate more with their own brand management teams. Extant research helps in terms of negotiation strategies, collaboration, and coordination processes.

Inventory Management

Managing product supply is critical to shopper marketing execution because retailer-unique stock keeping units (SKUs) are often involved in shopper marketing programs.[12] This not only means products unique to a retailer but possibly slightly altered products for an initiative within the same retailer where the original products are regularly sold. Manufacturer-retailer collaboration, communication, and information sharing between channel partners are crucial to shopper marketing execution success for this reason.[13] Inventory management must be coordinated between marketing and operations functions and between the firms in the channel to deliver the necessary product mix. Inventory management directly impacts retail customer satisfaction through order fulfillment accuracy and on-time delivery performance, which are critical for successful shopper marketing execution.

As part of supply chain management, effective inventory management is critical to retail channel shopper marketing success[14] and reflects (1) the impact of signaling, collaboration, and coordination on performance and (2) the impact of the product and service mix on the overall inventory management system of choice.[15] Information distortion in the supply chain creates a bullwhip effect in which the manufacturers' or suppliers' disproportionate responses to mixed signals sent from downstream in the supply chain result in stockouts and overstocks.[16] Due to a lack of coordinated inventory management, stockouts have a direct impact on store image and can result in product substitutions, store exits, or purchase delays.[17] From a shopper marketing perspective, in-store initiatives are heavily dependent on precise timing of inventory availability at specific locations within the store, and this depends on superior retailer-manufacturer communication.

Another important stream of inventory management research focuses on the type of supply chain structure that supports the flow of inventory. Inventory management has shifted from a manufacturer dominated "push" of inventory downstream to a more responsive "pull" system, in which manufacturers respond to the needs of retailers.[18] Pull supply chain strategies focus on the design of the supply chain structure to support lean, postponement, and supply chain agility strategies that increase inventory performance.[19] Like retail forecasting, effective inventory management is dependent on information sharing between a manufacturer and retailer. Shopper marketing requires a more responsive and agile supply chain to adapt product packaging, inventory levels, packaging, and merchandising displays as events happen.

Many firms struggle with shopper marketing execution because inventory management and retail forecasting become complicated by customization within the retail channel and retailer level. Retailers and manufacturers have a historically tense relationship that complicates coordination.[20] Marketing and logistics functions within organizations still operate in silos, hindering marketing execution.[21] For example, brand managers and account managers (that is, sales) often find it difficult to coordinate due to varying incentives and time horizons. Successful shopper marketing requires functional personnel to work closely together across their siloed boundaries. Research to-date does not explore the necessary integration within and across firms that enables better execution.

Retail Customer Satisfaction and Loyalty

Retail customer satisfaction and loyalty are dependent on the effectiveness and efficiency of the manufacturer/vendor. More loyal relationships facilitated by service quality enable more effective initiatives such as those created by manufacturers' shopper marketing managers.[22] Manufacturer service quality to the retailer is increased in part through successful inventory management and order fulfillment.[23] Similarly, efficiency is augmented when customer-oriented manufacturing companies proactively pursue collaborative relationships with their retail customers to reduce costs.[24] Improved collaboration and coordination in the supply chain also increase program effectiveness through improved inventory management.[25] While coordination and collaboration in the supply chain for the execution of product distribution and marketing strategies in the retailing context are important, little research has been conducted within the context of shopper marketing specifically.

Shopper Orientation

When it comes to involving supply chain management and other functional areas in the planning and execution of marketing programs, we find in research that a market orientation for the entire firm helps. As we move into shopper marketing, the integration of demand and supply management processes may suggest that the successful organizations, those planning and executing superior shopper marketing programs time and time again, possess a *shopper orientation*. Work at the University of Tennessee and Florida State University is currently exploring what a shopper orientation might look like. In short, it would suggest that there exists an overarching mindset and accompanying set of behaviors focused on understanding and serving shopper segment needs through the entire channel along the entire path to purchase. Stay tuned for research emerging in this area.

Endnotes

1   This chapter's content in large part is drawn from Stolze, H. (2012), *Shopper Marketing and Social Networks: The Path to Integration*, dissertation, University of Tennessee. We are grateful to Dr. Hanna Stolze and one of her dissertation chairs, Dr. Diane Mollenkopf for their contribution to this work. They are the supply chain experts.

2   Deloitte Research (2007), Shopper Marketing: Capturing a Shopper's Mind, Heart, and Wallet, New York: Deloitte Development, PLC; IBM Institute (2002), Ehancing the Customer Shopping Experience: 2002 IBM/NRF "Store of the Future" survey. Somers, NY: IBM Global Services; Piercy, N. F. (1998), "Marketing Implementation: The Implications of Marketing Paradigm Weakness for the Strategy Execution Process," *Journal of the Academy of Marketing Science*, 26, 222-236.

3   Flint, D. J. (2012), "Shopper Marketing's True Potential," in M. Stahlberg and V. Maila (Eds.) *Shopper Marketing: How to Increase Purchase Decisions at the Point of Sale, 2nd edition*, London: Kogan Page, 175-180; Flint, D. J., Lusch, R., and Vargo, S. (2013), "The Supply Chain Management of Shopper Marketing as Viewed Through a Service Ecosystem Lens," *International Journal of Physical Distribution and Logistics Management*, forthcoming.

4   Mathwick, C., Malhotra, N. K., and Rigdon, E. (2002), "The Effect of Dynamic Retail Experiences on Experiential Perceptions of Value: An Internet and Catalog Comparison," *Journal of Retailing*, 78, 51-60.

5   Boyd, D. E. and Bahn K. D. (2009), "When Do Large Product Assortments Benefit Consumers? An Information-Processing Perspective," *Journal of Retailing*, 85, 288-297.

6   Dréze, X., Hoch, S. J., and Purk, M. E. (1994), "Shelf Management and Space Elasticity," *Journal of Retailing*, 70, 301-326; Miller, C. M., Smith, S. A., McIntyre, S. H., and Achabal, D. D. (2010), "Optimizing and Evaluating Retail Assortments for Infrequently Purchased Products," *Journal of Retailing*, 86, 159-171.

7   Anon (2005), "Special Report: Retail Technology: Technology's New Role in the Retail Supply Chain," *Supply Chain Management Review*, 9, 53-56.

8   Barratt, M. (2004), "Understanding the Meaning of Collaboration in the Supply Chain," *Supply Chain Management: An International Journal*, 9, 30-42; Ireland, R. D., Hitt, M. A., and Vaidyanath, D. (2002), "Alliance Management as a Source of Competitive Advantage," *Journal of Management*, 28, 413; Ireland, R. and Bruce, R. (2000), "CPFR Only the Beginning of Collaboration." *Supply Chain*

Management Review, 4, 80-88; Moon, M. A., (2013), *Demand and Supply Integration: The Key to World Class Demand Forecasting*, Upper Saddle River, NJ: Financial Times Press.

9   Arcelus, F. J., Kumar, S., and Srinivasan, G. (2005), "Retailer's Response to Alternate Manufacturer's Incentives under a Single-Period, Price-Dependent, Stochastic-Demand Framework," *Decision Sciences*, 36, 599-626; Gauer, V., Kesavan, S., Raman, A., and Fisher, M. L. (2007), "Estimating Demand Uncertainty Using Judgement Forecasts," *Manufacturing and Service Operations Management*, 9, 480-491.

10 Kulp, S. C., Leem H. L., and Ofek, E. W. (2004), "Manufacturer Benefits from Information Integration with Retail Customers," *Management Science*, 50, 431-444.

11 Deloitte Research (2007), *Shopper Marketing: Capturing a Shopper's Mind, Meart, and Wallet*, New York: Deloitte Development, PLC; Hoyt, C. (2012), "Touching the Elephant," in Markus Stahlburg and Ville Maila (Eds.), *Shopper Marketing: How to Increase Purchase Decisions at the Point of Sale, 2nd edition*, London: Kogan Page, 161-168; Hoyt, C. (2013), "Shopper Crossroads," *The Hub Magazine*, Jan/Feb 42-45.

12 Flint, D. J. (2012), "Shopper Marketing's True Potential," in M. Stahlberg and V. Maila (Eds.), *Shopper Marketing: How to Increase Purchase Decisions at the Point of Sale, 2nd edition*, London: Kogan Page, 175-180.

13 Davis-Sramek, B., Mentzer, J. T., and Stank, T. P. (2008), "Creating Consumer Durable Retailer Customer Loyalty through Order Fulfillment Service Operations," *Journal of Operations Management*, 26, 781-797; Davis-Sramek, B., Germain, R., and Stank, T. P. (2010), "The Impact of Order Fulfillment Service on Retailer Merchandising Decisions in the Consumer Durables Industry," *Journal of Business Logistics*, 31, 215-230.

14 Dubelaar, C., Chow, G., and Larson, P. D. (2001), "Relationships between Inventory, Sales and Service in a Retail Chain Store Operation," *International Journal of Physical Distribution and Logistics Management*, 31, 96-108.

15 Fisher, M. L. (1997), "What Is the Right Supply Chain for Your Product.," *Harvard Business Review*, 75, 105-116; Sahin, F. and Robinson, E. P. (2002), "Flow Coordination and Information Sharing in Supply Chains: Review, Implications, and Directions for Future Research," *Decision Sciences*, 33, 505-536.

16 Lee, H. L., Padmanabhan, V., and Whang, S. (1997), "Information Distortion in a Supply Chain: The Bullwhip Effect," *Management Science*, 546-558.

17 Zinn, W. and Liu, P. C. (2001), "Consumer Response to Retail Stockouts," *Journal of Business Logistics*, 22, 49-71.

18 Fugate, B. S., Sahin, F., and Mentzer, J. T. (2006), "Supply Chain Management Coordination Mechanisms," *Journal of Business Logistics*, 27, 129-161.

19 Gligor, D. M. and Holcomb, M. C. (2012), "Understanding the Role of Logistics Capabilities in Achieving Supply Chain Agility: A Systematic Literature Review," *Supply Chain Management: An International Journal*, 17, 438-453; LeBlanc, L. J., Hill, J. A., Harder, J., and Greenwell, G. W. (2009), "Modeling Uncertain Forecast Accuracy in Supply Chains with Postponement," *Journal of Business Logistics*, 30, 19-31; Rabinovich, E. and Evers, P. T. (2003), "Postponement Effects on Inventory Performance and the Impact of Information Systems," *The International Journal of Logistics Management*, 14, 33-48.

20 Davis-Sramek, B., Fugate, B. S., and Omar, A. (2007), "Functional/Dysfunctional Supply Chain Exchanges," *International Journal of Physical Distribution and Logistics Management*, 37, 43-63.

21 Drucker, P. F. (1993), *Managing in Turbulent Times*, New York City: Harper Paperbacks; Ellinger, A. E. (2000), "Improving Marketing/Logistics Cross-Functional Collaboration in the Supply Chain," *Industrial Marketing Management*, 29, 85-96.

22 Biong, H. (1993), "Satisfaction and Loyalty to Suppliers within the Grocery Trade," *European Journal of Marketing*, 27, 21-38; Davis-Sramek, B., Mentzer, J. T., and Stank, T. P. (2008), "Creating Consumer Durable Retailer Customer Loyalty through Order Fulfillment Service Operations," *Journal of Operations Management*, 26, 781-797; Davis-Sramek, B., Germain, R., and Stank, T. P. (2010), "The Impact of Order Fulfillment Service on Retailer Merchandising Decisions in the Consumer Durables Industry," *Journal of Business Logistics*, 31, 215-230; Thirumalai, S. and Sinha, K. K. (2005), "Customer Satisfaction with Order Fulfillment in Retail Supply Chains: Implications of Product Type in Electronic B2C Transactions," *Journal of Operations Management*, 23, 291-303.

23 Eroglu, C., Williams, B. D., and Waller, M. A. (2011), "Consumer-Driven Retail Operations: The Moderating Effects of Consumer Demand and Case Pack Quantity," *International Journal of Physical Distribution and Logistics Management*, 41, 420-434; Mejias-Sacaluga, A. and Prado-Prado, J. C. (2002), "Integrated Logistics Management in the Grocery Supply Chain," *The International Journal of Logistics Management*, 13, 67-78.

24 Bolumole, Y. A., Knemeyer, A. M., and Lambert, D. M. (2003), "The Customer Service Management Process," *The International Journal of Logistics Management*, 14, 15-31; Zokaei, A. K. and Simons, D. W. (2006), "Value Chain Analysis in Consumer Focus Improvement: A Case Study of the UK Red Meat Industry," *The International Journal of Logistics Management*, 17, 141-162.

25 Sahin, F. and Robinson, E. P. (2002), "Flow Coordination and Information Sharing in Supply Chains: Review, Implications, and Directions for Future Research," *Decision Sciences*, 33, 505-536.

12

Conclusion

We began by asking the question: What in the world is this thing called *shopper marketing*? Now you know. You should now be aware of the following:

- Shopper marketing is not a fad. It is in fact a rather new way of looking at brand management, sales management, advertising, and retailing.
- Shopper marketing is not about in-store or out-of-store. It is about communicating with consumers when they are in shopping modes.
- Shopper marketing is strategic, involving strong collaborative relationships between brand manufacturers and their key retail customers. But it also involves partnerships with shopper marketing agencies and brokers.
- Shopper marketing programs should be designed to achieve one or more of six key objectives.
- Shopper marketing rests on eight foundational principles.
- Shopper and business insights drive shopper marketing programming.
- Doing shopper marketing can follow a four-phase process of opportunity identification, strategic planning, execution, and measurement.
- Execution of shopper marketing initiatives is difficult with success rates hovering between 20% and 50%. This needs to be improved. Supply chain management is critical to this execution challenge.

Those are merely a few of the highlights from what we have shared here. We hope that you now realize that by following a straightforward but disciplined process for your shopper marketing program development you can consistently create successful programs time and time again. If you do not, you may develop successful programs, but they are likely to be ad hoc and unreliable.

As we look into the future of shopper marketing, we see a number of issues arising. One has to do with the international nature of shopper marketing. Specifically, in what ways does shopper marketing change as we move from region to region or country to country? Related to this is the question of emerging markets. How do shopper marketing processes need to be modified to adapt to the structures and processes inherent in emerging economies like India's? The answer might very well be similar to modifying shopper marketing processes for highly fragmented markets such as Italy. A second issue deals with online shopping. In what ways does shopper marketing apply and in what ways does it differ when it is applied to online environments? Finally, a third issue deals with sustainability. Shopper marketing can be powerful, but it also has the potential of generating more waste. How can shopper marketing be conducted in a sustainable way? How can shopper marketing actually assist in global sustainability efforts?

Internationalization

Shopper marketing is alive and well in Europe. Agencies like Mars Advertising for one are sharing their vast expertise developed in the United States with retailers and brand manufacturers in Europe, either US organizations with European operations or European and other multinational firms. Retailers like Tesco and brand manufacturers like Unilever and Nestlé are all some of the best in class at this, and it is no surprise they can achieve great things in western Europe.

In many other parts of the world, though, shopper marketing is far less developed. The Path-to-Purchase Institute recently announced a book of case studies from around the world to compare and contrast shopper marketing globally. From what we know, several things are certain. Fragmented markets such as those in emerging economies like India or developed ones like Italy, involve many times more retailers and even brands and as such many smaller organizations. Shopper marketing processes all still work, but in many cases the budgets are less. So programs are on a smaller, more localized scale and are unlikely to involve customized elements for each and every retailer. However, due to the nature of fragmented markets, this is fine because the same programs can be run within many retailers as long as they are not in competing markets and still help those retailers and brands differentiate. That said, a great deal of work is being conducted at a rapid pace to apply shopper marketing principles and processes in many regions of the world. The potential for cross-pollination of ideas is exciting.

Here are a few things that we know about markets elsewhere:
- A majority of Chilean shoppers visited the mall with a well-developed plan and made purchases accordingly. US shoppers were more spontaneous: Nearly half of them made unplanned purchases. Chilean shoppers have different purchase patterns compared with shoppers in the United States; they are less susceptible to situational influence than US shoppers.[1]

- Although some universal behavior patterns exist, shoppers' motivation, selection criteria, and purchase behaviors were found to vary across cultures and/or the type of shopping facilities.[2]

- Chinese consumers perceived service quality in the regular supermarkets based on their purchasing process instead of from the tangible and nontangible aspects found in previous studies. Measurement and underlying structure of service quality perception was not only industry and culture specific, but also specific to the form of retail structures that may enter the cultural mélange of the Chinese marketplace.[3]

- Private labels are less prevalent in Thailand; Thai grocery shoppers enjoy shopping more than Americans do, are less time pressured, are likely to use price more to indicate brand quality, and tend to have more people accompany them on a shopping trip.[4]

- Examining economy, mid-quality, and premium private labels (PLs) in the UK: Economy PLs cannibalize standard PLs and premium PLs cannibalize both economy and standard PLs, partly due to brand-type similarity effect. Economy PL introductions benefit mainstream-quality national brands (NBs) because these NBs become a compromise or middle option in terms of quality in the retailer's assortment. The effects of premium PL introductions on premium-quality NBs are mixed: Their share improves in two of four cases but decreases in the other two cases.[5]

- Cultural values, as in Chinese versus the United States, do seem to affect emotional and behavioral responses to online store atmospherics.[6]

- Customers who buy across multiple product categories initiate more contacts with the firm, have past experience with the supplier through the online channel, have longer tenure, purchase more frequently, are larger and receive communication from the supplier through multiple communication channels, especially through highly interpersonal channels. Customers who shop across multiple transaction channels provide higher revenues, higher share of wallet, have higher past customer value, and have a higher likelihood of being active than other customers.[7]

Online Shopping

Shopping online has been explored for a number of years now. With respect to shopper marketing, managers of online shopping have not taken advantage of the concepts and processes presented here as aggressively as they could. For one thing, the entire path-to-purchase is often not considered. Second, insights to online shoppers have a long way to go. Third, concepts such as solution centers, purchase barriers, stop/hold/close, unique brand-retailer partnerships, and mostly programs and initiatives are not being demonstrated. The online retail environment has significant potential to apply shopper marketing concepts but has a long way to go. That said, here are a few things we know:

- Male and female online apparel shoppers show significant differences in their shopping orientations, online information searches, and purchase experiences.[8]
- Research suggests that online shopping and in-store shopping are complementary and not only about substitution.[9]
- Satisfaction with previous purchases, website security and privacy policies, and service quality are the main determinants of trust in retail websites.[10]
- Compulsive shoppers may tend to shop more online than in brick-and-mortar stores.[11]

Sustainability

Finally, sustainability cannot be ignored in business today. Shopper marketing programs have the potential to create, in the aggregate, far more waste in terms of marketing materials in the supply chain. From complex temporary display units to unique short run packaging to potentially more frequent deliveries of smaller lots and so forth, if not well planned, the impact in terms of waste and carbon footprint could be negative. But there is a much larger issue at stake. If shopper marketing is a powerful marketing tool, it should be used to "do good" for society. Figure 12-1 depicts a possible way to think about shopper marketing's potential in terms of social responsibility.

What Figure 12-1 presents is a chance to not only do shopper marketing well, but to master it and do well for society. We are nowhere near this in industry—yet. But we could be there eventually.

Our final thought is that we hope we have shown you how important shopper marketing is, how to identify best in class shopper marketing programs, and how to step-by-step create your own profitable shopper marketing programs. Certainly the media available to us will change over time and in some cases quite rapidly. In addition, shoppers, brands, retailers, and agencies will change. However, the thought processes for developing effective programs will remain stable for years. Take the time to master the processes outlined here and lead the discipline in the shopper marketing field. Then come join us at the many conferences, join us on LinkedIn groups, and share your knowledge with the rest of us—all in the name of continuous improvement of the industry. We wish you all the best of business success!

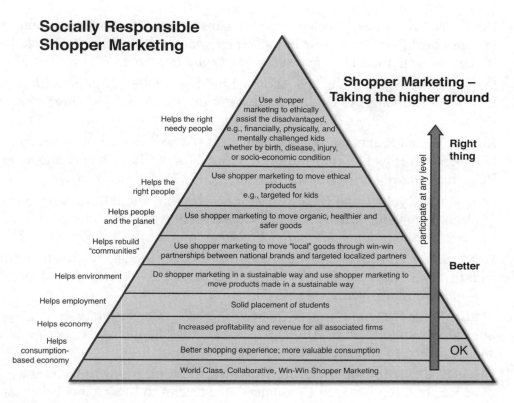

Socially Responsible Shopper Marketing

Shopper Marketing – Taking the higher ground

Helps the right needy people — Use shopper marketing to ethically assist the disadvantaged, e.g., financially, physically, and mentally challenged kids whether by birth, disease, injury, or socio-economic condition

Helps the right people — Use shopper marketing to move ethical products e.g., targeted for kids

Helps people and the planet — Use shopper marketing to move organic, healthier and safer goods

Helps rebuild "communities" — Use shopper marketing to move "local" goods through win-win partnerships between national brands and targeted localized partners

Helps environment — Do shopper marketing in a sustainable way and use shopper marketing to move products made in a sustainable way

Helps employment — Solid placement of students

Helps economy — Increased profitability and revenue for all associated firms

Helps consumption-based economy — Better shopping experience; more valuable consumption

World Class, Collaborative, Win-Win Shopper Marketing

participate at any level

Right thing

Better

OK

Figure 12-1 *Taking the higher ground with shopper marketing.*

Endnotes

1 Nicholls, J. A. F., Fuan Li, Sydney Roslow, Carl J. Kranendonk, and Tomislav Mandakovic (2001), "Inter-American Perspectives from Mall Shoppers: Chile-United States," *Journal of Global Marketing*, 15 (1), 87-103.

2 Nicholls, J. A. F., Fuan Li, Sydney Roslow, Carl J. Kranendonk, and Tomislav Mandakovic (2003), "Structural or Cultural: An Exploration into Influences on Consumers' Shopping Behavior of Country Specific Factors Versus Retailing Formats," *Journal of Global Marketing*, 16 (4), 97-115.

3 Meng, Juan (Gloria), John H. Summey, Neil C. Herndon, and Kenneth K. Kwong (2009), "Some Retail Service Quality Expectations of Chinese Shoppers," *International Journal of Market Research*, 51 (6), 773-796.

4 Shannon, Randall and Rujirutana Mandhachitara (2005), "Private-Label Grocery Shopping Attitudes and Behaviour: A Cross-Cultural Study," *Brand Management*, 12 (6) 461-474.

5   Geyskens, Inge, Katrijn Gielens, and Els Gihsbrechts (2010), "Proliferating Private-Label Portfolios: How Introducing Economy and Premium Private Labels Influences Brand Choice," *Journal of Marketing Research*, 47 (5), 791-807.

6   Davis, Lenita, Sijun Wang, and Andrew Lindridge (2008), "Culture Influences on Emotional Responses to On-line Store Atmospheric Cues," *Journal of Business Research*, 61 (8), 806-812.

7   Kumar, V., and Rajkumar Venkatesan (2005), "Who Are the Multichannel Shoppers and How Do They Perform?: Correlates of Multichannel Shopping Behavior," *Journal of Interactive Marketing*, 19 (2), 44-62.

8   Seock, Yoo-Kyoung, and Bailey, Lauren R., (2008), "The Influence of College Students' Shopping Orientations and Gender Differences on Online Information Searches," *International Journal of Consumer Studies*, Vol. 32 (2), 113-121.

9   Farag, Sendy, and Krizek, Kevin J. (2006), "E-Shopping and Its Relationship with In-Store Shopping: Empirical Evidence from the Netherlands and the USA," *Transport Reviews*, Vol. 26 (1), 43-61.

10 Martin, Sonia San and Carment Camarero (2008), "Consumer Trust to a Web Site: Moderating Effect of Attitudes toward Online Shopping," *Cyber Psychology and Behavior*, 11 (5), 549-554.

11 Kukar-Kinney, Monika, Nancy M. Ridgway, and Kent B. Monroe (2009), "The Relationship Between Consumers' Tendencies to Buy Compulsively and Their Motivation to Shop and Buy on the Internet," *Journal of Retailing*, 85 (3), 298-307.

Index

e-commerce, 47-48

ECR (efficient consumer response), 164

EDLP (Every Day Low Pricing), 47, 223

efficient consumer response (ECR), 164

emerging markets, 246-247

emotions and shopper behavior, 217

empiricism, 186-188

EMTP (eclectic marketing theory and
    practice). *See also* philosophical
    perspectives

  building eclectic teams, 198-199

  definition of, 180-181, 197

  designing studies, 201

  executing studies, 202

  learning and exploration, 200-201

engagement (creative copy), 159

environmental design, 135

environmental stimuli and shopper
    behavior, 215-219

equities summary (shopper marketing
    customer plan), 138-139

equity (brand), 209, 219-220

  aligning, 125

  brand equity pyramid, 96-97

  equities summary (shopper marketing
    customer plan), 138-139

  equity building (creative copy), 159

  identifying, 138-139

ethics and shopper behavior, 216

ethnographies, 113

evaluating

  creative copy, 158-159

  opportunities, 110, 140-141

  packaging, 133

Every Day Low Pricing (EDLP), 47, 223

executing studies, 202

execution

  agency relationships

    evaluating creative copy, 158-159

    reporting results, 159

    selecting partners, 157-158

    strategic briefs, 155-156

    tips for working with agencies, 154-155

  collaboration with customers, 148

    agreement on priorities, 150-151

    common subjects for collaboration,
      152-154

    final approval, 151

    follow-up, 151-152

    initial meetings, 149-150

    what retailers want, 148-149

  explained, 8

  messaging, 160-162

  overview, 147-148

  research findings, 164-165

  retail channel execution, 238

  successful execution, 160

  supply chain management. *See* supply chain
    management

existential phenomenology, 187, 191-192

expected impact

  expected impact over time, 172-173

  measure-learn-change process, 173

experiments, 115

exploration (EMTP process), 200-201

eye tracking, 114

F

falsificationism, 186-189

fast moving consumer goods (FMCG)
    firms. *See* manufacturers

feminism, 194

"fighter" brands, 69

final approval, 151

financial estimate (shopper marketing
    customer plan), 142-143

first moment of truth (FMOT), 26

"flanker" brands, 69